THE TRIUMPH
OF UNARMED FORCES
1914–1918

A FRIEND IN NEED

Germany. Who said 'God punish England!'? God *bless* England, who lets us have the sinews of War.

[*From "Punch."*

THE TRIUMPH
OF UNARMED FORCES

(1914–1918)

*An account of the transactions by which Germany during
the Great War was able to obtain supplies
prior to her collapse under the pressure
of economic forces*

BY

REAR-ADMIRAL M. W. W. P. CONSETT,
C.M.G.

NAVAL ATTACHÉ IN SCANDINAVIA 1912–1919
NAVAL ADVISER TO THE SUPREME COUNCIL 1920

ASSISTED BY

CAPTAIN O. H. DANIEL, R.N.

LONDON
WILLIAMS AND NORGATE
14 HENRIETTA STREET, COVENT GARDEN, W.C. 2
1923

Printed in Great Britain

PREFACE

With the causes that led to the outbreak of the Great War (1914–1918) this book is not concerned. That our statesmen did everything possible to avert the catastrophe is accepted as historical fact. Nor could this country honourably have held aloof. The war, however, was prolonged far beyond the limits of necessity. It is the causes that led to the undue protraction of this struggle that are made the subject of examination and comment in this book : for the exhaustion of war destroyed the fruits of victory by bringing economic defeat alike to victor and vanquished in the battle of arms.

When Germany drew the sword in August, 1914, it is beyond all reasonable doubt that its work was to be short, sharp and decisive; and that it was to be returned to its scabbard—for a time—pending preparation for a future task. It is certain that Germany was neither prepared nor equipped for a struggle of four years' duration.

> " If we don't get to Paris in thirty days, we are beaten," Wangenhcim had told me in August, and, though his attitude changed somewhat after the battle of the Marne, he made no attempt to conceal the fact that the great rush campaign had collapsed, that all the Germans could now look forward to was a tedious, exhausting war, and that all which they could obtain from the existing

situation would be a drawn battle. " We have made a mistake this time," Wangenheim said, " in not laying in supplies for a protracted struggle; it was an error, however, that we shall not repeat. . . ."[1]

England's entry and the battle of the Marne had placed all hope of an early decision for Germany out of the question; and the problem with which Germany was faced from the very beginning was an economic one: she was not self-supporting, and the supplies upon which she depended for feeding, clothing and munitioning her armies, and for supporting her civil population, had to come from oversea.

The four years' Great War was a struggle for the mastery of these supplies. The essence of war, it is generally held, lies in the application of force, and in the acts of unbridled violence to which licence is given. But in 1914–1918 the clash of arms, the destruction of cities and even the passing subjugation of smaller nations were not the sole determining factors of an issue in which one half of the more highly organised nations of the earth sought to impose its will upon the other half. In a war of lesser magnitude and shorter duration, and with the seas open, they might have been. The real struggle itself was un-accompanied by any single act of violence; yet it was more deadly in its passive relentlessness than the military forces and engines of war, on which the whole attention of the world was exclusively riveted.

For more than two years Germany maintained an unequal economic struggle with us: she suffered famine, but she won through. In 1917 she sealed

[1] " Secrets of the Bosphorus," by H. Morgenthau, American Ambassador at Constantinople. Hutchinson.

her own doom by declaring war upon all merchant vessels in the waters round the British Islands; for by this act trade with the outside world overseas was virtually stopped. British trade with Germany's neutral neighbours, which had continued throughout the war, ceased. America entered the arena and Germany was reduced to starvation: her troops left the fighting line in search of food.

It is the story of this unseen economic struggle that is here told. The story is as yet an unrecorded chapter in the history of the war. The very existence of the struggle is probably unsuspected by the majority of Englishmen.

The oversea supplies that reached Germany came mainly through Scandinavia [1] and Holland, passing through two stages in their journey: one by sea and one by land.

Taking these stages in order; over a certain part of neutral trade we possessed belligerent rights, sanctioned by international law, treaty and convention. The rules of naval warfare under which we had fought in the past gave us great power over neutral trade with the enemy; but at our own suggestion they had been made to suffer fundamental alteration in the long period of peace following on the Napoleonic wars, which ended in the early part of the nineteenth century: much of our belligerent

---

[1] For convenience' sake, when speaking of Scandinavia the author includes Holland in addition to Norway, Sweden and Denmark.

The remarks on oversea supplies to Scandinavia apply generally in principle to supplies to European countries bordering on the Mediterranean littoral. Neither these countries nor Holland, whose economic conditions resemble those of Denmark, have therefore been treated separately. The supplies through the Mediterranean were of far less importance than those through the North Sea.

power had been voluntarily surrendered; and the Navy, on the strength of which the power to enforce these rights depended, had therefore been rendered partially impotent. During the war, and while the enemy was receiving the benefit of our surrendered rights, a series of efforts was made to retrieve them and to bring into use the rules of the past for the conduct of our naval warfare. This policy brought us into conflict with America. The new rules, of our own making, are chiefly contained in the Declaration of Paris (1856) and the Declaration of London (1909).

Having passed the scrutiny of the British fleet and found sanctuary in Scandinavia, merchandise, in its second stage, was free from further belligerent interference. Nevertheless there were at our command very powerful and effective coercive measures by which it could be controlled, and which could not be disregarded with impunity. Oversea supplies came not only from neutrals, but from Great Britain and her Allies, including, it is to be remembered, Japan. Scandinavia was herself dependent upon oversea supplies for her industrial and economic existence. But she was dependent largely upon certain products of the British Empire and especially upon British coal. With our own goods we were free to do as we wished. Had there been certainty that our supplies would neither reach nor indirectly benefit Germany, there was every reason that trade with Scandinavia should have been encouraged. But from the very beginning goods poured into Germany from Scandinavia, and for over two years Scandinavia received from the British Empire and the Allied countries stocks which, together with those from neutral countries, exceeded all previous quantities and literally saved Germany from starvation.

Our trade with Scandinavia was conducted and justified on the accepted security of guarantees that Germany should not benefit by it : here it is sufficient to say that this security was worthless.

A two-fold form of economic pressure could thus be brought to bear upon Germany : that by belligerent right, to which recent custom applies, in a generic sense, the term "blockade"; and that by the control of goods from the British Empire and Allied countries.

It had been the author's wish to avoid meddling with subjects whose discussion is recognised to be the exclusive monopoly of lawyers; but during the course of a three years' struggle by correspondence on the subject of the supplies that reached Germany he was given to understand that there stood insuperable difficulties in the way of taking preventive measures for their restriction; and, of these difficulties, that the chief lay in the attitude of America towards the subject of maritime rights.

It must be pointed out that maritime rights are slippery and elusive affairs and not very amenable to amateur treatment. They rest upon an international legal basis and lend themselves, from their ambiguity, to the most extravagant form of quibbling. They are admirably adapted to contradictory interpretation : and it was thus that they were interpreted by American and English lawyers according to their interests. If the American conception of maritime rights was alleged by H.M. Government to constitute an obstacle in the way of their conducting the blockade of Germany with greater vigour, and of preventing excessive supplies from reaching her, it would have been a bold man that would have ventured to challenge this assertion.

It is partly for these reasons that the chapters

dealing with the correspondence that took place between H.M. Government and the Government of the United States have been included. The author has confined himself to a few cursory comments on the rival claims of the combatants during the course of the struggle. Unfortunately, before the climax has been reached, both combatants disappear from the paper, leaving it to the choice of fancy to pronounce upon the issue.

But during the course of this battle over our right to interfere with American trade—for that was the *casus belli*—the dispute assumed an unexpected and significant phase.

America, who had been very closely pressed on the subject of the alleged injury caused by our operations to her export trade, turned sharply round and requested information on the subject of British trade. While we were invoking the aid of maritime law in support of our right of interference with American commerce, we were ourselves competing in trade with America. American displeasure was understood during the war; but the cause behind it was not. It is not alone from the light thrown on this subject by the American correspondence that the author attributes the friction with America directly to our competitive trading : the nature of many of the commercial transactions that came under his personal observation in Scandinavia, not to speak of the personal opinions of Americans themselves both during and after the war, give strong support to this view.

It was not the friction caused by our trade and the consequent attitude of America towards the subject of our maritime rights; but it was chiefly our trade itself with Germany's neutral neighbours that under-

mined the power of the fleet, succoured our enemies
and nearly led to our defeat.

During the debates that took place in the Houses
of Parliament on our blockade policy great solicitude
was shown by H.M. Government for the Scandinavian
neutrals, whose cause was pleaded with considerable
eloquence in support of their claim to our good offices
in respect of trade.

But the sufferings of the Scandinavian communities
were not caused by the naval operations of Great
Britain, nor by the belligerent operations of any
country: they were the direct result of the deliberate
actions of their own people, who sent their goods to
the lucrative markets of Germany.

The war brought to Scandinavia a period of unprecedented prosperity. During 1915 and 1916 she
received supplies in excess of all previous quantities.
There was a double irony in the situation: for
although it was through our own trade only, whose
ostensible object here was the mitigation of hardship,
that the neutral profiteer was enabled to conduct
his thriving business, yet the scarcity thus produced
in the neutral country was attributed by the suffering
people to the harsh conditions of the British blockade.
There was a time when meat was so scarce in Copenhagen that butchers' shops had to be closed down:
special fast trains packed with fish, the staple article
of diet among many of the Danes, carried it to
Germany when fish was unprocurable in Denmark;
incidentally, be it mentioned, the trains were run on
British coal and the fishing tackle was supplied by
Great Britain: Swedish spindles were idle when the
wharves and quays of Swedish ports were choked
with cotton for Germany: and coffee, the favourite
beverage of the Swede, was unobtainable in Swedish

restaurants at a time when Sweden was exporting large quantities to Germany.

Germany's propinquity placed the Scandinavian States in a position that gave trading in any circumstances the character of a very hazardous enterprise, in which any doubt should have been resolved in favour of our fighting forces; but the magnitude of the traffic with Germany was notorious, and it left no room for doubt that it was the pure growth of all Scandinavian oversea importations.

It is most difficult to reconcile statements made from time to time by H.M. Government on this subject. Thus, at one time, when the country was uneasy on account of the extent to which supplies were being allowed to reach Germany, we are given to understand that not much was going through neutral countries; [1] and at another, when the occasion required it, as it did during the diplomatic discussion with America in order to establish a claim for interfering with her trade, we learn that " it is common knowledge that large quantities of supplies have . . . passed to our enemy through neutral ports "; and that they—the ports—" have, in fact, been the main avenues through which supplies have reached the enemy." [2]

Without apparent discourtesy to either one side or the other it is not possible here to make appropriate comment.

Moreover, the policy of H.M. Government towards these neutrals did not conduce to the good understanding which it was desired should be established

---

[1] From speech of Lord Robert Cecil quoting Lord Faringdon, who had visited Scandinavia. (See Part II, Chap. XIII.) Parliamentary Debates, No. 153, p. 3194, 26th January, 1916.

[2] Cd. 8234, p. 24. H.M. Government to U.S. Government.

with them. The neutrals were proof against flattery, which they assessed at its correct value : they took our goods, and such of them as could be spared, if not sold to Germany, they used for Germany's benefit.

The author, who served as Naval Attaché in Scandinavia for six years, including the four years of war, can, he thinks, speak with some knowledge as to the general trend of Scandinavian opinion on the blockade policy of this country. It was, in his opinion, the universal belief that, should England become involved in a European war, Scandinavia would have to be prepared to make sacrifices. That all supplies from England would be cut off was not expected; but it was felt certain that the bare requirements of domestic consumption would in no case be exceeded.

The prestige of this country probably never stood at so high a level, and our naval strength was never greater than in August, 1914. With the help of our Allies we were in a position of advantage which the most extravagant optimism could never hope again to reach. If the name of England was not uttered with bated breath, it was mentioned with real respect. But when war broke out the extent of our traffic, which helped to swell the stream that poured into Scandinavia, amazed the Scandinavians. It was equally injurious as well in its moral as in its material effects, for it gradually stimulated the belief that necessity quite as much as philanthropy lay at its roots. Our prestige waned, and the belief was encouraged that it was no longer England but Germany that was to be feared.

Trade with Scandinavia continued unchecked for over two years : agreements by which neutrals engaged that Germany should not benefit by our trade

were openly and continuously violated : representations, containing clear, authentic statements of facts,
supported by trustworthy analyses of figures relating to the manner in which the raw materials and
finished products from oversea passed in identical or
similar form through Scandinavia to Germany, were
disregarded.

When Germany was in the grip of famine and food
riots had to be put down by the military, disaster
was averted only by the prodigious supplies that
passed into the country through Scandinavia. It is
true that direct trade with Germany was forbidden,
and that certain restrictive measures for the prevention of indirect trade were provided for by
municipal legislation. Such measures, however, were
inadequate : they proved to be no protection against
their abuse. Moreover, the ulterior and dangerous
uses to which almost all merchandise can be put in
war time by a neutral bordering on enemy territory
are multitudinous, and little appears to have been
understood of the potential power for harm possessed
by merchandise when it had reached Scandinavia;
or of the manner in which it affected the economic
situation of Germany, which it was the object of the
blockade to exploit to our advantage.

The leverage that the control of our own supplies,
especially coal, gave us, had it also been combined
with a knowledge of the needs and the resources of
other nations, was a weapon that could not have been
resisted. ∤There is probably no case in history in
which the economic forces at the disposal of a nation
on the outbreak of war have been so great as those
that this country held in August, 1914.

It was only when, from sheer necessity, really
effective pressure was brought to bear, both from the

full exercise of our maritime rights and the right to control the distribution of the products of our own Empire, that the position of Germany—always desperate—became hopeless.

Whatever may be thought of the views of the author, it may be stated that his proposals for preventing supplies from reaching Germany were all carried out after the war had been in progress for two and a half years.

Although our entry into the war came as an unwelcome surprise to Germany, yet it was a contingency for which she had made certain well-considered preparations. General von Bernhardi in his " Germany and the Next War "—a pre-war publication, referring to which General Ludendorff[1] says, " It would have been better if it had never been written "—observes, " It would be necessary to take further steps to secure the importation from abroad of supplies necessary to us, since our communications will be completely cut off by the English."

Bernhardi's view, which, like that of the Scandinavians, had been based upon England's naval record of the past, was wrong. But, that Germany should be able to obtain her supplies in war time, especially food and the raw materials for munitions, due provision had been made.

In 1909 there had been drawn up at Germany's suggestion a set of rules by which commerce in war time was given so great a measure of freedom as to render the power of our fleet, through which the right over commerce was exercised, almost useless. Wonder and mystery seem to have accompanied the Declaration of London, which contains these rules, throughout

[1] " My War Memories." By General Ludendorff.

b

its career from the time of its inception up to the date of its final renunciation. It was brought into being in secrecy; its provisions, when known, were examined; and reasons so clear, forcible and convincing were brought to bear against it as to be unassailable. It was rejected by the House of Lords as being redolent of German suggestion and dangerous. Yet when this country became embroiled in war with Germany the Declaration of London, unratified and long considered dead, leaped into life, defied its detractors and started on a career of disaster which continued until the 7th July, 1916, the date on which it met its doom.

On 24th April, 1916, in a Memorandum presented to the U.S. Government it is stated :—

> The United States Government will, it is believed, agree with His Majesty's Government that no belligerent could in modern times submit to be bound by a rule that no goods could be seized unless they were accompanied by papers which established their destination to an enemy country. . . . To press any such theory is tantamount to asking that all trade between neutral ports shall be free, and would thus render nugatory the exercise of sea power and destroy the pressure which the command of the sea enables the Allies to impose upon their enemy.[1]

Article 35 of the Declaration of London tells us that the ship's papers are conclusive proof both as to the voyage on which the vessel is engaged and as to the port of discharge of the goods.

The one statement was made in war time, the other

[1] Cd. 8234.

in peace time : the latter under German suggestion, the former under German coercion.

There are one or two words, however, to be said in favour of the Declaration of London : they come from Germany and will be found duly recorded. They furnish unimpeachable evidence of the tenacity with which Germany was prepared, at least in one case, to cling to her plighted word.

In Part I an attempt has been made to present to the reader a short account of the origin and history of the laws of sea warfare, and of the principal changes that they have suffered up to 1914, in so far only as these matters may help to a better understanding of the real nature of the war in which we were engaged, and serve as a fitting, and, it is hoped, not uninteresting introduction to Part II.

The subject matter of Part II, which deals with the transit of oversea supplies to Germany during their second stage, refers to transactions that came under the author's personal observation and were embodied in his reports. After political considerations and the relative economic conditions of Great Britain, Germany and Scandinavia have been briefly outlined, the vicissitudes through which the passive forces at our command passed before they were placed in harness and their power was vindicated are illustrated by copious examples; which also serve to show the evil effects that were brought about by British trade with Scandinavia upon the blockade of Germany.

Such being its general features, the author would lay stress upon the necessity, to which this book seeks to give special prominence, for a realisation of the conditions under which we in these Islands live. We live mainly upon supplies that are brought to us from oversea; and the condition of existence is the security of these supplies. Until the waters recede from our coasts and our boundaries are in territorial connection with the continent of Europe, our marketing must be done under the protection of the Navy.

It is improbable that this country will soon again attain to the same position of naval supremacy that it held in August, 1914. The financial strain of the four years' struggle has depleted our resources and placed out of the question any present prospect of quick recovery; but all other considerations must yield to the paramount one of our existence, which is threatened if our sea-power is not upheld. Sea-power, with its adjunct air-power, cannot be bartered for the illusory advantages of paper security—those "rotten parchment bonds" spoken of by the poet, whose words have been borrowed to grace the half-title to Part I.

The Navy, we are told, has been reduced to help to avert national bankruptcy. It is devoutly to be hoped that when the country is in funds again immediate attention will be given to the safety of these Islands and the security of our hearths and homes.

The substance of what has been said on the subjects of the Declarations of London and Paris has been derived mainly from the two works of the late Mr. Thomas Gibson Bowles, M.P., "Sea Law and Sea Power" (John Murray) and "The Declaration of Paris of 1856" (Sampson Low, Marston and Co., Ltd.).

In the death of Mr. Gibson Bowles the country lost one of the stoutest champions of its national rights. A great part of his life had been devoted to a study of our sea history, and Mr. Gibson Bowles—himself a thorough and practical seaman—possessed a knowledge of maritime law and the meaning of sea-power greater, probably, than that of any living

man. It was due almost solely to the untiring
exertions of Mr. Gibson Bowles that the Declaration
of London was not ratified. For his public services
the country, and the Navy in particular, owes him a
debt which, alas! can now only be acknowledged
by the homage rendered to his memory.

The author has greatly appreciated the help and
encouragement that he received from many quarters,
and especially from officers of the Royal Navy, during
the writing of this book.

To Mr. Hugh Birrell, in particular, he would express
his grateful thanks for the very laborious work of
compiling a large part of the statistical information
upon which Part II of this book chiefly relies for any
value it may possess, and for the assistance Mr.
Birrell kindly gave in other directions.

To make the book more acceptable to the general
public its dimensions since it was first completed
have been greatly reduced. The work was seriously
retarded by the author's appointment early in 1920
as Naval Adviser to the Supreme Council in Paris.
It would have been further delayed but for the help
of Captain O. H. Daniel, R.N., a friend and old ship-
mate of the author's. Unfortunately, Captain Daniel's
co-operation could not be obtained at a time to have
enabled it to make an earlier appearance.

M. W. W. P. C.

Brawith Hall,
Thirsk.
12th March, 1923.

CONTENTS

LIST OF ILLUSTRATIONS AND DIAGRAMS

PART I

AN ENCHAINED NAVY

This precious stone set in the silver sea,

  .   .   .   .

This blessed plot, this earth, this realm, this England,

  .   .   .   .   .

Whose rocky shore beats back the envious siege
Of watery Neptune, is now bound in . . .
With inky blots, and rotten parchment bonds.

King Richard II.

PART I

AN ENCHAINED NAVY

THE
TRIUMPH OF UNARMED FORCES

1914-1918

CHAPTER I

INTRODUCTORY

THE freedom with which all nations in peace time can engage in their lawful sea-borne trade, in war time becomes subject to certain recognised limitations under powers vested in a belligerent. These powers, which are referred to collectively as "maritime rights," can be asserted only through sea-power : they are therefore mainly the prerogative of the stronger belligerent. Germany, for instance, had the full right to stop the supplies of munitions that reached us from America, but she was unable to exercise it. It is therefore the aim of the stronger naval Power to retain a maximum control by belligerent right over commerce in war time : it is for the lessening of such belligerent control and for its being regulated by international agreement that the weaker naval Power strives.

There are thus two distinct and antagonistic sets of belligerent interests in maritime rights : the interests that would secure the uninterrupted flow of sea-borne supplies free from the right of interference by an enemy; and those that would have them subject to all possible belligerent control. These are broadly the interests respectively of the European continental

3

nations on the one hand, and of Great Britain, the island Power, on the other. Into the separate interests of individual States in this subject it is not necessary here to enter. A belligerent will find that a law or rule, which at one time may operate to his advantage, in other circumstances will favour his enemy : a right, too, which favours a nation as a belligerent may do him untold harm as a neutral, and *vice versâ*.

In addition to the general conflicting nature of the interests of opposing nations in war time, and to the particular conflict of our own individual interests with those of our European neighbours in respect of the control of sea-borne supplies, there are the separate and distinctive interests of neutrals to be considered. It is obvious that if the operations of naval warfare could be exclusively confined in their effects to the belligerents concerned, there could be no restraints upon the use by one belligerent of all possible means at his disposal for injuring his adversary. But they cannot. The prosperity of nations is founded upon an inter-trading relationship : belligerent operations at sea have as their sole ulterior offensive object the stoppage of all supplies to the enemy : the normal flow of neutral oversea commerce, upon which neutral prosperity depends, is interrupted; belligerent and neutral interests come into harsh conflict, and the right to employ the full resources at the disposal of a belligerent becomes subject to restrictions due to the just recognition of neutral rights.

It is the object of the rules of naval warfare to determine and define these restrictions. The difficulty of conciliating the opposing interests of neutral and belligerent is one of the first magnitude and delicacy : no one can read the American correspondence without becoming impressed with this fact—nor, it is thought, without becoming more impressed with the futility of ever hoping to conciliate them. The rules have at all times been fruitful sources of friction between neutral and belligerent: they will always so be. On the outbreak of war on a scale such as that of the recent one, the whole civilised world becomes involved, and the diplomatic war between belligerent and neutral is scarcely less momentous in the gravity of its issues and the possibility of its consequences than the conflict of the nations themselves that are under arms. A belligerent would not willingly add to the number of his enemies, nor would a neutral wish to become involved. Neither the one nor the other will unduly press his views upon his diplomatic opponent. Germany failed to recognise this necessity in arguing debatable points with America, with whom later she became embroiled by a culminating act of open defiance of rules the propriety of whose observance had never before been questioned.

The rules of naval warfare are thus seen to be an expression of maritime rights, which may signify either the rights of neutrals or the rights of belligerents, the former being the passive and the latter the active expression of these rules.

Until the year 1856 the code of rules which had received tacit general acknowledgment, though not on all occasions universal acceptance, was based upon the traditional usage of the sea, precedent and general first principles of equity. These rules are not contained in any printed publication; they are referred to generally as the " Law of Nations."

In 1856 they suffered a fundamental change : in 1909 existing belligerent rights were further restricted and, moreover, were hampered with conditions that deprived them of most of their value to this country.

CHAPTER II

THE three principal rules, sanctioned by the Law of Nations, under which naval warfare was conducted in the past, referred to the right of visit and search, blockade and the capture of enemy goods at sea.

By the right of visit and search a belligerent war vessel was empowered to hold up and board any merchant vessel for the purpose of verifying her nationality, examining her papers and searching her cargo for contraband. The only modification suffered by this rule during the war was that, for safety's sake, the search was carried out in harbour instead of at sea. This innovation was challenged, but unsuccessfully, by America.

By the right of blockade a belligerent Power may forcibly prevent any neutral merchant ship from either entering or leaving an enemy port by stationing a cordon of ships off such port. Such blockade is recognised only when it is really effective, *i. e.* when the number of ships that form the cordon is sufficiently large to ensure there being no reasonable possibility that a ship shall be able to pass through unseen.

The old law of blockade, which will be spoken of more fully in another chapter, was of but little use to us during the war owing to the effective long range of modern guns and the dangers from submarine, mine and aircraft.

We come to the third rule, the most important of all

6

and that which has suffered the greatest change. A belligerent originally had the right to capture and confiscate enemy property wherever found upon the high seas. This right, which extended to the capture of enemy property in neutral ships, was frequently disputed.

The first to challenge the old law and to make a serious attack upon it were the Dutch. Towards the middle of the seventeenth century they put forward a new principle by which enemy commerce on the high seas received immunity from risk of capture when carried in neutral ships. This principle sought justification on the ground of its being identified with the sovereign rights of neutrals, upon which, so it was alleged by the Dutch, the application of the principles of the old law constituted an encroachment.

The Dutch arguments and principles were all contained in condensed form in the neatly packed formula " Free ship, free goods." This formula was launched on the world, elevated to the dignity of a doctrine and accepted by the Dutch school as a sound and exhaustive exposition of the Law of Nations in all matters relating to the subject of enemy property on the high seas. Not being easy of comfortable refutation, this doctrine held the field until a formidable rival appeared unexpectedly upon the scene. This was " Enemy ship, enemy goods," which argued that if the character of the cargo was to be determined by the nationality of the ship, then neutral cargoes on board enemy ships must partake of an enemy character.

Both these propositions may be perfectly sound, although in our personal opinion they are not; for if one belligerent cannot protect his own property on the high seas it seems only right that it should become lawful prize to the other belligerent; bearing in mind that the dispute, in which property at sea plays the most vital part, has by both belligerents been referred to the arbitrament of the sword and not to the good offices of the neutral. Be this as it may, the point is that, Dutch doctrines notwithstanding, we asserted our right and maintained it. Neither Frederick the Great of Prussia in 1752, nor the armed neutralities of Catherine of Russia in 1780 and 1800, succeeded in establishing their claim to the new doctrine in the face of the uncompromising resistance that it met with from our statesmen and seamen of those days; and on the outbreak of the French Revolutionary War the old law received almost universal acknowledgment.

But in 1856, after the Crimean War, we committed ourselves to the fatal act of setting our signature to the Declaration of Paris, Art. II of which paraphrases the Dutch doctrine as follows :—

> The neutral flag covers enemy's merchandise with the exception of contraband of war.

The immunity given by this Article to the general bulk of sea-borne merchandise struck a blow at the very heart of our sea-power. It is true that the protection which this Declaration gave to enemy commerce was given also to British; but this protection, being already provided for in our case by our fleet, extended only to the commerce of our enemies, and struck a vital blow at our sea-power.

Continental nations stand on an entirely different footing from that of Great Britain with regard to the security of their oversea supplies : they have therefore been compelled to seek protection for them in paper agreements. The illusory nature of a security that rests upon the assumed inviolability of a bond is supplied by Germany's actions during the war when, from the very outset, she violated Belgium's neutrality and proceeded to the perpetration of successive acts in contravention of every written and unwritten law that stood in the way of her objective.

In signing an agreement that will give alike to us and to others immunity to commerce from capture, or the transfer of naval power to international legal instruments, the whole of the advantage accrues to our potential enemies. This fact should always be borne in mind by those who live on islands, and have powerful and bellicose military nations as neighbours across the water.

" I believe," said the late Lord Salisbury, speaking in the House of Lords on 6th March, 1871, " that since the Declaration of Paris, the fleet, valuable as it is for preventing an invasion of these shores, is almost valueless for any other purpose." The hampering effect of the Declaration of Paris upon the power of England at sea may be judged from the fact that we found it absolutely necessary so early in the war as on the 11th March, 1915, to renounce its provisions completely in principle, though not in law, by our Reprisals Order of that date.

More than half a century elapsed before the next great surrender was made. The Declaration of Paris made it very important to us that the right over contraband goods should be as complete as possible. But during the nineteenth century very revolutionary changes had taken place in the conditions under which naval warfare had previously been conducted.

In the Napoleonic days the operations of war were confined almost exclusively to the armed forces, partaking somewhat of the nature of a gladiatorial combat. The civil population existed practically as a separate entity; its concern with the war was but slight (it is understood, however, that it was always allowed to pay taxes), and, as a military asset, it was almost negligible. There was, therefore, no real necessity for stopping supplies to the civil population.

Nations, too, in those days were nearly self-supporting and dependent far less than they are now upon sea-borne supplies. The contraband list was therefore small and simple, and there was then no difficulty in determining the contraband character of goods. As for evidence of proof that contraband found on board a ship was destined for the enemy, that was an equally simple matter to determine; for, there being no adequate land transport across adjoining neutral territory, a neutral port did not afford facilities for contraband traffic, and enemy ports only needed to be considered. But the operations of war have felt the full force of the impetus launched by the advent of steam; and the amazing fertility with which the resources of science and invention have been harnessed and adapted to these operations has greatly contributed to the enlargement of the contraband list. During the Great War, when the whole of the civil population became merged in the military, strictly non-contraband goods formed but an insignificant part of the bulk of merchandise.

The growth of railways and the facilities that they afford for the conveyance of goods between enemy and adjacent neutral territory has also added immeasurably to the difficulties of stopping the contraband traffic : for the complicated problem had to be faced of discriminating between *bonâ fide* neutral goods and goods destined for the enemy; both being contraband and both being stowed cheek by jowl in the hold of a ship that discharged its cargo in a neutral port; where neutral and enemy, as frequently as not, had a common interest in adding to existing complications brought about by the invention of steam.

The question, therefore, of determining what goods should be regarded as contraband and how they should be proved to have an enemy destination became very complex.

The tribunal to which such matters and all questions affecting the validity of captures at sea are referred is the national Prize Court of the belligerent. The judgments of Prize Courts have always been based upon a review of the evidence available and in accordance with precedent and the teachings of international jurists.

The Declaration of London arose out of a proposal by Germany for the establishment of an International Court of Appeal from the decisions of Prize Courts. The functions of our Prize Courts were thus to be handed over to an alien tribunal. This could not, fortunately, be done without the authority of Parliament. The Naval Prize Bill, embodying the German proposal, was therefore introduced : it passed the House of Commons, but, mainly through the untiring energy and patriotic devotion of the late Mr. Gibson Bowles, it was thrown out by the Lords; who, by this wise act, freed the country from the grave danger during the Great War that all decisions in the matter of prize and legality of our belligerent operations at sea should be made the subject of appeal to a foreign Court; a Court sitting in secret session, and to the impartiality of whose findings there would inevitably attach the taint of suspicion, arising from the conflicting interests of the represented Powers, prejudicial, in their residual effect, to our own.

It was necessary that the new Court should have a

law to administer. For this purpose a conference of ten States was convened in London in 1908; and the result of its deliberations is contained in the Declaration of London 1909, to the contraband clauses of which our remarks will be chiefly confined.[1]

The Declaration of London contains two lists : one of absolute contraband, which comprises articles of exclusive military utility such as guns and explosives; and one of conditional contraband, such as food, fuel and clothing, which are necessary for the civil population as well as for military purposes. There is also a Free List which contains articles that cannot be made contraband.

Now contraband in its very nature is not susceptible of being so listed, for the contraband character of goods must depend upon circumstances of varying conditions, such as time and place : there may at one time be a scarcity and at another a sufficiency of any particular commodity; which, again, might be obtainable or not according to the relationship of a belligerent with adjoining neutrals. But it is the Free List that constitutes the most mischievous feature here; for although the raw materials for our manufactures are to be found on this list, it also includes the ingredients from which munitions and the most potent forms of explosives are made, *e. g.* raw cotton, nitrates, metallic ores, ammonia, oil seeds and rubber.

Turning to the question of evidence of proof, the Declaration of London lays down certain presumptions of guilt. These presumptions assume a *bonâ fide* character to ships' papers : they seriously fetter the jurisdiction of Prize Courts, and are so simple of evasion as almost to amount to a notification of how the smuggler may avoid risk to his venture. Article 35

[1] See Appendix, p. 281.

virtually places conditional contraband on the Free List, for the mere fact of its being discharged in a neutral port is held to give it an innocent character.

Matters might well have been worse, for in the instructions to Sir Edward Fry, 12th June, 1907, it is stated that H.M. Government were ready and willing to abandon the principle of contraband, thus allowing oversea trade in neutral vessels between belligerents on the one hand and neutrals on the other to continue during the war without any restriction, subject only to its exclusion by blockade from an enemy's port. This project was overruled.

The Declaration of London, though not ratified, was adopted on the outbreak of war, and ran its course until it was superseded by the Maritime Rights Order.

Referring to the restrictions upon the right of blockade imposed by the Declaration of London, the *Hamburger Nachrichten* of 13th June, 1909, ingenuously observes, "in Germany we have received these decisions with exceptional pleasure."

For later pronouncements we call upon Admiral von Tirpitz and the late Herr von Bethmann-Hollweg.

From Admiral von Tirpitz :— [1]

> The kernel of our altogether too humble answer to America, which was dispatched on Feb. 17th, 1915, lay in the invitation to the American Government to find a way of ensuring the observation of the Declaration of London by the English, with the suggestion that in that case the German Government would be ready to follow out the logical results of the new situation thus created. That meant of course that in that case we should abandon the use of the submarines not

----

[1] Admiral von Tirpitz's Memoirs.

merely in the barred zone, but also against enemy vessels.

Germany's submarines had not on the whole been doing badly, but they had not quite the same numbing effect that the Declaration of London alone possessed.

From the late Herr von Bethmann-Hollweg, German Chancellor :—

> " Of special interest," says Mr. Cababé,[1] " in this connection is the statement of the German Chancellor, Herr von Bethmann-Hollweg, in July 1916, to the American journalist, Mr. W. B. Hale, as reported in *The Times* of July 11th, 1916. ' There was,' said the Chancellor, ' another Declaration of Independence which history will record as of import no less significant than the document signed at Philadelphia on July 4th, 1776—the manifesto issued by the Great Powers of the world upon the freedom of God's ocean to the people of whatever clime who set sail upon its bosom on lawful errands. The proclamation of the freedom of the seas is known as the Declaration of London. It was subscribed to in London, of all places in the world, on February 26th, 1908. To its enunciation of principles ten nations placed their " John Hancocks." ' " [1]

[1] " The Freedom of the Seas." By Michael Cababé. John Murray.

[2] That is, signatures. John Hancock was the first to inscribe his name on the Declaration of Independence.

THE CHIEF MOURNER

[From " Punch."

CHAPTER III

An Admiralty Memorandum published in 1910 stated that :—

> The really serious danger that this country has to guard against in war is not invasion, but interruption of trade and destruction of our mercantile marine.

. . . . . .

There was a time when this country was self-supporting and our fleet existed only for defence against invasion; but with the growth of our Empire and our dependence upon foreign trade for our existence, the main *rôle* of the Navy has been transferred to the protection of our commerce and long lines of communication, and its size has increased to meet new requirements. On sea-borne supplies these islands depend for their existence : our continental neighbours are not to such an extent dependent upon them for theirs. In addition to their land communications extending over Europe and Asia, they have facilities for obtaining supplies from oversea sources through neutral ports; we have none : our only neighbour is the sea. It is a mere truism, therefore, to say that our existence depends upon our ability to give security to our sea-borne supplies—that is to say upon our Navy. To us naval disaster signifies irretrievable national ruin; to our neighbours it has a far less limited meaning.

The fleet has an offensive and a defensive purpose to fulfil.   The advent of the submarine and its rapid development since 1914—though not before—has had a serious influence upon the original offensive function of a fleet, whose direct and immediate object is to destroy the enemy fleet.[1]

The destruction of the enemy fleet, however, is only the means to a certain end; it is the removal of a barrier that stands in the way of attack upon enemy commerce.

As a protection to its commerce an enemy fleet is rendered equally useless if, as was the case with the German High Sea Fleet, it can be confined to its harbours.

Having gained its immediate objective by removing the barrier or rendering it useless, the victorious fleet is in a position to reap the fruits of victory.   If, however, there is no commerce upon which to prey, or if it is under the protection of treaty, the destruction of the enemy fleet—still speaking of it only as a barrier or screen—has been little more than a Pyrrhic victory : it has been the destruction of so many lives and so much material; and the intrinsic loss suffered by the enemy, as measured by the standard of war values, has not been of great importance.

The significance of this offensive function of our fleet lies in its exposure of the *only* spot in the enemy's armour that is vulnerable from the sea; namely, his sea-borne supplies.   It is true that we ourselves are far more dependent upon sea-borne supplies than any continental nation; but in our own *special* case these supplies are safeguarded by our fleet.

We turn to the main defensive function of the fleet, which consists in the protection of our commerce and

[1] The submarine is briefly discussed later on in this chapter.

trade routes. We have bits of empire scattered all over the world and our lines of communication must be kept free from attack by units of the enemy fleet. A sufficient force must therefore be available for dealing with details that may be encountered anywhere in the various oceans, any one unit of which has the power to inflict incalculable injury on our mercantile marine, as witness the exploits of the "Emden" and "Moewe."

The defensive function of the German fleet, which was confined to the protection of German commerce, was undertaken in the first place by the Declaration of Paris, which gave the greater part of German commerce the protection of the neutral flag. Germany's commerce was further protected by our adoption of the Declaration of London, which made the capture of contraband exceedingly difficult, and in other ways weakened the power of our fleet.

There is no record in history in which a fleet has carried out the work of blockade so efficiently as did the British fleet in 1914-1918 : the number of ships that escaped its unceasing watchfulness was negligible ; the effectiveness of the work of the Navy was, unfortunately, seriously impaired by the release of many ships without the authoritative sanction of the Prize Courts. This matter was affected in no way whatever by the existence of the German High Sea Fleet, whose proper function it was itself to protect the sea-borne supplies of the German armies and to prevent our fleet from holding them up.

If the reader would know who won the battle of Jutland, let him make inquiry in the first place as to the objects that each of the contending fleets had in view, and then as to the results of the fighting as they affected those objects. He will find that the

c

object of the German fleet was to obtain command of
the sea with the special purpose of giving security to
Germany's sea-borne supplies, which had then passed
from the state of being a pressing need to that of
being a vital necessity to her; with the further object,
also, of cutting our communications with France and
preventing reinforcements from crossing the English
Channel. He will find that the object of the British
fleet was to prevent these purposes from being
achieved.[1] He will find also that, as a result of the
battle of Jutland, the blockade of Germany was
unaffected; that the number of ships which escaped
the vigilance of our fleet was as negligible after as
before the battle; that our communications with
France were maintained; and that our transports
passed to and fro in perfect security under naval escort
—one or two only were lost by direct enemy action
throughout the war. These results are further accentuated by the pregnant fact that the German fleet
never again challenged our sea-supremacy, although
the German nation was in the grip of starvation.

Although the German High Sea Fleet was unable to
justify its existence as a protection for its commerce
and as a menace to our trade and communications
outside the Baltic, nevertheless as a " fleet in being "
it exercised a far-reaching influence on the fortunes of
the war; mainly in two respects : it enabled the
Baltic trade to be kept open and, by containing the
British Grand Fleet, it prevented the latter from
operating elsewhere. Sweden was to Germany in a
lesser degree what America was to us; and the
destruction of the German fleet would have given us

[1] This was its immediate and imperative object. But the
British objective was also, if possible, to destroy the German
fleet, which was a serious obstacle in the path of other operations.

command of the Baltic.   These considerations furnish
a good instance of the meaning of sea-supremacy.

With regard to the submarine : the German fleet,
it is said, seldom or never went to sea; and, after
Jutland, it did not again put in an appearance.   This
is not quite the case.

A fleet, as has been shown, has an offensive and a
defensive part to play.   The submarine has placed
this distinction in a very clear light.   In the case of
Germany the two functions are to be seen in the two
separate arms of her fleet—her High Sea Fleet, whose
part during the war was mainly a passive one, and
her under-water fleet.   It was the offensive function
of the fleet that this under-water fleet was called upon
to perform, and the success achieved by the German
submarine placed this country in a critical situation.
The submarine was always at sea, and could prey
upon our commerce direct by evading the barrier
which alone gave it shelter.   Commerce therefore
could be, and was made its immediate objective.
The German submarine fleet had no opposing fleet
to destroy, and the barrier that we erected was of
necessity an extemporised one, consisting of under-
water obstructions, mines and explosive charges from
surface or aircraft.   We also developed the sense of
hearing the submarine, but the enemy came very close
to dealing us a mortal blow before the fortunes of war
turned finally in our favour.

The limitations imposed by international law upon
belligerent rights include the obligation on the part
of a belligerent to respect life in all interference with
commerce.   By treaty contraband goods only are
liable to capture, subject to the antecedent procedure
of visit and search being carried out and to subsequent
Prize Court proceedings being taken.   The German

submarine in its attack upon our commerce brushed aside all moral and legal obligations and sank ships at sight. Had Germany bound herself by any code of law, either moral or legal, this weapon would have been almost useless : it is unlikely that she would have succeeded in bringing into her ports a single prize. But she nearly effected her purpose. International law and treaty did not protect us from Germany, but we allowed them to protect Germany from us. This is a lesson it is well should be taken to heart.

The German submarine campaign has at least, it is hoped, served some useful purpose. It has taught us the futility of relying upon treaty obligations for the protection of our commerce and our food supplies; it has brought home to us in a very practical manner our dependence, as an island kingdom, upon sea-borne goods and the necessity for effectively safeguarding them; it has taught us that bread is not always to be obtained by the simple process of sending round to the baker's, nor through the sweat of the brow alone; it has to be fought for, and bled for, and died for.

The protection of our commerce against the probable engines of war of the future does not come within the scope of this work as a matter for discussion. We have only this to say about it. If our commerce is to rest for its protection upon treaty obligations, and if modern Declarations of Paris and Declarations of London are again to be foisted upon us, it is to be hoped that they will be backed up by the most powerful material forces that can be devised by the wit of man; that our ablest men will be invited to apply themselves whole-heartedly and unremittingly to the investigation and solution of this problem; and that no question of money shall be allowed to stand in the way of attaining success.[1] Mistakes, which nearly cost us our lives, are apt to occur, as has been seen, when dealing with international law and treaty; but no such mistakes have yet been made when it has been our fleet with which an enemy has had to deal. At the present moment we are living with a halter round our necks.

In 1914 the submarine menace existed, but not as a serious danger. Before it had time to assume the formidable dimensions that marked its rapid develop-ment in the later stages of the war, Germany, had we exercised our maritime rights unfettered by the Declaration of London and abstained from trade in dangerous areas, would, we think, have succumbed to our sea-power.

[1] The munificent gift of £100,000, recently made by Sir Alfred Yarrow to the Royal Society, for the purpose of promoting scientific research was accompanied by a letter in which Sir Alfred Yarrow states :—" It is doubtful whether even yet it has been realised how completely this country would have been at the mercy of our antagonists in the late war had it not been for the research work done by our scientific men before the war and during its course."

CHAPTER IV

THE REPRISALS ORDER

THE causes that predisposed the official mind to a policy in antagonism to the requirements of national defence are to be found in the false sense of security into which the nation had been lulled during the long period of peace following on the close of the Napoleonic Wars. The sinister and intermittent omens of war, the ominous rumblings which came from Agadir, the widening of the Kiel Canal, the increase of the German Army, but, in particular, the expansion of the German Navy were among the many disquieting warnings which, though unheeded by this country, were clearly appreciated by France. While Germany was making open preparation for the coming struggle, the fear of precipitating a crisis would override considerations governing the necessity for meeting it. It is impossible to conceive how by word or deed, were they never so rash, consequences could have befallen the world more appalling than those which it has suffered by the indulging of a reluctance to incur the displeasure of a political rival or provoke the wrath of a friendly though powerful State. The road to office was seen to lead along the pleasant path of economy, and in the artificial atmosphere of peace political judgment became warped.

Thus it came about that the possibility of our becoming a belligerent in the impending struggle was made subordinate to a desire to remain neutral. In this desire, or belief, are to be found the reasons for framing the rules discussed in a previous chapter. Under these rules immense wealth would have been amassed by the carrying trade brought to our mercantile marine—by far the largest in the world—in a European war in which this country was neutral.

But when war broke out, hypothetical considerations had to yield to facts : the belief that this country was to be neutral was shattered by the fact that she was a belligerent and, moreover, that Germany was our foe. In these circumstances the adoption of the Declaration of London (which had given birth to the expression " Sea Law made in Germany "), with slight modifications, cannot be defended. The Convention was the work chiefly of Viscount Grey (then Sir Edward Grey).

The greatest cataclysm in the recorded history of nations has left to the world an impression of unsurpassable deeds of prowess; and many a new name will be found inscribed on history's honoured page : but the topmost heights of fame remained unscaled; and the Great War is linked with the memory of no towering personality by which its fortunes were pre-eminently dominated.

The Prime Minister, who, with Viscount Grey, shared and courageously accepted the responsibility of committing this country to war, was Mr. Asquith, to whose skill in debate, profound learning and inimitable mastery of stately phrase we would respectfully pay our meed of homage. Nevertheless, as Prime Minister in the opening and early stages of the war, he will, we think, be best remembered for the magnificent things he said. There is, we feel sure, no living statesman who has said finer things than has Mr. Asquith. The graceful ceremonies of the art of statesmanship could not possibly have been in better keeping or in more accomplished hands. No one has ever obtained greater value from words. However depressed we might become under the news of successive reverses, Mr. Asquith kept our jaded spirits constantly revivified. In the heyday of their career the effect of some of his more telling phrases was nothing short of stupendous. The country got the belief firmly rooted into its very system that it could not, while such things lasted, be beaten. No more wry faces were then to be seen at the breakfast table. The morning papers were eagerly scanned, not so much with a view to ascertaining what Germany had done as to learn what Mr. Asquith had said. Under the effect of the words which poured from the Premier's lips the country became fairly hypnotised. But unhappily the propaganda work of his enemies began to make itself felt; and the mind of the country slowly but surely became impregnated with its deadly poison. The belief got about that Mr. Asquith's ordnance was defective; that Oxford in time of war is no match for Krupp's, and that the language of Woolwich should be given a trial. We often picture Mr. Asquith as pondering over the words of Merlin :—

> That, if to-night our greatness were struck dead,
> There might be left some record of the things we said,

and making provision for such an emergency. Think of the record there would have been left us.

His successor, Mr. Lloyd George, is also a master of words and, in particular, of metaphor. But he specialised also in deeds. Probably no man contributed a greater individual share to the winning of the war than Mr. Lloyd George. So vast, however, were its ramifications that it was beyond the power of any one man to grapple with the meaning and significance of many of its aspects. Even the superhuman energy and will-power of Mr. Lloyd George himself were not sufficient for such an herculean task. His labours, moreover, were identified only with the military and political side of the struggle; and we venture to say, with diffidence, that the part played by economics failed of necessity to gain the attention of his already fully-occupied thoughts. We do not for a moment think that the haunting spectre of " Too late," which dogged and crippled our every effort to meet emergency after emergency as it arose, was known, or even so much as suspected, by the Premier to be associated with any causes other than the uncertainties inseparable from all prognostics relating to military operations. He could not have been aware—of this we feel convinced—that the German fighting forces were sustained by ourselves, and that the munitions that reached Germany were brought over to her in ships which passed as freely through the waters of the English Channel and North Sea as those that carried our own troops; and that our Navy was these ships' common protection. He did not understand why it was that his feet were always in the clay.

The Fates were in ironic mood when they retained at the head of Foreign Affairs in August, 1914, another great personality, the author of the Declaration of London. In striking contrast to the previously formed views of Viscount Grey on the subject of contraband is the action taken after the opening of hostilities. The Free List was gradually unloaded, and goods were gradually moved up to the two lists of contraband until in the course of time these lists contained most of the principal articles of merchandise of contraband character. The want of organisation (which is frankly admitted), the inability to seize conditional contraband, and the difficulty of discriminating between *bonâ fide* neutral goods and goods with an enemy destination left us powerless to exercise effective control over sea-borne traffic. Such cargoes as were sent in for adjudication, before being brought to the Prize Courts, were subjected to a preliminary filtering process at the hands of a Contraband Committee, whose work was admirably carried out. But as this work was to free neutral traffic from all avoidable delay and inconvenience, it was clearly prejudicial to our interests by tending to the release of guilty cargoes.

The best part of the 3,000,000 tons of Germany's mercantile shipping was locked up in German or neutral ports, and German trade was carried on in neutral ships under Art. II, Declaration of Paris.

> The situation as regards German trade was as follows : Direct trade to German ports (save across the Baltic) had almost entirely ceased, and practically no ships were met with bound to German ports. The supplies that Germany desired to import from overseas were directed to neutral ports in Scandinavia, Holland, or (at first) Italy, and every effort was made to disguise their real destination.[1]

Goods poured into Germany viâ the neutral ports for several months until circumstances arose which enabled certain measures to be taken to bring the traffic under some sort of control.

In March, 1915, an attempt was made to cut off all commerce with Germany by applying the " principle " of the law of blockade but departing from the letter

[1] Cd. 8145.

of the law. The measures adopted by H.M. Government were framed as an act of reprisal against Germany.

The specific offence against international maritime law that led to the drafting of the Reprisals Order [1] was Germany's declaration that the English Channel, the north and west coasts of France and the waters round the British Isles were a " war area "; and that all enemy ships found in that area would be destroyed, and that neutral vessels might be exposed to danger.

Articles I and II of the Reprisals Order are framed for the purpose of cutting off all commerce through German ports.

External commerce consists of imports and exports. Exports have for a belligerent but one purpose to fulfil—to pay for imports. They represent in other respects a useless dissipation of energy.   In Germany's case exports were probably not of prime importance, for she had made arrangements with Scandinavian banks for making payment on a money basis.   In any case imports were of far the greater importance to her. Now with regard to the imports through Germany's own ports, we are in fact told in the " Statement of the Measures adopted to Intercept the Sea-borne Commerce of Germany " that " direct trade to German ports (save across the Baltic) had almost entirely ceased, and practically no ships were met with bound to German ports " : Articles I and II, therefore, appear to leave our power over the important part of enemy commerce, i. e. his contraband imports, much the same as before.

Articles III and IV attempt to stop all commerce with Germany through neutral ports.

[1] See Appendix.

Article III deprives conditional contraband of the immunity from capture which it previously possessed when destined for discharge at a neutral port.

In other respects the power conferred by these articles that was not previously possessed is that of stopping the import of non-contraband goods through neutral ports; which would seem to be a useless dissipation of energy.

The Reprisals Order is lenient to the point of tenderness to the enemy. The full force of its severities in the unnecessary interference with and detention of property which it is not intended to confiscate is felt by the neutral.

The Reprisals Order, which marks an epoch in the war, is of a very revolutionary character : it brought us into sharp conflict with America. A technical blockade could not be declared in practice in accordance with the provisions of the Declaration of London, which states that a blockade must not extend beyond the ports and coasts belonging to or occupied by the enemy; and that the blockading forces must not bar access to neutral ports or coasts.

For these reasons, therefore, the Reprisals Order did not profess to declare a blockade; its object was to intercept enemy commerce by an adaptation of the law of blockade.

There are two entirely different principles governing the two laws by which enemy commerce can be captured. With the law governing the capture of contraband we have already dealt. Contraband law requires that active measures be taken by a belligerent in order to effect the capture of contraband; and that the capture be submitted to the adjudication of the Prize Court for the determination of its validity.

By the law of blockade a belligerent has the right to

cut off all communication with the whole or any part
of an enemy coast.   By this law the absolute and prior
right of a belligerent to operate against the territory
of his enemy is placed before the trading interests of
the neutral world, which suffer from this blockade
operation.   A belligerent has the right to say, " No
one shall enter this port or approach this stretch of
coast-line : it is the port or coast-line of my enemy."

Under protest from America the word " blockade,"
which had been advisedly omitted in the drafting of
the Reprisals Order, was uttered : " for this end, the
British fleet has instituted a blockade. . . ." [1]

Thus a definite legal basis for discussion, which
did not exist before, was provided; and it is from
the standpoint that a legally constituted blockade is
in operation that the Reprisals Order was argued.
It was a most unfortunate change of standpoint that
the justified retaliatory character of the measures
should have been abandoned.

In a U.S. despatch of 2nd April, 1915, it was pointed
out as " novel and unprecedented features " of our
blockade that it embraced neutral ports and coasts
and barred access to them; and further that the risks
and liabilities placed upon neutral shipping were a
distinct invasion of the sovereign rights of neutrals.

In reply, Viscount Grey (23rd July, 1915) contended
that a belligerent violated no fundamental principle
of international law by applying a blockade " in such
a way as to cut off the enemy's commerce with foreign
countries through neutral ports if the circumstances
render such an application of the principle of blockade
the only means of making it effective." [2]

Admiring as we do the masterly manner in which
the many points raised by America in this controversy

[1] Cd. 7816.   [2] Cd. 8233.

were met by H.M. Government and the Foreign Office, we are unable to see how this point of view can be sustained : for it amounts to asserting a right to blockade neutral ports. Blockade law is very short and clear; and the principle of the law seems all to be contained in the letter of the law. In other laws principles may be applied by which the letter only suffers and not the spirit; e. g. where ships are taken into port for searching them in safety the neutral's interests suffer very little injury. But the claim to change the principle of the law of blockade after the manner of the Reprisals Order is a claim to alter the law radically and to alter it to the great prejudice of neutrals' interests.

> We are interfering with no goods with which we should not be entitled to interfere by blockade, if the geographical position and the conditions of Germany at present were such that the commerce passed through her own ports.

But they were not such, and America argued on conditions as they existed.

We find two sets of conditions, viz. firstly, that we cannot blockade Germany's ports by preventing communication with them by our armed forces—which is the condition of blockade—because Germany's own military measures prevent our doing so; secondly, that of the three parts that comprise enemy commerce, i. e. absolute contraband, conditional contraband and non-contraband, it is the first only of these three over which we have any real hold.

But how was this state of affairs brought about? The conditions here were created by ourselves; conditional contraband by the Declaration of London is virtually non-contraband, and non-contraband enjoys immunity from liability to capture under Article II of the Declaration of Paris. We invoke the protection of the Law of Nations, which we voluntarily surrendered in 1856 and 1909, in respect of the capture of enemy property under law other than that of blockade when the law serves our interests; but the law of blockade, which furthers the interests of our enemy, we find defective; and we invoke principles that are alien to it to take the place of surrendered rights.

Viscount Grey further contends that the one principle which is fundamental and has obtained universal recognition is that, by means of blockade, a belligerent is entitled to cut off by effective means the sea-borne commerce of his enemy.[1]

If America had thought the same, there would have been no ground for discussion; and it is permissible to suggest that this is more a question of opinion than of fact. The blockade, as already stated, is, in our opinion, a measure directed against enemy territory. Its object is certainly to cut off trade with the enemy; but to do so the belligerent must seal up the enemy's port: if he cannot do this, then the port is open to neutrals. If neutrals do not wish to use this port, it does not prevent a belligerent from exercising his right to blockade it to his heart's content if he wishes to do so; but the fact that neutrals do not use such port does not give the right to a belligerent to follow up the neutral with his blockade and transfer and apply it to neutral ports: blockade law simply lapses, and other laws come into operation—the laws governing the capture of enemy property at sea, and the rules governing trade with neutral ports in wartime, which we declared by Royal Proclamation that we would comply with. It is unfortunate for the

[1] Cd. 8233.

blockader but has its compensations from the point of view of the blockaded. It is hardly to be expected that America would acquiesce, to the infinite injury of her own interests, in our proposed rejection of principles to which we had agreed in peace time, because in war time we found they did not suit us.

Not only was the validity of the so-called blockade challenged, but the jurisdiction conferred by the Reprisals Order on our Prize Courts was pronounced by America to be illegal.

Under the rules of the Reprisals Order special provision is made for the investigation of neutral claims in respect of goods placed in the Prize Court. The anomalous position is created here that a jurisdiction for determining claims in respect of action taken under the provisions of the Reprisals Order rests for its authority on the Order itself. The Order in Council is made valid by the King in Council. The claims preferred by neutrals rest on the alleged invalidity of the Order : they dispute the very rule that the Prize Court is administering, and give rise to the question : Are Prize Courts bound by Orders in Council ?

America's attitude towards this question is thus stated :—

> The Government of the U.S. cannot recognise the validity of proceedings taken in H.M. Prize Court under restraints imposed by the municipal law of Great Britain in derogation of the rights of American citizens.[1]

The Declaration of London is valid only by virtue of an Order in Council (20th August, 1914). Were our Prize Courts bound by this Order ? The importance of this matter is our excuse for quoting at some length.

[1] Cd. 8233.

As illustrating further the attitude adopted by the judges of British Prize Courts towards these two sources of law, the municipal legislation of its Sovereign on the one hand and the principles of international law on the other, I should like to refer your Excellency to a classical passage in the judgment of Lord Stowell in the case of the " Fox," in which that famous judge observed :—

" In the course of the discussion a question has been started, What would be the duty of the Court under Orders in Council that were repugnant to the law of nations ?

" It has been contended on one side that the Court would at all events be bound to enforce the Orders in Council; on the other, that the Court would be bound to apply the rule of the law of nations adapted to the particular case in disregard of the Orders in Council. . . . This Court is bound to administer the law of nations to the subjects of other countries in the different relations in which they may be placed towards this country and its Government. That is what others have a right to demand for their subjects, and to complain if they receive it not. This is its unwritten law, evidenced in the course of its decisions, and collected from the common usage of civilised States. At the same time, it is strictly true that, by the Constitution of this country, the King in Council possesses legislative rights over this Court, and has power to issue orders and instructions which it is bound to obey and enforce; and these

D

constitute the written law of this Court. These two propositions, that the Court is bound to administer the law of nations, and that it is bound to enforce the King's Orders in Council, are not at all inconsistent with each other, because these orders and instructions are presumed to conform themselves, under the given circumstances, to the principles of its unwritten law. They are either directory applications of these principles to the cases indicated in them; cases which, with all the facts and circumstances belonging to them, and which constitute their legal character, could be but imperfectly known to the Court itself; or they are positive regulations, consistent with these principles, applying to matters which require more exact and definite rules than those general principles are capable of furnishing. The constitution of this Court, relatively to the legislative power of the King in Council, is analogous to that of the Courts of common law, relatively to the Parliament of this kingdom. These Courts have their unwritten law, the approved principles of natural reason and justice; they have likewise the written or statute law, in Acts of Parliament, which are directory applications of the same principles to particular subjects, or positive regulations consistent with them, upon matters which would remain too much at large if they were left to the imperfect information which the Courts could extract from mere general speculations. What would be the duty of the individuals who preside in these Courts, if

required to enforce an Act of Parliament
which contradicted those principles, is a
question which I presume they would not
entertain *à priori ;* because they will not
entertain *à priori* the supposition that any
such will arise. In like manner, this Court
will not let itself loose into speculations,
as to what would be its duty under such
an emergency; because it cannot, without
extreme indecency, presume that any such
emergency will happen. And it is the less
disposed to entertain them, because its own
observation and experience attest the general
conformity of such orders and instructions
to its principles of unwritten law."

The above passage has recently been quoted
and adopted by the President of the Prize Court
in the case of the " Zamora." [1]

In the opening sentences here it is stated in simple
language that a Prize Court is bound to administer
the unwritten Law of Nations to the subjects of other
countries. But the classical part of this passage
(which we assume to be the remainder of it) seems
clearly either to be at variance with this decision,
or to have no direct bearing upon the question which
it sets out to answer.

The question is : What is the duty of a Prize Court
—to obey an Order in Council or to disobey it under
circumstances which make it repugnant to the Law
of Nations ?

We are told that a Prize Court is bound to obey
such orders, which constitute the written law of the
Court; and that there is no inconsistency in its being

[1] Cd. 8234.

called upon to administer both the written and the unwritten law, because the orders and instructions of the former " are presumed to conform themselves " to the principles of the latter.

But they are not presumed to do this. The question to be answered specifically presumes the opposite. There would be no question at issue if it did not.

How, too, can the analogy, which is drawn here, of the relationship between the Courts of Common Law and Parliament be held appropriately to illustrate the relationship between Orders in Council and Prize Courts? To point the analogy it must in the first place be assumed that an Act of Parliament does " contradict those approved principles " of natural reason and justice which constitute the unwritten law of the Courts of Common Law; for it is on the supposition that Orders in Council contradict the principles of the law administered by Prize Courts, and on that supposition alone, that this judgment was delivered, or that there was any need for its being delivered.

It is argued—or rather presumed—that the supposition would not be entertained in Courts of Common Law, and that it would be extremely indecent to presume that such an emergency would arise in the Prize Courts. The presumption, nevertheless, is made; and it is scarcely sufficient a reply to America to say that it is indecent to make it.

Further, the analogy does not consider the fundamental difference which distinguishes Prize Courts from Courts of Common Law. Neither Parliament nor the King in Council has jurisdiction over the subjects of a foreign State : the analogy would hold good only if such jurisdiction did exist. A British subject cannot challenge the law of his own country; but the Head of a Foreign State can challenge the British law when applied to his own subjects. The sovereign rights of a State extend only over the subjects of that State, and not over those of another State. The fact that in the opinion of one State it may be indecent to contest this view will not prevent another State from contesting it. America disregarded propriety in the interests of her own citizens, and brought the issue to one as between the Heads of two States on the question of sovereign rights; and with undeniably good reason.

> The officers appear to find their justification in the Orders in Council and regulations of His Majesty's Government, in spite of the fact that in many of the present cases the Orders in Council and the regulations for their enforcement are themselves complained of by claimants as contrary to international law. Yet the very Courts which it is said are to dispense justice to dissatisfied claimants are bound by the Orders in Council.
>
> The principle, the note adds, has recently been announced and adhered to by the British Prize Court in the case of the " Zamora." [1]

Our comments, it must be noted, criticise the reply which the Foreign Office, quoting a famous judge, makes to America on a matter relating to a disputed right in a claim over enemy property; a right through which it was this country's only hope to end the war successfully.

There is another passage—also from the classics—which, though not entirely free from all trace of obscurity in respect of the exact conclusions that may safely be drawn from it, was, nevertheless, accepted

[1] Cd. 8284.

as a model of perspicuity, wisdom and learning. We take the liberty of quoting it :—

" My name's Jack Bunsby ! " (Commander of " Cautious Clara ").

.   .   .   .   .   .

" And what I says," pursued the voice, after some deliberation, " I stands to."

.   .   .   .   .   .

The Captain nodded at the auditory, and seemed to say, " Now he's coming out. This is what I meant when I brought him."

" Whereby," proceeded the voice, " why not ? If so, what odds ? Can any man say otherwise ? No. Awast then ! "

When it had pursued its train of argument to this point, the voice stopped, and rested. It then proceeded very slowly, thus :—

" Do I believe that this here Son and Heir's gone down, my lads ? Mayhap. Do I say so ? Which ? If a skipper stands out by Sen' George's Channel, making for the Downs, what's right ahead of him ? The Goodwins. He isn't forced to run upon the Goodwins, but he may. The bearings of this observation lays in the application on it. That an't no part of my duty. Awast then, keep a bright look-out for'ard, and good luck to you ! "

In this case also the world, though a smaller one, listened with breathless interest, drank deep of the waters of wisdom, and (though there were sceptics) felt much refreshed.

We are convinced that the Commander of the

"Cautious Clara" before being conveyed to Brig Place, where judgment was delivered, had made himself acquainted with the same famous passage that Viscount Grey uses for clinching his argument with the United States of America.

The "Zamora" case stood thus: the "Zamora" (a Swedish ship) was carrying copper, which is contraband of war, from New York to Stockholm. The ship was brought in and her case was made the subject of Prize Court proceedings. Pending the final decision of the Court the President of the Admiralty Prize Court made an order giving permission to the War Office to requisition the copper, which was then in the custody of the Marshal of the Court. The rules of the Prize Court, under which this order was given, derive their authority from Orders in Council. The order was appealed against, and the Lords of the Judicial Committee of the Privy Council decided that there was " no power in the Crown by Order in Council to prescribe or alter the law which the Prize Courts have to administer."

The decision of the Judicial Committee of the Privy Council was given in April, 1916, whereas the reference to the "Zamora" case in the American correspondence is dated 31st July, 1915, at which time Viscount Grey was citing the decision of the President of the Prize Court in support of his argument in ignorance of the impending appeal and the reversal of the decision by the Judicial Committee of the Privy Council.

The importance of the judgment delivered in the appeal in the "Zamora" case can scarcely be exaggerated.

How it should come about that our Prize Courts should have been unaware of the state of the law they were administering, and that it should have been left

for the casual circumstance of the "Zamora" judgment
to give to the Law of Nations the clear and natural
meaning and independent character which only—as
stated in the first part of Lord Stowell's judgment,
quoted by Viscount Grey—it is susceptible of bearing,
is a great mystery. The wrong procedure had apparently been in operation to Germany's advantage from
4th August, 1914, to 7th April, 1916.

But this mystery is only one of a series in which
our Prize Courts were enshrouded. We have made
inquiries as to whether the Judicial Committee of the
Privy Council had any part in the drafting of orders
upon whose validity in international law it might
become their duty to pronounce; or if their views
were elicited as to the probability of the orders
becoming the subject of international dispute; and,
if so, as to the consequences that would be likely to
ensue. We are advised that they were not; they
simply acted as umpires. So, in this curious game that
was being played, it was the umpire only who knew
the rules; and the umpire, apparently, would speak
only when spoken to.

The Reprisals Order, besides provoking the resentment of America, is open to further very serious
criticism.

The order seems to be admittedly illegal, for Mr.
Asquith stated that it was not intended that our
efforts should be " strangled in a network of juridical
niceties "; an expression which, without such illegal
meaning being assigned to it, can have no meaning
whatever.

To the objection that the U.S. " cannot submit to
the curtailment of its neutral rights by these measures,
which are admittedly retaliatory, and therefore
illegal," H.M. Government state :—

But although these measures may have been provoked by the illegal conduct of the enemy, they do not, in reality, conflict with any general principle of international law, of humanity, or civilisation; they are enforced with consideration against neutral countries, and are therefore juridically sound and valid.[1]

It is not easy to understand why these very orthodox and legal measures should be described as retaliatory. No other legal measures have been so described, *e. g.* Orders in Council of 20th August and 29th October, 1914. But it is incomprehensible why measures that were considered to be juridically sound and valid, and that did not conflict with any general principle of international law, should not have been put in force on the outbreak of war.

[1] Cd. 8284.

CHAPTER V

On the outbreak of war America stood aloof for a few months to watch events, and was " not disposed, in view of the unexpected outbreak of hostilities and the necessity of immediate action, to prevent contraband goods from reaching the enemy, to judge this policy harshly or protest against it vigorously."

We are bound to confess that this disposition took strong hold of her in December, when the American Ambassador's first despatch to Viscount Grey was penned; nor was it easily to be shaken off.[1]

The main ground of America's complaint was founded on the alleged serious injury caused by our naval operations to her export trade : the situation was described as pitiful to the commercial interests of the United States and as threatening financial disaster to steamship and insurance companies. Here we find H.M. Government on firm ground.

Viscount Grey, in his reply, quoted such figures as were available in respect of American exports in support of the contention that it was not the action

---

[1] The American Ambassador, the late Mr. Walter H. Page, was as staunch a friend to us during the war as he was loyal a servant to his own country. It has recently been proposed to commemorate his services by a suitable memorial to be erected in the neighbourhood of Westminster. Among the signatories of the memorial appeal, in which Mr. Page is described as " one of the best friends Great Britain ever had," are the present Prime Minister and three of his predecessors.

of H.M. Government in particular, but the existence of a state of war and consequent diminution of purchasing power and shrinkage of trade, that was responsible for adverse effects upon trade with neutral countries.

Here are some of Lord Grey's figures, admittedly incomplete, and not put forward as conclusive :—[1]

	November 1913	November 1914
	Dollars	Dollars
Exports from New York for :—		
Denmark	558,000	7,101,000
Sweden	377,000	2,858,000
Norway	477,000	2,318,000
Italy	2.971,000	4,781,000
Holland	4,389,000	3,960,000

The export of copper up to the end of the first three weeks of December is as follows :—

	1913	1914
Italy	15,202,000 lb.	36,285,000 lb.
Norway Sweden Denmark Switzerland } . . .	7,271,000 ,,	35,347,000 ,,

" With such figures," it is stated, " the presumption is very strong that the bulk of the copper consigned to these countries has recently been intended, not for their own use, but for that of a belligerent who cannot import it direct."

Of a total of 773 ships which had left the U.S. for Holland, Denmark, Norway, Sweden and Italy between the 4th August, 1914, and 3rd January, 1915, only forty-five had been temporarily detained to enable particular consignments of cargo to be discharged for the purpose of Prize Court proceedings, and only eight had been placed in the Prize Court.

[1] Cd. 7816.

It is further shown from an examination of the general statistics for the export of all merchandise that there had been a decline in the export trade of the U.S. before the war, the effect of which had been " not to increase but practically to arrest the decline of American exports which was in progress earlier in the war."

The first paragraph of a circular issued by the Department of Commerce at Washington on 23rd January, 1915, (which is noted by H.M. Government " with great satisfaction ") is then quoted. This circular speaks of the marked improvements in America's foreign trade, the figures for which (in millions of dollars) were as follows :—

August	.	.	.	110
September	.	.	.	156
October	.	.	.	194
November	.	.	.	205
December	.	.	.	246

Further figures show that the total volume of the trade of the United States with Scandinavia and Holland had increased by 300 per cent.

The conclusions that are drawn from an examination of these figures seem to us to be fully convincing. The naval operations of this country were certainly not directed against our own trade with America, yet the exports to Great Britain fell during the first four months of the war to the extent of 28,000,000 dollars; whereas the American exports to neutral countries and Austria increased by over 20,000,000 dollars.

Further figures are given which suggested, as stated by Lord Grey, that a substantial part of the American trade was trade intended for enemy countries going through neutral ports by routes to which it was previously unaccustomed. The only comment made by the United States upon these figures was to point out that their comparative values failed to take into account the increased price of commodities resulting from a state of war, or to make any allowance for the diminution in the volume of trade which the neutral countries in Europe previously had with the nations at war; a diminution which compelled them to buy in other markets.

It must be pointed out here that it was (very properly) on the ground that our operations interfered very seriously indeed with American trade that America challenged the legality of the measures we employed; it was therefore very important that she should herself bring forward figures clearly disproving the facts to which those produced by Lord Grey pointed; or else that it should be shown that by reason of the incompleteness of these figures (which is admitted), or for other reasons, which should be given, the value of Lord Grey's figures was discounted, and the conclusions which he drew from them were erroneous. This is not done; and with regard to the statement of a general vague nature quoted above, it may be said that the diminution in the volume of neutrals' trade owing to the war is an argument which would certainly seem to have force, though it does not necessarily vitiate the results sought, to be indicated: but as to comparative values' failing, as it is stated, to take into account the increased price of commodities resulting from a state of war, we turn to the figures produced by Lord Grey and taken from American official documents showing the fall, in terms of money, of American exports to Great Britain and her Allies, and compare them with the figures showing the rise of exports to neutral countries and Austria.

The figures are as follows :—

TOTAL EXPORTS 1ST AUGUST TO 30TH NOVEMBER (IN THOUSANDS OF DOLLARS)

	1913	1914
Great Britain and Allies .	316,805	288,312
Neutral countries . .	103,401	123,802

(Austria-Hungary is unavoidably included.)

The significant purpose of the figures here was to show the rise in the one case and the fall in the other; and although it is not to a comparison of America's ante-war and war total exports that they are applied, they nevertheless illustrate the fact that it is only in the matter of the degree of magnitude of the results they show, and not in the general conclusions themselves to be drawn from the comparison, that they would be affected by any increase in price of the commodities whose value they represent.

But, turning to the specific case in which objection is taken to this method of drawing comparisons, that is to say to the employment of this method for the purpose of illustrating the effect of the war on the export trade of the U.S., it is permissible, in view of the immense differences shown in the figures referring to America's exports, to doubt whether, even if the increased price of commodities had been taken into consideration, the object of making the comparison would have been destroyed : moreover, we note that the same method is employed by America herself : for her Department of Commerce at Washington—whose statements, by the way, are allowed to pass unreproved by the American Ambassador—in order to indicate a marked improvement in the foreign trade of America, draws comparisons between the monetary values of her exports for the months of November 1913 and 1914, and for the months of December 1912, 1913 and 1914.

America's case in this important matter is not sound. The pitiful situation in which the U.S. found herself is one, we venture to think, for which some other countries would not have been unwilling to exchange places with her.

With regard to the detention of shipping in the search for contraband, it is pointed out that, as against the eight vessels placed temporarily in the Prize Courts (referred to on p. 43), twenty-five neutral vessels had been reported as having been destroyed by mines on the high seas, and that " there was far more reason for protest on the score of belligerent interference with innocent neutral trade through the mines scattered by the enemy than through the British exercise of the right of seizing contra-band."

While Lord Grey had been scrutinising figures dealing with the American export trade, America had turned her attention to the subject of our own trade.

On 3rd June, 1915, the American Ambassador, at the request of the American Consul-General in London, asked for information regarding the amount of raw cocoa and preparations of cocoa exported from Great Britain to Holland, Denmark, Sweden, Norway and Italy during the four months ending 30th April, 1915, as compared with the same period of 1914 and 1913.

The following is from a summary of the figures sent in :—

EXPORTS TO SWEDEN, HOLLAND, DENMARK, NORWAY AND ITALY

Raw Cocoa

	1913	1914
January	260,361 lb.	2,626,687 lb.
February	116,868 ,,	1,628,173 ,,
March	137,423 ,,	4,060,428 ,,
April	415,815 ,,	3,903,633 ,,

The despatch containing this information is dated 16th July, 1915. On 22nd July the following telegram was sent by the British Ambassador at Washington to Lord Grey :—

> Mr. Lansing draws serious attention to increase in export from United Kingdom to Northern European ports since the war which have formed the subject of unfavourable reports from the United States consul-general in London. Germans here are said to make use of these facts to create ill-feeling by circulating allegations that England is preventing American oversea trade with neutral countries in Europe with a view to capture this trade for herself, and that we are ourselves exporting the very goods which we have seized from Americans.[1]

On 13th August Lord Grey called the attention of the American Ambassador to this matter by letter; and statistics were furnished in which a comparison of the American exports with those of the United Kingdom during the first five months of 1915 was shown to be favourable to the United States. The results of this comparison we note with less concern than the extensive trade itself with Scandinavia and Holland, in view of the open knowledge that it was through these countries that Germany got her supplies; that the scale of such supplies, as officially admitted,

[1] Cd. 8233.

was unprecedented; and that the guarantees for preventing the supplies from reaching the enemy, as pointed out on more than one occasion by the author, were worthless. It could hardly be expected that America would look on unconcernedly while such things were taking place, and acquiesce in our claim, on the score of a privileged extension of belligerent rights, to interfere with her own legitimate trade with these countries. Nor can the fact be overlooked that the circumstances which led to these disclosures excluded the possibility of withholding them. We incline to the view that it is not by comparisons that these transactions are to be judged so much, perhaps, as by their morality.

Disregarding the periods covered by the transactions and the figures for the various commodities and dealing only with the question of comparison, we are told that there was in the case of :—

Cotton	.	.	. 6 times an increase of American over British
Lubricating oil	.	5 ,,	,,	,,	,,
Tobacco .	.	. twice	,,	,,	,,
Cocoa	.	nearly 1½ times	,,	,,	,,

Other commodities show similar comparisons favourable to the U.S. trade.

In many cases, we are told, increases in United Kingdom re-exports were due to the fact that the products of British India and colonial products which formerly went direct to continental ports, such as Hamburg, Rotterdam or Copenhagen, were sent to the United Kingdom, and thence distributed to old customers in Scandinavia and the Netherlands. Says Lord Grey :—

Everything in the statistics I have quoted tends to show that the mercantile community

E

of the United States has made profits pro-
portionately equal to or greater than those of the
mercantile community of Great Britain, in respect
to all those demands which have inevitably arisen
in Scandinavia and the Netherlands as a con-
sequence of the closing of German ports.[1]

The closing of the German ports diverted German-
destined goods to neighbouring neutral ports.   The
demands that had arisen in Scandinavia and the
Netherlands   were   to   meet   the   requirements   of
Germany.   While   we   were   endeavouring   to   stop
the American part of this traffic, we learn with some
surprise that the mercantile community of Great
Britain were trading pretty much to the same extent
as America—and to all intents and purposes with
the enemy; for trade with Germany's neighbours
was trade with Germany, as will be made clear in
Part II.

With regard to the goods that passed to Hamburg,
Rotterdam and Copenhagen from the British Empire,
they passed through in peace time.   The alteration
of the route owing to the war may have affected
customs returns and official statistics relating to the
British exports of these goods; but no explanation
is given for the export itself of merchandise to the
dangerous Scandinavian and Dutch areas in war
time; nor can the interests even of old customers in
Scandinavia be held to be paramount over the interests
of the British Empire, which demanded the stoppage
to these States of all supplies that might reach and
benefit our enemy.   How could it be otherwise but
that to the extent that the Scandinavian and Dutch
requirements were satisfied by one country, by so

[1] Cd. 8233.

much the less would they require to be satisfied by another country? To the extent that we supplied these European neutrals with commodities, by so much the less would American supplies be required by them.

Yet while straining the international code in favour of our maritime rights and adversely to American interests, we refrained from adopting the full legislative powers that we possessed over the commerce of this country.

"It is a matter of common knowledge," we are told by America, "that Great Britain exports and re-exports large quantities of merchandise to Norway, Sweden, Denmark and Holland, whose ports, so far as American commerce is concerned, she regards as blockaded."

We draw very particular attention to the following passage in one of the United States despatches :—

> Before passing from the discussion of this contention as to the presumption raised by increased importations to neutral countries, my Government desires to direct attention to the fact that His Majesty's Government admit that the British exports to those countries have also materially increased since the present war began. Thus Great Britain concededly shares in creating a condition which is relied upon as a sufficient ground to justify the interception of American goods destined to neutral European ports.[1]

On what possible ground of equity could presumptions of enemy destination be applied to American cargoes in face of so manifestly inequitable a practice on our part? We were fighting for

[1] Cd. 8234.

presumptions of proof of enemy destination : we had them fully and firmly established by admirable reasoning : they are thrown into hopeless confusion by America's *tu quoque* references to our own trade.[1]

The good-will of this powerful and friendly neutral, which it was most important that we should secure, was not best obtained by asking her to regard us as a neutral in respect of our own trade but as a belligerent in respect of hers.[2]

[1] See also Appendix for extract from a letter on this subject written by the author in December, 1918, to Sir Esme Howard, British Minister at Stockholm.

[2] The following extract is taken from " The Life and Letters of Walter H. Page," by Burton J. Hendrick (Heinemann) :—

"The situation was alarming for more reasons than the determination of Germany to force the peace issue. The State Department was especially irritated at this time (September, 1916) over the blockade. Among the ' trade advisers ' there was a conviction, which all Page's explanations had not destroyed, that Great Britain was using the blockade as a means of destroying American commerce and securing America's customers for herself."

CHAPTER VI

THE methods, challenged by America, by which we sought to obtain presumptive evidence of enemy destination for imposing a contraband character upon cargoes bound for neutral ports was justified by H.M. Government on the ground that new devices for despatching goods to the enemy must be met by new methods of applying the fundamental and acknowledged principle of the right to intercept such trade.

Consignments of meat products, we learn, were addressed to lightermen and dock labourers, to a baker, to the keeper of a small private hotel and to a maker of musical instruments. Several thousands of tons of such goods were documented for a neutral port and addressed to firms which did not exist there. At one time, when it was found necessary to hold up certain cargoes of cotton on their way to Sweden, it was discovered that though the quays and the warehouses of Gottenberg were congested with cotton, there was none available for the use of the spinners in Sweden. Nor did ships' papers convey any suggestion as to the ultimate destination of goods.

The position in which this country found itself during the war was in some respects analogous to that of the United States in the American Civil War. This fact was not lost sight of in the correspondence, and it was brought to bear with considerable force.

Into the able and learned disquisition on the all-important subject of evidence of proof of contraband we have not space to enter. The official despatches show the ability with which our case was maintained in the teeth of very powerful opposition.

In an appendix to the U.S. note of 5th November, 1915, particulars are furnished regarding vessels detained by the British authorities. The length of time during which each vessel was detained is given, and various alleged irregularities are noted. The number of offences committed, that is to say the number of vessels to which reference is made, is about 420. The work that must have been entailed in the drawing up of this record is rewarded with the following notice :—

> These lists are a strong testimony to the vigour and effectiveness with which the naval forces are carrying out the measures which the Allies have deemed it necessary to take against the commerce of their enemies.
>
> Perhaps the most striking conclusion which can be drawn from these lists is the rapidity with which the vessels are released and the very small amount of loss and inconvenience to which they are, as a rule, exposed.[1]

The firm ground on which H.M. Government and the Foreign Office had established themselves is here abandoned : for the matter referred to is clearly one of congratulation for neutrals and the enemy and not for this country; moreover, the release of these ships would seem to show the futility of the vigorous action taken by the Navy.

[1] Cd. 8284.

It was not with London alone that Washington found herself in correspondence on this subject : we imagine that her diplomats were engaged in similar business with Berlin, whence, as is known, came angry protests against America's contraband traffic. It must be remembered that a neutral State is under no obligation to interfere with the contraband traffic of its citizens, who deal in it at their own risk. It was for Germany to prevent the munitions from America from reaching England : the matter was one as between London and Berlin only. America had to bear the weight of Germany's displeasure, and the contraband traffic of her citizens was not calculated to conciliate German prejudices.

If America was a thorn in our side, Germany was a greater thorn in America's side; and America's lot was not an enviable one. This, possibly, may account for what, we cannot but think, was an utter inability on the part of America to see that this war was a conflict between human beings with human passions : she seemed to see in it only a test of rules : before speaking she looked to see what said the book. The old law in its letter obviously could not apply to the conditions of modern warfare; although in its broadly accepted meaning in many cases it could. But this was not to be allowed.

America herself seems to have been a little uncertain as to the justice of the grounds of some of her protests : for instance, in our search for contraband we are told that " mere suspicion is not evidence " [1] on which to justify seizures and detentions of American ships : but at a later date, when it was desired to magnify the concessions enjoyed by a belligerent, we are told : ". . . it is even conceded the right to

[1] Cd. 7816.

detain and take to its own ports for judicial examination all vessels which it suspects for substantial reasons to be engaged in un-neutral or contraband service, and to condemn them if the suspicion is sustained." [1] This, however, is a very slight and perhaps an excusable inconsistency of which there are certainly not many instances.

America was least happy when enacting the *rôle* of self-appointed referee. For instance, when our ships were being sunk wholesale and in open defiance of law; when they were sunk without the required formality of visit and search and of preliminary inquiry being observed; when no quarter was given to innocent passengers, including women and children; and when, moreover, we stood fair to lose the war by these illegal practices, America sees and reviews the matter thus :—

> If the course pursued by the present enemies of Great Britain should prove to be in fact tainted by illegality and disregard of the principles of war sanctioned by enlightened nations, it cannot be supposed, and this Government does not for a moment suppose, that His Majesty's Government would wish the same taint to attach to their own actions, or would cite such illegal acts as in any sense or degree a justification for similar practices on their part in so far as if they can affect neutral rights.[1]

The implied doubt as to the actual fact of Germany's notorious atrocities, and the terms in which the most barbarous acts ever perpetrated by a

[1] Cd. 8233.

so-called civilised nation are referred to as possibly being " tainted with illegality," can hardly be expected to be viewed by those against whom Germany's acts were directed with the same cold philosophy and serene detachment that characterised the unimpassioned utterances of America.

We cannot but regretfully reflect upon what would have been the attitude of the late Mr. Roosevelt towards these German outrages; for neutral shipping was being sunk as well as British.

The passage we have quoted was, we suppose, technically correct : nevertheless we regard it as furnishing an infelicitous example of a set determination on the part of America to identify herself only with a conception of the written letter of the law; a conception limited to the circumstances contemplated by the law at the time that it was written. There seems to have been an inability to realise that where right is transparently being abused it must so continue to be abused but for interference from human agencies; for laws cannot alter themselves. Neither Law of Nations nor convention ever sanctioned, nor was ever intended to sanction, the taking of innocent life; nor did they ever contemplate that their literal meaning should be held to condone the violation of their unwritten implied principles. None will dispute this; nor will the facts of the outrages themselves be disputed. But the spirit of the law found but little human championship at White House, whose uncompromising and stubborn attitude in one or two instances seemed incapable of yielding to any form of reason.

Although the British operations were proved not to have acted injuriously upon the normal American export trade, that is far from saying that they did not prevent an abnormal increase in trade due to the abnormal requirements of Germany.

Both in America and in some of the northern European countries huge fortunes were amassed during the war; it was the amassing of this wealth that evoked the determined opposition to anything that stood in the way of its attainment. This is not said in disparagement of the motives for this opposition; for such motives are common to all nations : nor would such a suggestion have any meaning; for if there were no neutral interests affected, there would be no necessity for neutral opposition; and, moreover, it is for no other purpose than the protection of neutral trade and neutral interests that international maritime law exists. No matter what measures might have been adopted to prevent contraband from reaching Germany, it was to have been expected that they would be met with the full force and weight of international law; for the stoppage of contraband was the stoppage of a goodly part of neutral commerce. Official opposition was directed against method : it had to be; but behind it was the thing itself—the delivery of the goods. The neutral wished to get his goods to market; and if a belligerent prevented him from doing so, it would be in the prevention itself and not in the method by which it was brought about that the germ of objection would lie. Such at least is our view, though H.M. Government thought differently :—

> The wording of this summary suggests that the basis of the complaint of the United States Government is not so much that the shipments intercepted by the naval forces were really intended for use in the neutral countries to

which they were despatched, as that the despatch of goods to the enemy countries has been frustrated by methods which have not been employed by belligerent nations in the past.[1]

The summary referred to is the following :—

> I believe it has been conclusively shown that the methods sought to be employed by Great Britain to obtain and use evidence of enemy destination of cargoes bound for neutral ports and to impose a contraband character upon such cargoes are without justification; that the blockade, upon which such methods are partly founded, is ineffective, illegal and indefensible; that the judicial procedure offered as a means of reparation for an international injury is inherently defective for the purpose; and that in many cases jurisdiction is asserted in violation of the law of nations.[1]

Up to this point in the debate honours may be said to have been easy. The consummate skill with which thrusts have been dealt and parried by both sides must compel admiration. But the debate, like our blockade, had its " novel and unprecedented features." Lord Grey had brought his figures to bear with irresistible force on the subject of America's export trade, but America adopted the plan of severely ignoring them, and, moreover, produced four pages of ships, each ship with its offence, date and place shortly recorded. H.M. Government, who enter the lists at this stage, treat the ships much on the lines of the American plan, but greatly improved; for the ships are made to speak up for

[1] Cd. 8234.

ourselves : and the valuable midnight oil has been burned in vain. We were lost in amazement at the masterly ingenuity of this stroke, for the sight of this formidable fleet had filled us with misgivings.

But now America, who has already been badly shaken over the Bunsby episode, receives a thrust for which, as far as we are aware, there is no known defence.

The paragraph quoted above shows that the American summary had evidently been very carefully examined by H.M. Government, who could make neither head nor tail of it. It suffers from the bad defect of vagueness; a weakness (very noticeable in the American utterances) which H.M. Government are not slow to detect. But they are disposed to show a friendly disposition towards America : they do not contradict, nor are they rude : they simply tell America that they understand her complaint to be something quite different from what America herself understands it to be, and what, to the best of her ability, she states it to be; and that they are going to argue on this understanding.

It must not be supposed that this correspondence contains many oversights due to the haste with which it was conducted : the present reply of H.M. Government, 24th April, 1916, referred to an American despatch of 5th November, 1915. In any case, even if America had chosen to cable back a message, she must have seen the utter futility of such a proceeding; and, indeed, the futility of any measure which could possibly prevent H.M. Government from placing its own construction upon anything America might choose to say. America had got her neck fairly into a noose, and had no more chance of getting it out than she had of avoiding getting it in. In this

diplomatic battle, as in maritime law, we searched for
" principles " : and here was one worth the finding.
Possibly this discovery may have caused America to
resign, for no further despatches are published.

Two or three facts which emerge from the American
correspondence will, it is thought, be generally
admitted. America's objections to the Reprisals
Order are, in the first place, most difficult to refute.
Her contention that our naval operations were
destroying her export trade is disproved outright by
figures; but her implied charges against our own
trade are unfortunately only too well founded.

On this subject we invite the reader's careful
attention to what has been said in our introductory
chapter, where it will be found that maritime rights
refer exclusively to trade, and concern the rules for
its control in time of war.

Let him then approach the correspondence with
America and note this : that the stoppage of oversea
supplies to Germany (*i. e.* to Scandinavia and Holland) was imperatively demanded by our national
safety; that it was on this ground alone that H.M.
Government debated with America to the extreme
allowable limits of diplomacy the strict rules relating
to the rights of belligerents; and that in doing so
they made the fullest acknowledgment that it was
only in the economic reduction of Germany that there
lay any hope of defeating her. Let him particularly
take note that it was not on the stoppage of American
trade only, but on that of all trade, that our national
safety depended; and that the attention of H.M.
Government is called to this significant fact by
America.

Let him put himself in America's place and, regarding the origin of belligerent rights as concessions to a

belligerent at the expense of a neutral solely to enable him to injure his enemy, he may well question the soundness, or even the justice, of the law, which places the belligerent under no legal obligation to apply its principles to himself.

The question of our own trade with the Scandinavian neutrals did not form the subject of debate in the Houses of Parliament on any single occasion, either in respect of its benefit to Germany directly or indirectly, or with regard to its bargaining power. Discussion focussed on the subject of others' property, not of ours. Those who pointed to America as the obstacle in the way of our blockade of Germany cannot have been aware of the intense feeling of resentment against this country that was aroused in America by the magnitude of our trading transactions, and that it was herein that lay the origin of America's stubborn opposition.

American feeling generally was, we believe, strongly sympathetic towards us and towards the Allied cause. There was, it is true, a section of the population of America which was pro-German; but that section was not representative of America : its pro-German sympathies were partly the direct outcome of the work of German agents, who abounded in the country; they were partly spontaneous sympathies. The offers from important firms of American exporters on the outbreak of war testify in a practical way to the real regard in which we were held. A mutual respect between Great Britain and America has existed since the time when the United States ceased to be a British colony : it is a respect which has sprung from an honesty of purpose and from the straightforward dealing which has always characterised the transactions between the two countries.

But it was with official America that we had to deal during the war; with the America that was neutral, not only to Great Britain and her Allies, but to Germany and her Allies. Washington could not identify herself with the views either of the one or the other of the belligerents. We imagine that in the correspondence that passed between Berlin and Washington German views on international maritime law are reflected in some of the protests that reached London from Washington. It may be taken for granted that there was no single action of Germany's that escaped the notice of America. America well knew what were Germany's ambitions, what her methods — that they were tainted with illegality, but that it could not be said so by America—and what were the momentous consequences involved in her own future were Germany to realize her aspirations, and obtain dominion over Europe and the waters of the Atlantic. Her own fortunes were closely identified with the fortunes of this country : and nothing short of wanton disregard of her national susceptibilities or her sovereign rights could have caused her to withhold in her own interests all support, moral and material, that her neutrality would legitimately allow. The official despatches are firm and in parts curt in tone : but they are marked throughout on both sides by a fine courtesy and frankness of expression, and with a punctilious regard for the traditional amenities of diplomatic discussion, well calculated to soften the asperities of bitter controversy : contentious debate was conducted on the common ground of friendship. The arrogant conduct of Germany towards America is too well known to need recapitulation here. Both from the German embassy at

Washington and from Berlin came blunder after blunder, both in phrase and in the exercise of the faculty of discernment : disillusionment came to Germany too late. America was moved neither by veiled threat nor open taunt from her stiff attitude of neutrality, except on one occasion, in April 1917, which Germany has good cause to remember. We will say this for Germany : her inordinate desire for new enemies seemed to have amounted to a positive passion. Having exhausted all the possibilities of Europe, she turned her eyes westwards. The importunity with which she pressed her right to a prior claim on America's services — a claim which was finally acknowledged—would alone, it might be thought, have rendered abortive any similar claim we might ourselves have preferred, had we wished to do so. That the friendly relations between Germany and America were continuously in a highly attenuated state admits of no question : the risk of a rupture was an ever-present reality; and the circumstances of the war did not favour the supposition that this risk could at the same time be held to exist in the relationship between America and Great Britain. Such a supposition is belied by America's own national interests, by her private interests, by traditional friendship, and by the part that America took later on in the war.

That America in April, 1917, took up arms against Germany is true; but " is the noble Earl quite sure that the U.S. would be on our side at this moment if we had outraged her feelings at the beginning of the war by treating her in an inconsiderate or cavalier manner ? " [1]

Thus the Marquess of Lansdowne on 4th July,

[1] Parliamentary Debates, No. 53, p. 789.

1917. Of this we cannot be sure, but had the Gordian knot of trade been cut on the outbreak of war there would, we submit, have been neither time, opportunity nor above all cause for America's displeasure to foment : for Germany's neutral neighbours could not support themselves without the resources of the British Empire; much less could they have rendered assistance to Germany.

That America did not view with marked favour our methods of conducting naval warfare we are ready to admit after reading what she said : nor does an analysis of the methods we employed give any special reason for surprise that this should be so; but that technical matters alone of international law were the cause of friction with America, and that America stood in the way of our stopping supplies from reaching Germany cannot be accepted as a correct presentment of the case. By the exercise of maritime rights we could and we did stop a certain proportion of Germany's supplies : with America's good-will we could have stopped a larger proportion; but we also held a very powerful weapon in our hands which international law could not touch, a weapon more potent than the fleet, though useless without it; this was the weapon of economic advantage.

Some particulars of the traffic that clogged the broad open neutral highway leading into German territory during the first years of the war before full use was made of our economic weapon, which finally brought such disastrous results to Germany, will be found in Part II.

F

PART II

TRADING WITH THE ENEMY

"I hope I may be pardoned if these Discoveries inclined me a little to abate of that profound Veneration which I am naturally apt to pay to Persons of high Rank, who ought to be treated with the utmost Respect due to their sublime Dignity, by us their Inferiors."

SWIFT.

PART II

TRADING WITH THE ENEMY

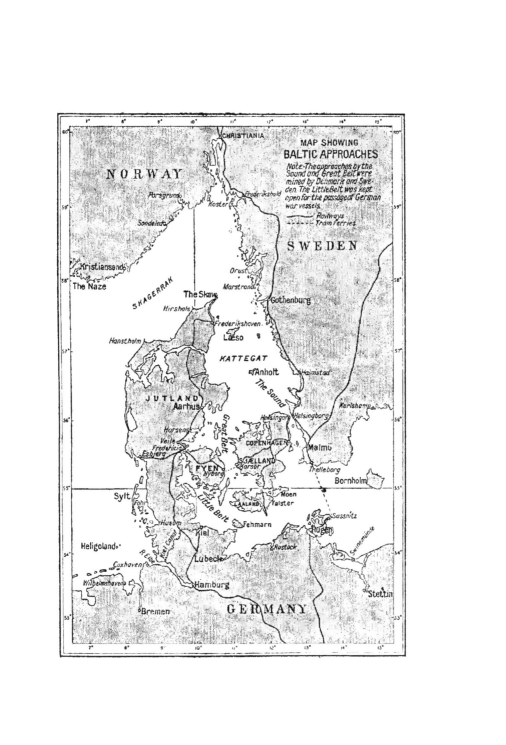

MAP SHOWING
BALTIC APPROACHES

Note.-The approaches by the
Sound and Great Belt were
mined by Denmark and Swe-
den. The Little Belt was kept
open for the passage of German
war vessels.

—————— Railways
- - - - - Train Ferries

CHRISTIANIA

NORWAY

Porsgrund

Koster

Frederikshald

Sondeled

SWEDEN

Kristiansand

The Naze

SKAGERRAK

The Skaw

Hirshals

Hanstholm

Orust

Marstrand

Frederikshaven

Læso

Gothenburg

KATTEGAT

Anholt

Halmstad

JUTLAND

Aarhus

The Sound

Horsens

Helsingor Helsingborg

Karlshamn

Veile

Fredericia

Esbjerg

Great Belt

COPENHAGEN

SJÆLLAND

Malmö

Sylt

Fohr

FYEN

Nyborg

Korsor

Trelleborg

Bornholm

Little Belt

AALAND

Moen

Falster

Husum

Fehmarn

Sassnitz

Heligoland

Kiel Canal

Kiel

Rugen

Swinemünde

Cuxhaven

R.Eider

Rostock

Wilhelmshaven

Lubeck

Stettin

Bremen

Hamburg

GERMANY

CHAPTER I

SCANDINAVIANS were not slow to discover that the reality of war could be faced with far greater composure than the prospect.

Candles and other illuminants, fuel and foodstuffs, had been hastily acquired to meet a shortage, especially in coal, anticipated from the impending naval operations of Great Britain: but when war broke out coal and merchandise poured into Scandinavia in greater quantities than ever before, and the energies of all concerned were directed to the work of handling the cargoes that came crowding in on to the wharves of Copenhagen, Gottenberg, Christiania and other ports, loading them on to German trucks and receiving payment. The slight assistance that Great Britain was able to offer in the way of supplies of coal for hauling the trucks to and from Germany was greatly appreciated, particularly by the Germans.

The Scandinavian countries, Norway, Sweden and Denmark, during the war were technically neutral, and formed bases of supplies for Germany. Denmark is in direct territorial communication with Germany, and although Sweden is cut off from Denmark by a narrow strip of water, communication is maintained by train-ferry services, thus virtually completing the direct connection between Germany and the three Scandinavian States.

No difficulties stood in the way of the transport of goods from Scandinavia to Germany. Local steamers plied to and fro in the Baltic for many months with immunity from risk, but the operations of British submarines later on in the war stopped during a short period the contraband traffic in these waters.

Having seen what powers were possessed and acquired to prevent goods from reaching the Scandinavian ports and Germany from oversea, we turn now to other means possessed by Great Britain and the Allies of controlling the oversea traffic to Scandinavia and restraining the Scandinavian States from disposing of their goods to Germany.

Scandinavia, whence Germany obtained the bulk of her supplies, depended for her own economic and industrial existence upon oversea importations, over the British and Allied portions of which we had full control, and part control over the remainder.

The chief objections to an embargo on all British exports on the outbreak of war were the moral obligation, under appropriate safeguards, to continue a trading relationship with friendly States, and the obvious advantage of trade to ourselves. But there was also the question of expediency. Here both economic and political considerations are involved. An embargo on British exports might be met with counter measures of a similar character. How would the Allies stand if such measures were put in force by Scandinavia? Could they have carried on the war with any good prospects of success? The counter measures raise a counter question: How would Germany stand as to her prospects of success with only the existing resources of Scandinavia upon which to draw, supplemented by such others as could be obtained from oversea in face of the determined efforts of Great Britain to stop them? On whose side would the economic advantage remain in an economic struggle between Great Britain and her Allies and Scandinavia? It will be seen that the advantage was immeasurably in favour of Great Britain.

As to the political expediency of imposing an embargo, if the resentment that would undoubtedly have been provoked throughout the Scandinavian States by such measures were the only evil to be reckoned with, then we should have had to endeavour to support the weight of Scandinavian displeasure. But there was more. There were two main political questions to be considered. How would the course of the war be affected if Sweden joined our enemies or if Germany were to occupy Denmark?

A consideration of the possible political consequences to which the adoption of drastic measures, however lawful in themselves, might expose us, leads to the conclusion that Germany would inevitably have been the loser from any change of the *status quo* in Scandinavia. This assumption is made in the succeeding chapters when discussing many of the transactions that are there recorded.

One of the chief difficulties with which H.M. Government had to contend in their lawful control over sea-borne goods was to distinguish between *bonâ fide* neutral trade and trade carried on with the enemy. The exercise of belligerent rights bore with considerable severity upon genuine neutral trade. Neutral importers were glad, therefore, in exchange for the certain and expeditious delivery of their goods, to give guarantees that the latter should not reach or benefit the enemy. Such agreements were made with representative associations of merchants, and certain classes of goods were protected by the guarantee of neutral Governments that they should not be re-exported. Since, however, neutral Governments reserved to themselves the right to grant exemptions from such prohibitions, the prohibitions themselves were of very little value.

Examples of the abuses to which guarantees were exposed are given particularly in the case of the Danish traffic with Germany, which, after coal, ranks first in importance among the commodities, British, Allied and neutral, that have been selected to illustrate the effect of our trade policy and administration during the first two and a half years of the war.

The figures for the year 1917 in the Scandinavian statistics [1] are the best testimony to the power of our unarmed forces after they had been placed in harness.

[1] See Appendix.

CHAPTER II

DENMARK is an agricultural country, and many years ago her agricultural industry was organised for the supply of her own needs. She is one of the few countries in Europe that can be made self-supporting.

With the growth of Great Britain's requirements for butter, bacon, eggs and dairy produce in general the Danish agricultural system was re-adjusted and the land so developed as to meet Great Britain's needs. A great industry was thus built up, based almost entirely upon British markets. In order to satisfy Great Britain's requirements, it was necessary, the soil of Denmark being of an indifferent quality, to import immense quantities of fertilisers for the soil, and fodder and cake for the stock. In addition, the land, which in former times had been used for growing wheat for domestic consumption, was now used for pasturage and for growing maize, oats and rye for feeding cattle : it therefore became necessary to import large quantities of foodstuffs to make up the deficiency. Thus there was created an entirely artificial state of affairs, whereby the over-stocked land became entirely dependent upon oversea supplies; and the country, instead of growing its own food, became largely dependent, especially for farinaceous foods, upon imports from oversea. Were these imports to have been stopped, then the land allotted to the live-stock which the imports maintained would, after the live-stock had been disposed of, be available for growing the natural foods required by the people. Denmark, therefore, in time of stress had nothing to fear from threat of starvation—she could always manage to exist. Other countries could not, and Denmark was singularly favoured in this respect.

Of the Danish produce exported, the quantity taken by Great Britain before the war was about 60 per cent.; Germany took about 25 per cent., and other countries the remaining 15 per cent. Looking at the question of the disposal of Denmark's produce during the war from the broad point of view as to what was fair to Great Britain and equally fair to Denmark, it was only just to Denmark that her trade should not suffer from the vicissitudes of war; it was also just from the point of view of Great Britain and Germany that Denmark should not favour the one at the expense of the other; and, if she did so, that she should be subjected to all lawful pressure from the country that suffered.

With regard to Denmark's trade, it never flourished so much as during the first two years of the war. In the matter of trade, therefore, Denmark had done more than full justice to herself. In the matter of the distribution of her produce, the figures 60 per cent. and 25 per cent. for Great Britain and Germany suffered a very rapid and significant change. The state of affairs will best be understood from the following table, which shows the number of tons of food lost by England and gained by Germany from Denmark during the years 1915, 1916 and 1917 as compared with 1913.

	Lost by England	Gained by Germany
1915 . . .	59,356	150,854
1916 . .	100,654	190,781
1917 . . .	154,331	73,360
Total . .	314,341	414,995

It must be noted that not only was Germany favoured in the matter of the percentage of the produce of Denmark, but also in the matter of the absolute quantities to which the percentage applied, and which, during the war, were very much in excess of those prior to the war.

Thus it came about that Great Britain, who commanded the avenues of approach to Scandinavia, who possessed the largest mercantile fleet for carrying purposes in the world, who had acquired also the control of the greater part of the Norwegian shipping, and whose home and colonial possessions, together with those of her Allies, contained stocks of goods indispensable to Scandinavia, should find these resources insufficient to attain any result better than that shown in the above table.

Denmark's fishing industry was unimportant to Great Britain as compared with Norway's. From Norway we took about 50,000 tons of fish a year before the war, whereas Denmark sent us only some 4,000 to 5,000 tons. Denmark's best customer was Germany, who took about 25,000 tons of fish a year. Fish constituted a very important item of food in the restricted German diet, and as its value to Great Britain was comparatively slight, it was an industry that she could afford to " kill " without the fear of bringing any evil consequences upon herself.

The lines upon which the Danish fishing industry was conducted resembled closely those of the agricultural industry. The bulk of Denmark's fish went to Germany, Great Britain supplying the fishing materials, which in this case corresponded to the fodder and fertilisers that she supplied for agricultural purposes.

Danish shipping worked mainly in Germany's

interest during the war.   In 1914 Denmark possessed a mercantile fleet of 750,000 tons gross, and although prolonged negotiations took place to press Danish shipping into the Allied service, they were not successful.

The principal shipping company in Denmark was the East Asiatic.   It was this company's ships that made the long journeys, and brought over the fodder and fertilisers, and the oil beans from the Far East. It is noteworthy that not one of the ships of this company was sunk by a submarine throughout the war.   In 1916, in spite of the dangers of the sea, the East Asiatic Company was able to pay a dividend of 30 per cent.

. Denmark's principal exports to Great Britain were agricultural produce and a mineral known as cryolite, which is used in the manufacture of aluminium for Zeppelins.

During the years 1915, 1916 and 1917 about 22,000 tons of cryolite reached Denmark from Greenland, British coal, it is almost needless to say, being used for its transport.   After being refined in Denmark—a simple process which could have been carried out quite well in England—the bulk of the cryolite was exported as follows :—

EXPORT OF CRYOLITE FROM DENMARK

Years 1915, 1916 and 1917

Germany	7,000 tons
France	4,200 ,,
England	3,700 ,,

In addition to the above, Sweden received a considerable amount (the quantity is not known : probably about 2,500 tons), the bulk of which was undoubtedly used for the benefit of our enemies.

Very little pressure would have compelled Denmark to forgo this traffic altogether, when the whole amount could have been brought to England for distribution as we thought best.

Although we were not dependent upon Denmark for agricultural produce, Denmark was dependent upon oversea supplies from the Allies and neutrals for coal, cereals, fodder and fertilisers, animal and vegetable oils and fats, petroleum for lighting and power, fishing gear, cotton and cotton piece goods, wool and woollen goods, copper, tin, tanning materials, rubber, binder-twine (for harvesting) and groceries of all sorts.

Germany sent Denmark potash manures, steel for shipbuilding, steel rails, wheels and axles, coke, dyes, chemicals and medicines.

SWEDEN

Sweden is a forest and mining country. Unlike Denmark, she was not self-supporting, but depended to a large extent upon supplies from oversea; she obtained very little from Russia. Her chief industries are the production of paper, cellulose and timber, and the mining of iron ore. Her fishing industry is much on the same scale as Denmark's : agriculture is on a much smaller scale.

Sweden's greatest asset was her iron ore.

Ludendorff speaks of the " paramount importance " of the iron ore from Sweden, and says, " Had England won such a battle " (meaning a naval victory) " she would have made it almost impossible for us to import iron ore from Sweden and the submarine warfare could never have assumed proportions so dangerous to herself."

The high-grade steel used, among many other purposes, in the construction of submarines, came in large quantities from Sweden. When war broke out Germany was deprived of her supplies of Spanish and French ores. The Spanish ores run very high in iron, and their loss was a serious blow to Germany. This loss was made good by the Swedish imports, which increased at once in 1915.

Germany took from 4,000,000 to 5,000,000 tons a year of iron ore from Sweden; this represents a quantity of metal for which a far larger quantity of ore in Germany would have had to be mined, varying with the rates of the German to the Swedish percentage of iron contained. Germany, to obtain the equivalent value of Sweden's ore, would have had to employ two or three times the number of men employed by Sweden : hence the value of Sweden to Germany.

The haulage of the ore from the mines to the coast was carried out to a large extent by the Swedish railways with British coal; its further transport by steamer across the Baltic was also (certainly for the two first years) effected by British coal.

Nothing would have hastened the end of the war more effectively than the sinking of ships trading in ore between Sweden and Germany in the Baltic, or by economic pressure brought to bear on the Swedish ore industry.

The greater the importance of any commodity to Germany, the less importance it would be made to assume through the subtle German propaganda agencies, which formed one of the most insidious and effective weapons in her armoury. This is particularly well illustrated in the case of her shortage of iron ore. When, at the beginning of 1918, negotiations were on foot for the restriction of Swedish ore to

3,000,000 tons per annum, it came to the knowledge of **H.M.** Government, " on good authority," that Germany held sufficient to meet her requirements for two years. The German refusal to entertain the Swedish proposal under pressure from Great Britain was on this account set down as a matter of prestige, and the point was waived by us. I had myself also received information to the same effect, and, it is more than probable, from the same authority as **H.M.** Government. It came from a patriotic Swede, who was himself financially interested in the export of iron ore to Germany, and whose business it was to represent Germany's stock of iron ore as very large and Swedish importations as of but little account. I had previously formed the opposite view, a view which was confirmed in a very unexpected and wonderful manner a few weeks later, full particulars being sent to **H.M.** Government. At that time not only was the Swedish ore of great importance, so far as it concerned the German steel industry, on account of the high quality of the ore and the furnace arrangements in Germany, but it was intimately connected with the question of man-power, than which nothing was of greater importance to Germany in the later stages of the war.

In the southern part of Sweden there is an extensive tract of land which is given up to agriculture. Although short of foodstuffs, Sweden exported meat and other foodstuffs to Germany, her agricultural system being framed for the purpose of the export of butter, meat, bacon and pork which it produced.

By suitable pressure Sweden could have been compelled to adjust her agricultural system during the war to meet the food requirements of the country, thus saving valuable shipping space allocated to the

G

use of imported cereals and other foodstuffs, throwing Sweden more on her own resources and reducing the quantity of food available for export to Germany.

The following table shows the export of food from Sweden to the United Kingdom and Germany and Austria during the years 1913–1917 : this table includes cattle, fish, pork and bacon, meat, milk, cheese, butter and eggs :—

	To U.K.	To Germany and Austria.
1913	26,567 tons	37,043 tons
1914	28,526 ,,	56,685 ,,
1915	8,563 ,,	104,203 ,,
1916	115 ,,	90,835 ,,
1917	—	16,451 ,,

The subject of fish is dealt with fully in Chapter VI. Before the war the United Kingdom took some 5,000 tons of fish yearly from Sweden. In 1914 this quantity dwindled down to 1,950 tons and then to nothing. Germany's supplies from Sweden were as follows :—

1913	30,000 tons
1914	43,000 ,,
1915	53,000 ,,
1916	51,000 ,,

In respect of Sweden's agricultural produce and foodstuffs, which depended upon oversea imports, it is seen that the pre-war percentages were not maintained ; supplies to the United Kingdom virtually ceased, whereas Germany received, not only the balance, but a largely increased quantity of foodstuffs ; for Sweden's total supplies to Great Britain and Germany in 1913 was (roughly) 63,000 tons, but in 1915 this total was 112,000 tons.

His Majesty's Government were advised that Sweden was practically independent of wheat supplies from oversea. As against this view, however, there was very good evidence from other quarters to the opposite effect.

When war broke out there were in the Baltic some sixty-five Àllied vessels, mainly British, of about 150,000 tons gross. At that time the scarcity of shipping was not felt and the necessity for clearing this tonnage was not realized. The ships were therefore laid up for the time. Presently, however, shipping space had become very valuable, and it was desired to free the tonnage laid up in the Baltic. Although the entrance to the Baltic had been mined, there was a small passage known as the Kogrund Pass on the S.W. coast of Sweden through which this shipping could have been navigated with safety. To prevent it from leaving the Baltic the Kogrund Pass was mined, presumably by order of Germany, though the point is immaterial. So pressing had become the demand for shipping that Sweden was unable to maintain her imports in sufficient quantity to enable her to supply Germany's requirements; and so urgent had these requirements become that about 450,000 tons of Scandinavian tonnage was engaged in bringing supplies from America and elsewhere to Scandinavia *free from German attack.*

At this time Germany was staking her chances of victory entirely upon the depletion of shipping. She was sinking ships at sight, whether passenger, cargo or hospital ships : she was running imminent risk of adding America to the number of her enemies : she had induced Sweden to commit the almost hostile act of mining her territorial waters, that Allied shipping might not be released; no consideration, therefore, short of necessity would, it may be assumed, have induced her to agree to the release of this Baltic shipping. Nevertheless the Baltic shipping was released in exchange for about 85,000 tons of wheat, which just sufficed to enable the Swedish industrial machine to struggle on and saved the State from being compelled to accept almost any terms that the Allied Powers cared to impose.

Mr. Dahlberg, the Swedish Minister for Agriculture, in a public speech delivered in September, 1917, referred to the serious position with regard to food-stuffs, aggravated by the lack of fuel and illuminants. He advised his audience to indulge in no illusions as to the impending food situation. During the next twelve months, said Mr. Dahlberg, Sweden could not reckon on more than 50 per cent. of bread corn or 40 per cent. of fodder actually needed. If it should prove that cereal supplies upon which the authorities were counting were withheld, the position was such that Sweden might regard herself as lost.

This ingenuous confession was extorted from Mr. Dahlberg by the necessity of having to stimulate the farmers to the production of cereals for home con-sumption instead of other foodstuffs for German export. It was in violent contrast to the beliefs held by the British Minister and H.M. Government and so carefully fostered by Sweden to buttress the counterfeit foundations upon which they rested.

Being wrongly informed of the economic situation of Sweden, we bribed her with food to obtain our ship-ping. Our shipping could and should have been released with the bare knowledge alone of Sweden's situation : with this knowledge and with our power there was nothing in reason in addition to the ship-ping that could not have been extorted from the country.

In addition to food Sweden supplied Germany with munitions, iron ore, sawn timber, zinc, steel wire, machinery, electric motors, and many important metals : probably also with torpedoes and torpedo air cylinders.

Sweden's mercantile fleet in 1914 amounted to about 1,000,000 tons gross : of this, only one or two ships were pressed into the Allied service.

Among the most important of Sweden's requirements from the Allies and neutrals were :—

Coal, cereals, lubricants, petroleum, fodder and fertilisers, cotton and woollen goods, animal and vegetable oils and fats, copper, lead, tin, tanning materials, bleaching powder, jute, rubber and groceries.

Germany sent Sweden potash manures, iron and steel for building purposes, steel rails, wheels and axles, conduit pipes (for conveying water under pressure), coke, electrical machinery, dyes, chemicals and medicines.

Sweden's principal exports to Great Britain were timber, pit-props and wood goods, paper and wood pulp, iron and steel (including tool steel) and ball-bearings, ferro-silicon and butter.

Regarding the economic balance as between Great Britain and the Allies and Sweden, Great Britain was very favourably placed. Sweden possessed no single commodity deprived of which Great Britain would suffer more than inconvenience. During the war, when the Swedish supplies of pit-props and paper fell short, the deficiencies were made good either at home or from the resources of the Empire or from neutral sources. This was also the case with steel and ball bearings. Sweden had nothing that was vital to the Allies, whereas, in addition to coal, Great Britain's large control over the raw materials for agricultural purposes was a source of great power.

NORWAY

Fish, wood and the production of cellulose and paper are Norway's principal industries. Like Sweden, she is a forest country, and, in the south, part of her soil is appropriated for the purpose of agriculture for export : hence fodder, fertilisers and cereals are among her principal imports from oversea.

The Norwegian fish industry is one of the largest in the world. It comprises the two separate operations of canning and exporting as fresh, dried or canned. The cans in which fish are packed are of tin, and the preservative used is either olive oil or tomato pulp. Hence tin, olive oil and tomato pulp play a very important part in Norway's economic life, and it was to Great Britain that Norway looked as the main guarantor of these and other requisites for her fishing industry. Her export trade in fish was dependent almost entirely upon coal, with which also we supplied her; the coal being used to boil down the fish for the extraction of the oil. In South Georgia and South Shetland (in the South Atlantic) are situated the bases of the most valuable whale fisheries in the world. These fisheries belong to Great Britain, but in nearly all cases the fishing concessions are held by Norwegians at our pleasure.

The Norwegians are a seafaring nation whose interests are closely identified with those of Great Britain. The gross tonnage of Norway's merchant shipping in 1914 was 2,400,000 tons, or a ton per head of population : no other nation has so relatively large a merchant fleet. With this vast amount of tonnage on the waters it was in the interests of Norway to fall in with the views of the nation in command of the seas : national interests and traditional friendship—the coastal population of Norway was pro-British almost to a man—both favoured a sympathetic attitude to British shipping policy, and H.M. Government were successful in obtaining control of practically the whole of the Norwegian shipping, the only notable exception being the Norwegian-American line, which was under Government subsidy; there was, however, an agreement with H.M. Government with regard to this line.

In addition to our success in the shipping policy, two important agreements were made with Norway respecting fish and copper, by which the supplies to Germany were greatly restricted.

Germany benefited from Norway's foodstuffs : she also obtained minerals on a modest scale, copper pyrites and nickel being the most important. Smuggling was checked, though not prevented; nor would it have been possible entirely to defeat the ends of the army of German agents that infested the country.

Although our economic policy did not reach the standard of idealism and did not, and could not, prevent the leakage of important supplies, yet it enabled Great Britain and the Allies to reap far greater benefit from Norway's resources than did Germany.

From the Allies and neutrals Norway imported as her principal items :—

Coal, cereals, fodder and fertilisers, animal and vegetable oils and fats, petroleum, tin, fishing gear, cotton, wool, rubber, electrolytic copper, salt and groceries.

From Germany she took much the same as did Sweden.

Her principal exports consisted of fish and fish oil, timber, pit-props and wood goods, paper and wood pulp, ferro-silicon, calcium carbide and cyanamide : and nitrates.

The whole of Scandinavia contained but one article of vital importance : this was the nitrates of Norway, on the supply of which the French at one time depended for 90 per cent. of their ammunition. These nitrates gave Norway a very powerful economic advantage, which, had she been sympathetic to the German cause, would have proved an exceedingly formidable obstacle in the way of successful negotiations.

As in the case of Sweden and Denmark, so also did Norway depend for her industrial existence largely upon British coal, of which she took from 2,500,000 to 3,000,000 tons a year.

In Copenhagen the German was at home, in Stockholm he was not comfortable, but in Christiania he was out of his element.

It will be conceded that the British Empire possessed very real and very great economic advantages over Scandinavia, and through Scandinavia over Germany.

The ideal policy was to keep all commodities of whatever description, but particularly foodstuffs, out of Germany. Failing this, the next best thing to do was, if commodities had to go into Germany, to see that as far as possible it was as component parts, and not as finished articles, that Germany received them, so that Germany should have to expend labour, *i. e.* man-power, of which she was so short, and land in producing the article required.

In addition to economic, Scandinavia possessed important strategic assets in her command of the entrance to the Baltic. The Baltic enabled Germany to import war material and foodstuffs from Sweden, for which the train-ferry services were inadequate. Sea transport in the Baltic was a very present help and relief to the congested Scandinavian and German transport systems. The Baltic forms a water route to Russian ports and provides a direct means of keeping open communication with Russia : from these advantages we were cut off. It is approached by three possible channels, known as the Sound, the Great Belt and the Little Belt. Of these, the Great Belt forms the main channel for heavy draught vessels, and was the only one of the three navigable to our fleet. During the Russo-Japanese War, the Russian fleet under Admiral Rahsjàstvensky, and, later, Admiral Nebogàhtoff's squadron, were not only allowed free passage by Denmark through the Great Belt, but the services of a Danish pilot were placed at the Russian Admirals' disposal : in 1854 the British fleet also passed through under Sir Charles Napier.

Denmark's first act in August, 1914, was, under pressure from Germany, to mine and block this channel to all traffic and to undertake the work of guarding it. This act was, as far as is known, unresisted by Great Britain, whose fleet was thus prevented from entering the Baltic.

The Little Belt is a narrow and tortuous deep-water channel whose southern end is controlled by Germany : for this reason it was impracticable of navigation to Allied shipping. Its main channel and northern approaches are within Denmark's control. Denmark, however, who had blocked the Great Belt and closed the Baltic to the British fleet, did not mine the Little Belt, which was thus made a safe and magnificent channel for the exclusive use of the German fleet. It proved to be a valuable alternative route for German submarines.

The Sound carries a depth of water sufficient for the vessels that trade in the Baltic, but not for the British fleet. With the Great Belt closed, it was the only alternative route for Allied shipping. Although Germany was prepared to block the southern approaches to this channel, which, these approaches being outside territorial waters, she was entitled to do, the necessity for doing so did not arise until British submarines penetrated into the Baltic. A very elaborate arrangement of mines, nets and under-water obstructions was then laid down in the deep waters of the southern approach. The defences were guarded by German destroyers, gunboats and other craft, all of which were based upon Denmark, from whom supplies on a very handsome scale were received. The supplies, it need scarcely be said, had come, directly or indirectly, through the British fleet.

There still remains a little gate of which Sweden possessed the key: this is the Kogrund Pass, a Swedish extension of the German mine-field. The circumstances under which this gate was locked have already been given.

The German obstructions and the Swedish mine-fields were not closed barriers; they were free for the passage of ships through " gates " opened only at the will of their guardians.

Thus the main strategic features of Denmark and Sweden in their command of the entrance to the Baltic, and thence to the command of the German Baltic trade and of the Allied Baltic communications with Russia, were already in German hands. They were lost to us : they could therefore be disregarded as factors having any place in the considerations governing the exercise of economic pressure.

CHAPTER III

LORD GREY, speaking of the functions of the Foreign Office on 26th January, 1916, said :—

> What is the work the Foreign Office has to do? The Foreign Office has to do its best to retain the good-will of the neutrals. Now, supposing you know at the Foreign Office that the War Office, the Admiralty, the Ministry of Munitions, and perhaps one or more of our Allies are specially anxious that you should maintain open communication with some particular neutral country for strategical reasons, or for the sake of supplies which you get from them. We are constantly being told that certain supplies which come from abroad are absolutely essential for the Ministry of Munitions. The Board of Trade know that certain other supplies from abroad are absolutely necessary to carry on the industries of this country. The business of the Foreign Office is to keep the diplomatic relations such, that there is no fear of these supplies being interfered with.[1]

That is one point of view, but the necessity in which Scandinavia stood of the good-will of Great Britain and of the produce of her Empire is overlooked. The

[1] Parliamentary Debates, No. 153, p. 3131. 26th January, 1916.

demands of the German Minister of Munitions and the German Board of Trade made it necessary to Germany that the diplomatic relations of Scandinavia should be kept open with the Power through whose good-will only it was possible for Scandinavia to obtain supplies and to send them to Germany. It was surely not beyond the resources of Sheffield and America to supply the steel ball-bearings which were obtained from Sweden. Our own trees were felled to supply a deficiency in the timber of Scandinavia, and besides the fact that Denmark's food was not necessary to us, it was only capable of being grown by the raw materials that we allowed into Denmark and which could as well have produced food on our own soil.

The nitrates of Norway excepted, there was nothing else, relatively, of importance to the Allies that Scandinavia alone could give us.

In considering what were the possible political consequences that would be likely to result from the application of economic pressure, there are two contingencies which may be ruled out of court as not coming within the sphere of practical politics. Under no circumstances was it ever likely that Sweden would take sides against Germany or Norway against the Allies : of the general Scandinavian sympathies it may be said that Sweden was pro-German, Norway was pro-English and Denmark was pro-Danish. The only possibilities that have to be considered are a German invasion of Denmark and a declaration of war by Sweden against the Allies, together with the possibility that in either case Norway would become involved.

DENMARK

The military assistance that could be given by any of these States would be available only at a sacrifice of the man-power by which their resources were developed and became of advantage to Germany. This question in no case arises with regard to Denmark.

Wherein lay the possibility that Germany might send an army of occupation into Denmark? What would be its object? And what the consequences?

Denmark was Germany's larder, Sweden her workshop. Denmark's agricultural and fishing industries were worked at high pressure for Germany throughout the war: both these industries depended for their existence upon oversea supplies. Denmark's shipping worked mainly in Germany's interests: the whole country, as neutral, was working at its maximum efficiency: an occupation of the country would have retarded production, not promoted it; it would have worked against the existing forces, not with them.

With an enemy in occupation of Denmark, her territorial waters and her ports become hostile, that is to say the whole of Denmark's imports become subject to the confiscable penalties of blockade: her accumulated stocks will last for some months, after which the Danish population and the army of occupation will have to subsist on the resources of the country, supplemented by such supplies of a very precarious nature as can be obtained through Norway, who, if also involved—and this must be considered— would finally shut the door on the only remaining possible source of supplies. Germany, bear in mind, who was in the grip of starvation, and who was at her wits' end to know how to stave off famine, was receiving from Denmark about 300,000 tons of food a year (in 1915 and 1916).

It must be pointed out that, in much the same measure that Germany should lose, we ourselves should gain.

Germany, besides being cut off from Denmark's resources in food, munitions and man-power, and having to make good the deficiencies elsewhere, would have to draw upon her military *personnel* for the necessary troops; she would have to lengthen her lines of communication and supplement the Danish diet with supplies from the scanty stocks for her own half-starved people. It seems incredible that an invasion of Denmark could ever have seriously been contemplated by Germany, or that it should have been seriously entertained as a possibility by responsible authority : it was, however, made the pretext for Danish requests for supplies on the ground that only by propitiating Germany could this alleged danger be averted. But why avert this danger? If the danger *was* real and an invasion of Denmark would bring trouble only to that country and Germany, it would constitute the best reason for withholding supplies from Denmark, and for turning the Danish pretext to our own account until Denmark should see fit to recognise our prior right over Germany to preferential treatment in the distribution of her agricultural produce.

If the danger was *not* real, surely we could do as we wished until at least it was real.

On two grounds only could the possibility of invasion be entertained : the threat of a landing by the Allies on the Danish peninsula would have had to be met : but since this contingency never arose it may be dismissed. The other ground has some small claim to plausibility. The immense sacrifices that an invasion would entail would not at once be felt, and if Germany could have been reasonably certain of obtaining a decision before the effects of Denmark's being cut off from her raw materials were felt, she might have thought it worth while to seize the existing Danish stocks. Obviously, though, unless she were faced with *certain* starvation without these additional supplies, this supposition had no special place outside the general argument given above.

What strategic advantages were there to justify a German occupation of Denmark?

Denmark had closed the Baltic to Germany's enemies and she had kept it open (by not mining the Little Belt) to Germany herself. Reflect upon what the use of the Little Belt meant to Germany; the greater the pressure off Kiel or the Heligoland Bight from mines or other causes, the greater became the importance of the waters of the Little Belt as a means of egress or ingress for Germany's ships, especially submarines and destroyers, and, indeed, for her High Sea Fleet if necessary. Denmark was already bled of her main strategic advantages : Germany had obtained them as a gift, and incidentally not a word of protest appears to have been raised by us against this flagrant breach of neutrality on the part of Denmark. An invasion of Denmark would certainly have strengthened Germany's hold over the approaches to the Baltic, but at what a cost ! What Germany obtained from Denmark she obtained and held without the expenditure of a single shot or the sacrifice of a single man. She obtained all these priceless advantages, not by the preponderance of military strength or the application of economic pressure, but by the benevolent neutrality of Denmark.

As already said, the idea of invasion may be dismissed when Germany was receiving 300,000 tons of food a year from Denmark. With regard to its possibility at a later date, Ludendorff says :—

> Only with extreme regret could we refuse to pronounce in favour of unrestricted submarine warfare on the ground that, in the opinion of the Imperial Chancellor, it *might possibly lead to war with Denmark and Holland.* We had not a man to spare to protect ourselves against these States, and even if their armies were unaccustomed to war, they were in a position to invade Germany, and give us our death blow. We should have been defeated before the effects, promised by the Navy, of an unrestricted U-boat campaign could have made themselves felt.
>
> The discussion, however, afforded an opportunity of overhauling our *defensive* arrangements on the Danish and Dutch frontiers.

Here, then, was Germany actually in fear of being attacked by this ferocious little State, who had been representing the extremity of her peril as a pretext for drawing upon us for supplies with which to conciliate a hungry and bloodthirsty neighbour.

Denmark's recent history is a sad and unfortunate one. She has never forgiven us for bombarding Copenhagen in 1801, nor for remaining a passive spectator to the filching of Schlesvig-Holstein by Germany in 1864. Hatred of Germany is ingrained in the very soul of the Dane. There is no love lost among any of the Scandinavian States, and the truth about any one of them during the war was best arrived at by searching for it outside : but the

Danish hatred of Germany was a truth to be discovered best in Denmark. Since 1864 this aversion had become very intense, and when war broke out Denmark felt she could trust nobody, her past experience telling her that it was to herself only she must look for salvation unless Great Britain should assume the *rôle* of protector, a circumstance which the existing situation did not favour.

Denmark's population in 1914 was about 2,800,000. Her army existed for defensive purposes only; the rank and file are smart and well disciplined, being under fine and efficient officers. It was said that no Danish soldier would level his rifle against an Englishman : whether or not this was the case, we undoubtedly held his respect. With my personal impressions of the Danes this book is not concerned : this, however, I must record, that nowhere is there to be met a greater unaffected courtesy and kindliness of disposition than among all Danes, whatever the class to which they may belong.

SWEDEN

There was one reason why the political consequences that might attend the exercise of economic pressure in the case of Sweden could not be lightly disregarded —it was Germany's wish and Sweden's wish that they should not be : but better reasons than this there were none, bearing in mind always the economic advantages we possessed and Sweden's dependence upon oversea supplies.

Sweden was frankly pro-German (politically) : she was Germany's *protégé*. From her German patron she had learned the lesson that there were two dangers

II

to be apprehended and to be guarded against in case
of war : from the East an invasion by Russia, and
from the West the seizure of a base on her west coast
by Great Britain; but Germany had also taught her
that it was to her, Germany, that Sweden would have
to look for protection in the hour of danger.

Much as Sweden liked Germany, the friendship was
of a platonic character only. It might have ripened
into a closer tie if Germany could have convinced
Sweden that she would emerge victoriously from the
war into which she herself had so callously plunged
Europe. But Sweden, although she very properly
stuck to her powerful patron throughout, was obliged
to consider the possible alternative of Germany's
being defeated; in which case it would be to England
that she would have to look for protection. Thus,
with the future shrouded in uncertainty, it was in
Sweden's interest to remain neutral, and she had to
trim her sails to the uncertain breezes.

The political outlook with regard to Sweden was
embarrassed by Sweden's geographical position as
standing athwart the direct line of communication
with Russia. The main line through the Black Sea
had been finally cut off by the exploits of the
" Goeben " and " Breslau." There was an alternative means of communication by the lengthy trans-
Siberian railway with its terminus at Vladivostok in
the Far East; and precarious facilities were afforded
through the port of Archangel in the White Sea when
not frozen. During 1917 a military railway was
completed joining Murmansk in the Kola Gulf—the
only Northern Russian port that is not icebound
in the winter—with the Russian railway system.
Reindeer transport was largely resorted to, and the
Russian supplies were maintained on a moderate

scale in face of the almost superhuman difficulties that were encountered in this bleak and inhospitable region. But the Swedish was the best remaining route.

Thus it came about that we found ourselves enmeshed in negotiations with Germany's friendly neighbour on the question of transit of stores to Russia, Germany's unfriendly neighbour.

The whole question of the transit of stores through Sweden, which was placed in the hands of a private Company, the " Transito," was made one of the greatest difficulty to us, though Germany encountered no difficulties in the transit of her goods : transit to Russia for us was allowed only when the " compensation " was deemed adequate—that broadly and fairly states the case.

The sacrifices that were made for the Swedish transit were enormous, though the traffic itself was comparatively unimportant in amount and much of it was diverted to Germany. Sweden herself supplied Russia with munitions. To enable her to do so, certain raw materials were allowed into Sweden which otherwise would have been withheld : Sweden obtained them only on the pretext that they were required for Russia. For instance, in Norway a firm under French control, the Norske Hydro-Elektrisk Co., of Notodden, produced concentrated nitric acid, most of which went to Sweden. A certain Swedish firm which worked in important war material for Germany took part of the nitric acid; and when the question was raised as to whether the acid should be allowed into Sweden, we were informed that the firm was supplying large quantities of materials to Russia. This was doubtful, but it could not be disproved. We knew for certain that Sweden was sending war material to Germany, and we knew for certain that Sweden *said* she was sending war material to Russia; but that was as far as our knowledge went, and it just fell short of satisfying curiosity in a slight particular affecting the journeyings of the Russian stores only.

I pressed for Russian statistics, that every transaction might be verified. Russia was our ally, and there was every reason in the Allied interests that these statistics should be produced; but they were not. Of this it can be said that a certain quantity of war material from Sweden reached Russia. I can safely assert that a certain amount did not : it reached Finland, whence it returned and was sent over to Germany. So it was with the stores that we sent in transit. The forwarding agent of the Transito Company took receipts from the agents in Finland : but the Finns were not very particular about their accounts; nor were the Russians to whom they were rendered. The rascality and all-round corruption connected with these stores is well-nigh incredible : I have personally met and spoken to one or two of these Finnish agents, and am tolerably well acquainted with the devious methods of this fraternity and the intermediate agencies through which the goods were diverted to Germany. Across the Gulf of Bothnia a service of motor-boats might be seen running their cargoes of Russian stores back to Sweden.

Mr. James W. Gerard, U.S. Ambassador at Berlin, in his " Face to Face with Kaiserism," referring to this traffic, says :—

> Smuggling is winked at, and at Lulea, on the Swedish coast near the head of the Gulf of Bothnia, great quantities of rubber, block tin

and oil arrive from Russian Uleaborg across the Gulf.

The French wanted to send a consul to Lulea, but their request was refused, doubtless because the Swedish authorities did not care to have any official foreigners see this traffic.

Not only was Russia miserably armed—her soldiers fought with sticks and fists at times—and therefore was it necessary to supply her with military equipment, but from the very first there was a strong peace-party in the country.

Were Russia to have been cut off from supplies through Sweden, disaffection would have been encouraged among the Russian troops, inclining Russia to abandon the Allied cause and to make a separate peace. Of the negotiations that took place for a separate peace something is said in another chapter : they were brought to nought by the unflinching loyalty of his late Majesty the Czar.

The possibility that Sweden might throw in her lot with Germany was skilfully exploited by Germany and Sweden, and the apprehensions that were entertained in the Legation and at home had their origin in German propaganda. The air in Stockholm was constantly charged with rumours the general purport of which was that Sweden had her hand on her sword, which was kept sheathed only by imports. Representations made by the Russian Minister could not be disregarded by the British Minister, on whom the responsibility for the consequences would rest. If the Russian Minister pressed for stores and munitions to be hastened through Sweden to meet a possible emergency, it is reasonable that Sir Esme Howard should not have felt justified in suggesting a policy that would delay the transit of supplies through Sweden.

With regard to the possibility of Sweden's attacking Russia, as already said, Germany had not reckoned upon the entry of Great Britain into the war. Our entry completely changed the political situation in Scandinavia : it made Sweden and Germany dependent upon us for supplies. Had the war been a purely military one, and a short one, Sweden might have employed her well-trained and well-disciplined troops to better advantage than turning out iron ore for Germany : they would have been a formidable force to be reckoned with on the Russian frontier; but to attack Russia during the Great War was to declare war upon England.

The only other case in which Germany might have required the use of Sweden's army was in the event of there being declared a real and absolute blockade : in which case adjacent neutrals would have been useless as dumping grounds and workshops. This contingency, however, had been provided for by Germany in the event of a naval war by the Declaration of London.

Sweden, let us suppose, has declared war. The first thing that strikes us is that, if such a contingency had arisen, we should have been sending military goods into a country with which at any moment we might be at war—Denmark was also a dangerous zone in this respect. The effect of this policy was to give Sweden the ability to conduct a campaign only by means of the stocks thus accumulated in the country : for British coal would be at once stopped and her industries would live only so long as the existing stocks held out except for help from Germany. Sweden would be cut off from all supplies under British control :

her army on a war footing would draw all the man-power from her mines and industries : she would be useless to Germany as a workshop : Germany would lose the best part of 5,000,000 tons of iron ore a year and the food with which Sweden supplied her : in addition, she would have to feed and clothe Sweden. Sweden has her hereditary enemy Norway to watch. A force of (say) 100,000 men—half her army—would have to be detached for this purpose, and a further force would have to be despatched to the west coast, i. e. away from the Russian frontier, to meet a possible British descent there. The seizure of a Swedish base would place us in a favourable position off the Sound and give us command of the entrance to the Baltic : it would restore to us part of the strategic value of these waters.

With Sweden's entry into the war there must also be considered the great probability of Norway's entry on the side of the Allies, and of the ensuing consequences. The magnificent harbours of Norway would become available for the British fleet, her territorial waters would be closed to the passage of the German U-boats, and the command of the waters of the Skagerrak and Kattegat would close the back door to Kiel, making the North Sea the only available route for German ships. The maintenance of a Norwegian base and the protection of its lines of communication would absorb shipping and naval forces employed in other services : but this notwith-standing, Norway's entry would give greatly increased striking force to our Navy and would accentuate the risk to all German war vessels that put to sea. With all these hard facts and possibilities staring her in the face it was not probable that Sweden would embark upon a venture beset with grave risks, of dubious advantage even if successful against Russia, but in which failure would entail certain and irreparable disaster.

Important as it was to the Entente Powers that communications with Russia through Sweden should be kept open, it was of far greater importance to Germany and to Sweden that Sweden should remain neutral : which she did. Outside Sweden the fantastic rumours that were put in circulation were treated with open derision : but they were taken very seriously at Stockholm, where it was difficult to make headway against the ingrained idea that Sweden was a very bellicose nation. Rumours of an invasion of England were frequently heard, but they were most prevalent at a time preceding big operations on the Western front : they kept an army at home.

By the Swedish Constitution war can be declared only by consent of the Ricksdag (Swedish Parliament). A " neutral diplomat "—I regret this discretion, which is unwillingly forced upon me—who knew many members of the Ricksdag, stated that the majority were by no means pro-German. " I can't make out," he said to me on one occasion, "what is the cause of the British anxiety." Indeed, outside Stockholm nobody could.

I expressed the opinion throughout the war, and I hold it now, that Sweden had never at any time either the intention or the power to take up arms : to have done so would have thrown the whole of Scandinavia into a hopeless state of turmoil; whereas, look where you will, and it will be seen that, German rumours apart, all other evidence tends to show that Germany's policy, her intentions and her interests, from the first to the last day of war, were to maintain the *status quo* in Scandinavia, and that her only hope of

victory lay in the successful accomplishment of this
policy, which, it must be remembered, also brought
to Sweden great wealth.

Of the Swedes, the Court, the Services and the
upper classes, as well as the official and professional
classes and the Conservative party, were strongly pro-
German. Men from these classes had to a large extent
received their education and training in Germany;
they had imbibed German habits and customs,
adopted German fashions, taken Germany for their
model and become thoroughly Germanised. There
were, however, many Swedes in high positions who
loathed the German and all his works. The poorer
classes, who are very intelligent, had, on the other
hand, strong pro-Ally sympathies, sympathies which
were also shared by many of the mercantile classes
and leading men of science. The thoughts of these
were turned towards America, to which country
their brothers had emigrated to make their fortunes,
and where one day they hoped to join them. Existence under the thraldom of German government was
held in abhorrence by these, whereas the free in-
stitutions of Great Britain and America made strong
appeal to their imaginations and sympathies. Many
Swedes offered their services to us during the war.

Sweden's population in 1914 was about 5,500,000.
The Swedes are a scrupulously clean people, well set
up, with a fine carriage and the dignified air proper
to the pride of race which the Swede possesses in an
intense degree.

The Napoleonic-Potsdam air occasionally to be
encountered in the streets of Stockholm was probably
an importation from Prussia, and doubtless now has
been put aside for the time being.

NORWAY

Norway, who was our best friend, and from whom there were no political consequences to be feared, received the worst treatment of the three Scandinavian States at the hands of the British Government. A suggestion has been advanced that if Norway had thrown in her lot with us Sweden would have given passage to German troops through her territory. Even if Germany had possessed the troops to spare for such a purpose, nothing was more improbable than that the high-spirited Swedes, whose affection for Germany was really nothing stronger than a political preference, would for a moment have tolerated a German soldier on the soil of Sweden. Norway is Sweden's hereditary enemy; in no circumstances would these two countries be found fighting side by side; and the political consequences of any disturbance of the *status quo* in Scandinavia that should embroil Norway could not but have been favourable to the Allies. There is little else to the purpose to be said on this subject. It was the opinion of staff officers in Norway that Sweden would take up arms with the object only of attacking Norway, who in 1905 threw off the Swedish yoke and became an independent sovereign State, for which Sweden has never forgiven her.

Towards the latter end of the war Norway mined her territorial waters, thus completing that stupendous operation, chiefly the work of America, of laying down a mine barrier across the North Sea.

Norway's population in 1914 was about 2,400,000. The bulk of the people were strongly attached to the Allied cause, about 70 per cent. of the Norwegians and the whole of the fishing community being pro-British.

Norway's small navy is smart, efficient and well disciplined : her army, however, cannot be regarded as a reliable instrument of war.

Norway was the only country in which we succeeded in establishing Consuls. In Sweden there were difficulties, which, however, might easily have been overcome.

One of the first matters that engaged my attention on the outbreak of war was the appointment of Consuls or Consular Agents of British nationality to the principal ports of Scandinavia. With the suppression of the Scandinavian statistics the services of Consular Agents became a matter of national importance; and, moreover, with the progress of the war and the growth of an abnormal trade relationship between Great Britain and Scandinavia, as between belligerent and neutral, the necessary work of supervision that our interests required became far too great for the Legations to cope with. In the early part of 1915 I wrote home, pointing out the desirability of having a Consul or Vice-Consul *de carrière* at every port of importance. With regard to Sweden, a Consul-General was subsequently appointed to Gottenberg, and a British Consul to Malmo, but already at Gottenberg there was established a fairly efficient Consulate, and our interests were well represented at Malmo. These appointments, therefore, brought about very little change, and no reliable information about trade could be obtained in Sweden throughout the war.

Having made a cursory review of the assets, economic, strategic, political and diplomatic, we can now assemble our arguments and take stock. Economic are with us, political are with us, strategic are against us, but the two former still stand to our good, having been considered with the accepted loss of the strategic assets. Diplomacy must regretfully be placed to the debit side of the account.

Norway's nitrates, by a great piece of good fortune, did not chance to be in Sweden, or nothing could then have saved us under the diplomatic treatment to which assuredly they would have been subjected.

Ludendorff ranges himself on our side in these arguments, but, above all, subsequent facts give the *coup de grâce* to the supposition that any obstacle ever stood in the way of applying all economic pressure at our command with any risk except to our enemies. For when America had entered the arena and the Scandinavian States were cut off from all supplies that were not necessary to them, nothing happened to disturb the *status quo* in Scandinavia : it was, indeed, made the more stable; for nothing further was heard either of Swedish threats or of the German invasion of Denmark. Nor was it America's entry that gave us the power to cut off supplies; for our power to say " Yea " or " Nay " had long before been demonstrated, notably in the case of the wheat that had reached Sweden only at our pleasure, and of the petroleum that was cut off from Denmark (see Chapter VI). America may have put us on a certain allowance of maritime rights—not by any means an ungenerous one—but she never put any obstacle in the way of our stopping our own produce from reaching Scandinavia.

When war broke out Scandinavians and the British and foreign Legations began to take in supplies :

there was every reason to think that Scandinavia in all seriousness expected trouble from us. Such little assets as she possessed she naturally turned to the best account. Denmark was insinuating, Sweden blustering, both scheming : but these States were not made to prove what they should say until necessity compelled it. In Sweden's case the political situation was to some extent complicated by the Russian transit, and at least there was a military question to be considered; but in Denmark's there was none.

With Germany in occupation of Denmark, and with Sweden allied to Germany, we should have suffered certain economic losses, but only temporarily : the Danish and Swedish coasts being hostile territory, Germany would have been permanently cut off from all outside sources of supply and her days would have been numbered.

To Sweden's threat to join Germany the proper reply was " Join."

To Germany's threat to invade Denmark the proper reply was " Invade."

There is no action that can be placed to the credit of these two neutral States entitling them to considerate treatment at the hands of the Allies. The suppression of the Scandinavian statistics, the outcome of the Malmo meeting, was a well-directed blow at the Allies calculated to keep them in ignorance of the Scandinavian traffic with Germany.

Malmo is a port on the west coast of Sweden where towards the end of 1914, at Sweden's suggestion, but at Germany's instigation, the three Scandinavian Kings with their Ministers for Foreign Affairs met in secret conclave. Norway's part was purely formal. Germany had made very efficient arrangements before the war for the regular delivery of goods from oversea, and her most sanguine expectations had probably been more than realized. It was necessary that knowledge of the Scandinavian traffic with Germany should be withheld. With characteristic German thoroughness the Malmo meeting was convened and a bolt from the blue was shot. The edict went forth that no further Scandinavian statistics were to be published during the war. This order enabled Scandinavia to conduct her trade behind a screen, and emphasised the importance that Germany, Sweden and Denmark attached to the necessity for concealment.

The Malmo decision was in order : there was no breach of neutrality committed : it told us merely what was the character of the neutrality of Sweden and Denmark.

Many readers will recall with horror the stranding of one of our submarines on an outlying shoal off Copenhagen, and how fifteen of her crew were killed by fire from a German destroyer either on Danish soil or while swimming helplessly about in the water. The survivors were interned by the Danish Government in fear of Germany; the British Government failed to obtain their release, although this cowardly and shocking outrage was in flagrant violation of international law. By the Danes themselves it was regarded as an indelible disgrace to their flag.

The case of the Swedish cipher messages, which brought Sweden to the verge of a rupture with America, will also be fresh in many readers' memories.

During the war it was discovered—it is said by America—that the Swedish Minister at Buenos Aires had received in cipher from the German Chargé d'Affaires, Count Luxberg, messages which were forwarded by the Swedish Minister to the Foreign

Office in the guise of official Swedish messages. From Stockholm they were sent under similar false guise to Berlin. Through the good offices of Sweden messages were transmitted from Berlin to the German representative at Buenos Aires and communications through Swedish official agency were established with most parts of the world.

An extract from one of these messages runs as follows :—

> I beg that the small steamers " Oran " and " Guazo " . . . which are now nearing Bordeaux, with a view to changing flags, may be spared if possible, or else sunk without a trace being left (spurlos versenkt).—LUXBERG.

In another message the amiable Count recommends, as regards Argentine steamers, either compelling them to turn back, sinking them without leaving any trace or letting them through.

It was in the highest degree probable that the Swedish Foreign Office knew that these messages referred to submarine piratical operations against the Allied naval and mercantile forces, which Germany was doing her utmost to destroy. It appears, however, that this practice had been going on since the early days of the war, that it was known to H.M. Government and that formal promises had been obtained from Sweden to discontinue it. The affair expended itself on paper. It led to the removal of the Head of the Swedish Foreign Office, who, however, was shortly afterwards appointed as Minister at Vienna, one of the most coveted posts in the Swedish Diplomatic Service. It is only fair to say that among Swedes this affair of the cipher messages was universally reprobated.

The foregoing incidents are placed on record for the purpose, not of perpetuating their memory for all time, but only that they may be recalled when the emotions are apt to be too strongly stirred by allusions to the pitiable lot of the " weaker " States.

CHAPTER IV

COAL

In addition to supremacy at sea we held the next greatest and most effective weapon for use in war time in our hands—coal-power.

Scandinavia has no coal. Prior to August, 1914, the Scandinavian countries imported annually about 10,000,000 tons of coal, practically all of which came from the United Kingdom. The following figures for 1913, which was a normal year in the Scandinavian coal trade, will illustrate the exact position :—

Total imports . . . . 10,308,238 tons

of which 9,813,389 were from the United Kingdom and 354,917 from Germany.

Very early in the war Germany began to suffer from a shortage of coal. Anticipating a short war, she had accumulated large surface stocks from which it was her intention to have covered her increased war requirements; and, based upon this consideration, many men engaged in the coal trade, both on the surface and below, were sent to join the colours. But the war on the two fronts entailed such an enormous and unforeseen strain upon Germany that her estimated war requirements in respect both of coal and men were soon found to be inadequate, and German coal exports to Scandinavia decreased both in quantity and quality soon after the commencement of hostilities.

The shortage of coal in Germany soon became a question of extreme gravity. Italy was making insistent demands for German coal in return for sulphur and other commodities of great war value. Moreover, it was necessary for Germany, in order to conserve her gold, and thereby prevent an adverse exchange, to export as much as possible to the Scandinavian countries in return for their imports of food, iron ore and other commodities. But the most serious aspect of the case was that, as the war progressed, certain firms in Scandinavia on account of their dealings with Germany were placed on our Black List; [1] they were thus unable to obtain British coal. It became obvious therefore to Germany, that as time went on it would be absolutely necessary to make good the deficiencies caused by the withdrawal of British stocks.

When matters were rapidly approaching a crisis Germany found partial relief in Belgium. In pre-war times Belgium produced about 23,000,000 tons of coal per annum, and since none of the mines had been destroyed or even damaged, the normal production of Belgian coal depended only upon the reorganisation of Belgian labour. This work was carried out by the Germans very thoroughly, and by the end of 1915 the production of coal in Belgium was not far short of the pre-war output.

In this way Germany was able to extricate herself from a very difficult situation, and in September, 1915, cargoes of Belgian coal began to reach Scandinavia. That the Scandinavians were aware of the fact that the coal they were importing came from Belgium admits of no doubt. Indeed, with the view of putting a stop to the traffic, Scandinavian officials

[1] The Statutory Black List was a sort of commercial " Coventry."

were warned on several occasions that on the return
of the Belgian Government to Brussels they might
possibly be compelled to compensate the rightful
owners.[1]

As will be seen from the following figures, the
amount sent to Scandinavia gradually increased until
1916, when, on account of the increasing shortage
in Germany due to loss of man-power, it decreased.

Without doubt Germany made every effort to
supply Scandinavia—especially Sweden and Denmark
—with as much coal as possible; yet, in spite of all
the advantages to be gained by exporting coal, the
Germans were able to make only the following contri-
butions, nearly the whole of which came from Belgium,
towards Scandinavia's annual requirements of over
10,000,000 tons :—

	1915	1916	1917
Coal	1,200,000	2,920,000	1,480,000
Coal briquettes	240,590	885,781	300,827

The figures for Belgian coal, which do not include
any by-products such as coke and briquettes, are as
follows :—

1915	1916	1917
881,425	2,617,885	1,129,682

These figures, however, convey but little meaning
because the value of coal for industrial and commercial
purposes depends altogether upon its quality.

Reports are almost unanimous in stigmatising the
Belgian coal that Germany sent to Scandinavia as
little better than worthless rubbish for steam-raising
purposes unless mixed with British : to use it at all
furnaces had to be altered.   Consumers complained
that it could not be used in steamers, locomotives

[1] See Chapter on Finance, pp. 246, 247.

or manufactories; in some cases ships that had bunkered with Belgian coal and put to sea had to return for British.

Up to the spring of 1916 no coal expert had been sent to Scandinavia, and, pending his appointment, I endeavoured to carry out the necessary work myself. Without the help of powerful Scandinavian friends of strong British sympathies, this would have been impossible. Special and excellent sources of information were available to me, and most of the reports that I sent home on the subject of coal have since been confirmed by the evidence of German writers.

The following extract from the *Aberdeen Journal* by a curious coincidence came under my notice when the above paragraph was being written. It bears out the substance of my reports. The vessels referred to had gone to Belgium during the great coal strike in 1921 :—

ABERDEEN FISHING
FOREIGN COAL USELESS FOR STEAM-RAISING

The local vessels which went across recently to Belgium for bunker coal are not likely to repeat the experiment. The stuff with which they were supplied, at a cost of £2 18s. per ton, was found to be absolutely useless for steam-raising purposes, and went up the funnel at an alarming rate.

The " P. Fauum " (Messrs. Stroud and Connon) had her bunkers filled at Ghent some days ago, and intended making a trip to Iceland before returning, but, finding that four miles an hour was the speed limit, she had to return to port without having commenced fishing operations. It took the vessel two days to make the voyage home.

German coal may be classed roughly as West-phalian and Silesian. Westphalian is good coal though inferior to Welsh : with the exception of a few cargoes its export ceased entirely during the war, Scandinavia being supplied with Silesian and Belgian coal only, and of the worst quality. The calorific value of this coal according to expert reports was about 50 per cent. of the normal value of English " smalls "; it was possible to burn it only when mixed with British coal in the proportion of three parts British to one part German. Many cargoes were said to contain a large percentage of earth, and in most cases they were 10 per cent. short in weight.

In addition to coal Germany sent Scandinavia briquettes. These were of bad quality, but, unlike the Belgian coal, they could, though of low calorific value, be made to burn alone : of all the fuel exported by Germany the briquettes were the best of a bad lot.

The other source of coal, America, was inaccessible to Scandinavia on account of distance, freights and scarcity of shipping : either British or German (including Belgian) coal had to be taken.

Frequent reference is made by General Ludendorff in his " Memoirs " to the importance of exporting coal to neutrals. It may therefore be assumed that the quantity of coal obtained by Scandinavia from German sources was the maximum.

Up to the year 1914 the Scandinavian countries had been accustomed exclusively to use British coal, which is by far the best in Europe.

The boilers in all classes of their men-of-war were designed for burning Welsh coal, their railway loco-motive boilers for English coal, and in the large industrial works—for instance, the majority of the pulp and paper mills—the furnaces were arranged for English " smalls " (called in the trade " D.C.B.,"

Yorkshire Slack, Newcastle Prime and Broomhill Smalls). Moreover, many large works in Scandinavia had installed patent mechanical stokers, which necessitated the use of small coal for which the furnace arrangements were designed. There was hardly an industry, large or small, in the three countries that was not entirely dependent upon coal, and, what is more important, upon *British coal*. The following is a list of some of the consumers in Denmark, an agricultural country, who were dependent upon British coal : State railways, gas works, electrical light and power stations, manufacturers of food such as lard, dairy produce, meat and fish conserves, breweries and oil mills. It is from the gas and electrical power stations that manufacturers of meat and fish preserves and tinsmiths engaged in preparing the tins for con- - veying the food abroad chiefly obtained heat and power. Indeed the economic life of Denmark depended almost entirely upon British coal.

Without discussing the situation in Norway and Sweden in detail, it may be stated that these countries in spite of water-power were perhaps even more dependent than Denmark upon British coal.

Great as was our power within these three countries it can hardly have been exceeded by the power we could bring to bear from without by withholding British coal from Scandinavian ships throughout the world. If properly applied no Scandinavian ship-owner could withstand bunker pressure. The bigger the shipping company the more vulnerable it became.

In coal, therefore, we had a fine, efficient and up-to-date weapon : not for any arbitrary and indiscriminate use against friendly, or rather be it said non-belligerent, States, but for lawful use against our enemies and for self-preservation.

There can be no doubt whatever that Scandinavians, who expressed their opinions quite openly, expected British coal supplies to be cut off abruptly, or at least to be issued only under strict conditions and in limited quantities. They were well aware that complete industrial and military disorganisation would rapidly ensue from the adoption of any drastic coal measures.

Yet scarcely any use outside bunker pressure was made by us of this incomparable asset. It is true that as the war progressed coal pressure was gradually brought to bear; but with the progress of the war knowledge and experience combined with good organisation helped our enemies to overcome obstacles which in its early stages would have been insurmountable. It was in the very first days that the curtailment of coal supplies would have had its most deadly effect. Circumstances were favourable. The great strikes in England had caused prices to rise, merchants and consumers were waiting for a drop, and stocks in Scandinavia had fallen below the normal. These stocks rapidly regained bulk. British coal poured in freely, Sweden alone obtaining in September, 1914, 633,000 tons—a seventh of her whole yearly requirements—although H.M. Government appeared to expect that she would join Germany. The amounts obtained by the three States in the last four months of 1914 were all above the average, Sweden's supply exceeding that for any period of four months in the past.

Coal was supplied without there being imposed any restrictions on its use; the trade in coal continued as in peace time. Moreover, soon after the outbreak of war, Scandinavian ships, using British bunkers, commenced to pour goods into Germany viâ Scandinavian ports. These goods came from all parts of the world.

For instance, a ship bringing cotton to Sweden from America bunkered with British coal before leaving Scandinavia, and returned for the next cargo with the least possible delay. As a Norwegian shipowner said to me, " This is a splendid game, in fact the finest I've ever played. I can almost pay for a new ship every trip across the Atlantic."

It is impossible to overestimate the loss of power and prestige which this policy entailed, especially when it is remembered that these countries expected nothing.

After the war had been in progress for three or four months rumours were heard that, in the event of coal supplies from England failing, Scandinavia would be able to cover her requirements from Germany. These rumours, which originated in most cases in Sweden, were difficult to refute, the more so because they received credence at the British Legation in Stockholm. In the early part of 1915, seeing the trend that events were taking, and feeling certain that these rumours were put in circulation by Germany in order to prevent Scandinavians from forming the impression that so far as coal was concerned they were completely in our power, I took up the coal question in earnest. Evidence had to be collected from various places in Germany—from the German Press, Swedish coal importers and consumers, captains of ships visiting German ports, and in short from every source available. The information obtained from all these sources was embodied in a series of exhaustive reports, which commenced in March, 1915, and continued well on into 1917.

The evidence collected confirmed fully what has already been said with regard to German coal—its wretched quality, its short weight and the insuperable difficulties of transport and man-power experienced by Germany in providing even such meagre supplies as were possible.

This evidence was not accepted by H.M. Government, who continued to supply Scandinavia with coal in strict accordance with the directions contained in German rumours.

Early in 1915 steps were taken by the British Legation in Christiania to control the use of British coal in Norway in order that ships trading to German ports should not use it, and that firms working for the enemy should not be able to obtain it. Once started, the organisation for this control was gradually perfected until at the end of the year it was almost impossible for a ton of coal to escape the vigilance of the Legation. One of the most astute commercial men in Norway, and probably Norway's largest fish exporter, who had been engaged exclusively from the outbreak of war up to about August, 1916, in supplying Germany with fish, had on that account, in the early days of coal control, been placed on the Black List, where he remained until August, 1916. He then left the German camp and, coming over to our side, rendered us great services in connection with the purchase of Norwegian fish. Some time after his removal from the Black List he stated to a British Foreign Office official, who had come to Norway in connection with the Norwegian Fish Agreement, that in spite of his being on the Black List, with the exception of coal he had been able to obtain all the commodities he desired. Coal he had never been able to obtain.

As a result of the efficient control of British coal in Norway several important factories and workshops, which formerly exported part of their output to

Germany, ceased to do so, and a considerable amount of shipping was therefore diverted from German to British trade. At the same time the relations between the British Legation and the coal importers were excellent. The Legation drew up lists, which were kept corrected up to date, of reliable coal merchants and firms importing for their own use. The Licensing Authorities in England had only to adhere to those lists in order to safeguard British interests. Unfortunately, much of the work of the Legation was at times rendered useless owing to the fact that licences were granted—some freely—to coal importers on the Black List and other firms not on the list of consignees compiled by the Legation.

The success of the coal control in Norway was due in large measure to the fact that from the very beginning it was made quite clear to the Norwegian importers that transactions with German coal merchants would debar them from receiving British aid. Success was also due to the fact that the control was entirely in the hands of the British Legation.

The total amount of coal from German sources exported to Norway from the beginning of the war up to the end of 1917 was only about 160,000 tons, the greater part of which went to one shipowner who ran a line of four or five ships between Norway and Germany.

Although Swedish industries were in the main working for Germany, yet no attempt to establish control of coal in Sweden was made until the end of 1915.

Sweden's intractable attitude had decided H.M. Government in June, 1915, to send a mission to Stockholm for negotiating certain commercial agreements.

The very presence of this English mission in Stockholm after the many affronts we had received from

Sweden showed clearly—and this was quick to be noticed in other neutral countries—the success of the Swedish high-handed policy. Soon after the arrival of the Mission in Stockholm rumours were circulated to the effect that Germany had promised Sweden 600,000 tons of coal : later the Swedish Government announced that arrangements had been made with Germany whereby Sweden would receive coal from Germany to the amount of 400,000 tons per month and that it was possible that this supply might commence in August. Had this been true it would have meant that Sweden could have covered her whole annual requirements independently of England.

Again I instituted exhaustive inquiries. All the evidence collected went to show that these German promises were hollow and made for the purpose of strengthening the position of Sweden, and therefore of Germany, at the conference table. The result of these German promises and Swedish threats was that H.M. Government lost faith in the power of British coal to wring concessions from Sweden. In 1915 Sweden got considerably less, it is true, than her normal quantity, but the one million tons of coal and the quarter of a million tons of briquettes which she received from Germany in that year just enabled the British coal to be eked out. These half measures had enabled Swedish consumers gradually to adapt their furnaces to the use of the mixed German and British coal; they had driven them also to the adoption of other expedients such as the burning of wood and the economising of coal where possible : thus the benefit of prompt application of coal pressure was lost.

During 1916 an endeavour was made to establish some sort of control in Sweden, but the control never became effective. The absence of British Consuls of British nationality on the Swedish coasts made it impossible to ascertain to what extent British coal was being made use of in Swedish ports for bunkering purposes.

During the period when Sweden was supplied with these millions of tons of British coal the official view prevailed that she might at any moment have joined Germany.

About the beginning of 1916 a foreign expert in coal, after making a tour of Sweden, stated that :—

> but for supplies having reached Sweden from England during the last six months the situation, now difficult, would have been desperate. Yet little apprehension as regards the future existed, as quite piteous appeals to ship pit-props had been received from England, and the coal importers expected to be able to get much more favourable terms in exchanging props for coals than hitherto.

Towards the end of 1916 it became apparent that the principal exports from Germany, including coal, were rapidly decreasing. It was no secret in Scandinavia that these reduced exports were due to lack of man-power in Germany. During 1917 German supplies became scantier : the total export of coal from Germany to Sweden in that year amounted to 600,000 tons, and 300,000 tons of briquettes, in each case almost exactly one-third of the amounts exported in 1916. Obviously pretence could then no longer avail, and, although undeserved, another opportunity occurred for England to compel obedience from Sweden to her wishes. [Our coal controlled the transport of Sweden's valuable iron ore, yet it was not until the spring of 1918 that any serious attempt was made to compel Sweden to reduce her exports to Germany. Our efforts were unsuccessful, and Germany received all she required to the end of the war through the prodigal supplies of coal from her foolish and gullible enemy.

"I found it very difficult," says Ludendorff, "in May and June, 1917, when we were under the influence of the great Entente offensive in the West and the extraordinary high rate of wastage it involved, to weaken the army further by releasing 50,000 workmen at the request of the Coal Controller. . . . The army never recovered the men thus released, and labour output even fell off considerably. That was, of course, a heavy blow to us."

On 4th July, 1917, in the course of a speech on the blockade in the House of Lords, Lord Milner said (in all good faith) :—

> At the same time it must be remembered that Germany has means of pressure, too. To give only one instance, the industries of some of the neutral countries adjacent to Germany are almost entirely dependent upon coal supplies from Germany for their continued activity. Germany is able to furnish them with coal at very much more favourable rates than they can get it from this country, and in that and in other respects Germany is just as well able to bring pressure to bear on them to induce them to send their goods into Germany as we are to bring pressure to bear on them to try and prevent their sending those goods into Germany.[1]

While Lord Milner was making this speech the

[1] Parliamentary Debates, No. 53, p. 784, 4th July, 1916.

Swedish Government informed H.M. Government that she would like to obtain from the United Kingdom 100,000 tons of coal a month, freight being £15 to £20 per ton.

In Denmark the control of British coal was placed in the hands of the Danes.

About June, 1915, H.M. Government sanctioned the establishment in Copenhagen of what was known as the " Coal Bureau." To the formation of this bureau, which was composed of Danes, I was strongly opposed. In the first place the bureau was extremely popular in Denmark : that in itself was a very bad sign. The popularity was due entirely to the fact that it was free from British supervision. But its most objectionable feature appeared to be that responsibility for observing conditions of sale was shared to a certain extent by both the bureau and the merchant, who would therefore have a mutual interest in preventing irregularities from coming to our knowledge. During the first four months of its existence not one firm had been denounced by the bureau for not complying with conditions of sale : in Norway there had been several.

A great effort was made to establish a coal bureau in Norway on the same lines as the Danish bureau. Investigation brought it to our knowledge that the moving spirits in this project were black-listed firms and two prominent pro-German Norwegians, one of whom was heard to remark, with a sad appreciation of its Utopian character, what an impetus such an arrangement would give to their trade with Germany.

In August, 1916, *i. e.* two years after the opening of hostilities and fourteen months after the establishment of the Coal Bureau in Copenhagen, a British Consul was sent out from England to make investigations. In addition to the universal use to which our coal was put in furtherance of the Danish trade with Germany, the Consul reported that the evasion of guarantees under which coal was supplied was looked upon as " good sport," and that the breaking of a bond was justified by profits made out of Germany. [Consumers could purchase as much British coal as they cared to pay for, and were under no obligation not to use it for any purpose that might be to the advantage of the enemies of the Allies. /

The above, be it again said, is from a report made two years after the outbreak of war.

With Denmark there was only one question to be considered : Was she supplying Great Britain with agricultural produce in appropriate quantity? If not, there was a practical reply without even a risk.

The results achieved by the Coal Bureau in Copenhagen may be seen from the following tables :—

British coal received by Denmark (in tons).

1913	1914	1915	1916	1917
3,034,240	3,059,162	3,130,642	2,305,409	856,037

Danish food (in tons) received by

	1913	1914	1915	1916	1917
United Kingdom .	256,754	277,579	197,398	156,100	102,423
Germany and Austria	123,547	134,105	274,401	314,328	196,907

The lavish supplies of British coal to Denmark became so notorious as greatly to increase the difficulties of exercising coal pressure in Norway. Norwegian shipowners and other coal consumers in Norway, while admitting that we were within our rights in looking after our own interests, bitterly resented our action in exerting coal pressure only against themselves.

Throughout the war, and particularly during the

first two years, large numbers of German railway trucks were to be seen in all three countries. These trucks were hauled to and from Germany with British coal. According to various newspaper reports the State railways were handling so much traffic to and from Germany that local requirements had frequently to be neglected. Not only were we actively assisting German trade in Scandinavia, but we were performing valuable transport service for the enemy and supplying him with the British man-power employed to win this coal from the mines, transport it to the coast, and thence across the North Sea at a time when shipping was scarce and had never possessed greater value.

Gas coal, of which we have almost a monopoly in Europe, was also supplied to Scandinavia during the war in very large quantities. The problem that here presented itself was how to control the gas and the by-products. Very little could be done with the gas, though a limited control was partly established in Norway.

Of the by-products only the liquid ones, tar and ammoniacal liquor, were of military importance, both being used for the production of high explosives : the latter is also used as a fertiliser.

In December, 1915, I suggested that these by-products should, as a condition for obtaining gas coal, be held at our disposal. This proposal bore no fruit until March, 1917 : until then our enemies obtained most of the benefit from the by-products.

A limited control over tar was established by obtaining Government prohibition of its export. The disposal of ammonia was by far the more important question, being intimately connected with the explosive supplies of France and England.

In Norway there is a large works, the Norsk Hydro Co., which obtains nitrogen from the air. This company during the war was under French direction, and almost the whole of the output of nitrate of lime and nitrate of ammonia—both very valuable ingredients for high explosives—went to Great Britain and her Allies. At one time the French were dependent upon the Norsk Hydro Co. for 90 per cent. of their explosives. In order to produce the large quantities of nitrate of ammonia, the Norsk Hydro Co. required a very large quantity of ammonia. They obtained the greater part of this ammonia from cyanamide and the balance direct from England in the form both of ammoniacal liquor and sulphate of ammonia.

The cyanamide was produced in Norway by an English company, the whole of whose output, with the exception of what was sent to the Norsk Hydro Co., was sent to England, where it was urgently required for the production of ammonia.

In England ammonia is produced almost entirely from coal in gas works. As the war progressed and coal miners were sent to join the colours the supply of ammonia and coal-tar produce became more and more difficult, until finally the Controller of Coal Mines issued an appeal to the gas industry with a view to increasing production.

Since Great Britain was supplying large quantities of gas coal, which could not be obtained elsewhere, to the gas works in Scandinavia, and since all gas works of any size produce ammoniacal liquor, it was clearly in our interests that all the ammonia recovered in Scandinavia, or a large part of it, should be sent to the Norsk Hydro Co. in order to take the place of the English supplies. No steps, however, were taken

K

in this matter until 1917, when, the export of gas coal from England to Scandinavia having fallen by 550,000 tons, the question was no longer of great importance.

In the meantime, during the years 1915 and 1916 only about 700 tons of ammoniacal liquor, out of a total production in Scandinavia of 18,000 tons, reached the Norsk Hydro Co. The whole of this 700 tons came from Norway. All the remainder was sold as in peace time, the great bulk of which was used in the form of sulphate of ammonia by Danish agriculturists.

The position may roughly be summed up by quoting an extract from a letter which I wrote to Sir Ralph Paget, H.M. Minister at Copenhagen :—

> It seems to me that when we are so hard pressed these valuable by-products should, in return for our coal, be placed at our disposal in order to help us to kill Germans, instead of being used by neutrals as a fertiliser for producing, amongst other things, grease for our enemies from which they obtain glycerine for their explosives in order that they may kill Englishmen.

The total amount of British coal exported to Scandinavia, from the outbreak of war up to the end of the year 1917, was 21,632,180 tons.

The total amount of German and Belgian coal and coal briquettes exported to Scandinavia during the same period was 7,196,208 tons.

In addition to the above, Scandinavia, during the same period, obtained from England 1,317,000 tons of coke, and from German sources 14,149,603 tons of coke.

A few words about coke.

Certain sorts of coke are used in blast furnaces for melting iron and steel, but, with this exception, it is of no use for industrial purposes and cannot take the place of coal for steam raising in any of the great industries. Its chief use is for household purposes, especially in connection with central heating.

Out of the 14,000,000 tons of coke that Germany sent to Scandinavia, 10,840,000 tons went to Denmark during the years 1915, 1916 and 1917. This is a very large amount, and therefore needs some explanation.

Throughout the war the German Government was haunted by the fear of food shortage. Denmark and Holland were the principal adjacent food-producing neutrals, and it was therefore of great importance for the Germans to maintain the good-will of these two countries.

It is not intended to enter into the particulars of the pretty story connected with the achievement of this object. Briefly stated, the Germans bought the extremist Press and the labouring classes with coke, hundreds of thousands of tons of which were given away or sold at a nominal price. This coke was used for household purposes, particularly in Copenhagen and other closely-populated areas in Denmark.

Such are the principal features connected with the subject of coal.

Our success in the great struggle depended almost entirely upon two factors: (1) man-power; (2) the blockade. That is to say, upon utilising the working capacity of our population to its utmost extent for war purposes, and upon pitilessly reducing the enemy's productivity and resources of every kind by means of the blockade.

Our policy in respect of the export of coal conflicted with both these conditions. It resulted in a large portion of our man-power being employed indirectly for the benefit of the enemy; and in assisting, in spite of the blockade, to maintain the enemy's productivity and to carry out service which was indispensable to him.

It was not until 1917 that the full pulverising effect of the superb weapon that Nature herself had placed in our hands was made felt and the blockade of Germany became effective.

CHAPTER V

DANISH AGRICULTURAL PRODUCE

THE decisive economic battle was fought in Scandinavia, but the centre of effort throughout was Denmark.

Germany's first concern was to exploit the strategic possibilities of the ground and see what could be done to turn them to good account. As has already been seen, she obtained all the strategic advantages that Denmark and Sweden possessed. From Denmark she obtained the key to the main entrance to the Baltic; from Sweden the key that closed the approaches entirely.

To Copenhagen as her diplomatic representative she sent Rantzau, one of the most efficient and astute of her public servants, whose services to his country were afterwards rewarded by his being appointed Minister for Foreign Affairs. The Head of the British Mission in Copenhagen on the outbreak of war was Sir Henry Lowther, who in August, 1916, was succeeded by Sir Ralph Paget.

The Naval Attaché's position in Scandinavia was unique in that, being accredited to the three Scandinavian countries and free to travel from one capital to another, he had opportunities possessed by no other Englishman of keeping in touch with current opinion throughout the whole of Scandinavia. During the war I availed myself fully of this freedom of movement and visited the three capitals periodically.

My headquarters were at Christiania, whence soon after hostilities broke out I proceeded to Copenhagen.

For the predictions of Bernhardi bade fair to become fulfilled. The Allied armies were being pressed back by the Germans, merchandise was pouring in from oversea to Scandinavia and through Denmark into Germany. The trend that events were taking and were likely to be taking in the future was made unmistakably clear very soon after the outbreak of war by many signs, but particularly by the abnormal and heavy traffic in horses and cattle from Denmark. During the last six months of 1914 Denmark alone sent to Germany 68,000 horses in excess of the normal number. I had been urged by many Scandinavians and by members of the Allied Legations to use my influence to get this traffic with Germany stopped, or controlled and kept within normal bounds so far as this might be possible. To this end I proceeded to Copenhagen and discussed matters with the British Minister, but was unable to obtain the necessary figures relating to the Danish imports from the United Kingdom and the distribution of the Danish produce to the United Kingdom and Germany. Without some definite and trustworthy data on which to work it was impossible to attack the Danish traffic. I succeeded, however, after the lapse of many months, in procuring from a private source a batch of figures, untabulated and roughly recorded on several sheets of foolscap, showing the actual quantities of food sent by Denmark and landed in various ports of the United Kingdom between 1st October, 1914, and 30th September, 1915. The work of disentangling this mass of figures, getting them into intelligible form and sifting them so that what was necessary might be separated from what was unnecessary occupied much time, pressure of other work preventing me from dealing with them except at odd moments : [1] and it was not until 1st February, 1916, that I was able to embody the result of my labours in a report, which was duly forwarded to the Foreign Office.[2]

Attached to this report were two tables,[3] one of which showed an all-round heavy drop in our supplies of Danish produce, and the other that it was an increasing one. Further, since the Danish produce was proportionate to the fodder and fertilisers that were imported, the decrease in the produce sent to the United Kingdom should have indicated a corresponding decrease in the imports of the fodder and fertilisers. But the latter were seen to have increased in quantity since the outbreak of war, thus accentuating the significance of the losses suffered by the United Kingdom. It would therefore appear that as scarcity and consequent high prices increased in Germany, so did the exports of agricultural produce to England decrease.

The importance of these figures lay in their providing clear proof for the first time that since the outbreak of hostilities Germany had been favoured in the distribution of Danish produce which oversea imports alone had made possible. The produce to us should, in view of the increase in the import of raw materials to Denmark, have been greater than the pre-war supplies. Had these supplies only been

[1] I had no assistants. The French Naval Attaché had two.

[2] The importance with which my report was regarded by the Foreign Office is amply borne out by the official intimation I received to the effect that instead of being sent through Christiania it should have been addressed to Sir H. Lowther at Copenhagen in accordance with paragraph 6 of the instructions issued to Naval Attachés upon their appointment.

[3] See Appendix.

maintained there would have been legitimate ground for complaint : but the quantities fell short of the pre-war figures, and by the substantial amount of 50 per cent. or thereabouts. The figures referred to a few items only : they might fairly have been assumed to indicate the scale on which the Danish traffic with Germany was being conducted.

In the summer of 1915, when the question of coal control arose, it had been represented by the British Minister that as only a comparatively small portion of Danish agricultural produce found its way to Germany, it was not considered desirable, in spite of the fact that British coal was being used in the agricultural co-operative factories in Denmark, to force the Danish agriculturists to forgo their German trade : nevertheless the facts brought to light by my report did not lead to the imposition of coal restrictions. The terms of the agreement, however, under which Danish imports were allowed into the country formed the subject of negotiations during the greater part of 1916.

Trading agreements with neutrals were sound in principle, but not in practice. The Danish agreements suffered in many cases from serious defects in their drafting, which was ambiguous; they did not set out in full and precise terms the meaning to be attached to certain vital phrases such as " benefiting the enemy "; so that in many cases they contained loopholes which enabled the sole purpose of an agreement to be frustrated without departing from the letter of the agreement. Was Denmark properly entitled to receive a consignment of one sort of foodstuffs which would release another sort for export ? The thousands of live cattle that Denmark exported to Germany every week contained the raw

materials for many articles, especially leather goods :
was Denmark to be supplied with raw hides, boots
and shoes, thus enabling her to export the cattle
which otherwise would have been required for her
own leather needs? The fodder and fertilisers that
were sent to Denmark were the raw materials of the
agricultural produce itself and the soil itself of Denmark; they represented the basic root of Denmark's
soil and of everything produced by the soil. If
imported goods were to be allowed to release other
goods, what purpose was served by attaching any
condition to their importation? For the principle
on which agreements were based had in view the
restriction of supplies to an amount necessary only
for the neutral's home requirements and the prevention of abnormal traffic with Germany.

What was the security on both sides in these
Agreements?

The steady arrival of ships and cargoes in the ports
of Denmark was Denmark's security for Great
Britain's pledge : that was good security. The
British security, however, rested on the somewhat
slippery ground of good faith on the part of those
who guaranteed that imported goods should not
benefit the enemy.

The system of rationing, which was an extension
of the principle of agreements, was an unjustifiably
generous one, being based upon Denmark's requirements before the war when these requirements in
their turn were based upon British markets. But
since the outbreak of war our share of the Danish
produce had fallen by 25 per cent. During the last
six months of 1914 Denmark had sent 68,000 horses
to Germany in excess of the normal number. Horses,
when in work, require in addition to other things

about 10 lb. of oats a day : these horses, therefore, released in the following year about 120,000 tons of oats for other purposes. The abnormal export of other live-stock further very much reduced the amount of fodder necessary for their upkeep. These matters were not taken into account. It was the common interest both of Denmark and Germany that the principle of rationing should be defeated; and agreements, which left matters such as the above undefined, merely provided these countries with the means of furthering their own interests. Germany reaped such benefits from the abuses to which they were open as enabled her to stem the tide of starvation and to pull through 1916 and 1917. In some respects she gained more than Denmark : for whereas Denmark consumed the imported raw materials, Germany obtained the finished article produced on Denmark's soil by Danish labour.

The negotiations that took place with representatives of the Danish agricultural industries had in view an improvement in the relative distribution of the Danish produce to Great Britain and Germany.

The chief of these delegates and their recognised spokesman was Mr. Andersen. Mr. Andersen was a gentleman who had risen to a position of extraordinary influence in Denmark, where, from his great wealth, great business ability and diverse interests, he was known as the uncrowned king. He was managing director of the East Asiatic Company, one of the two most important shipping companies in Denmark, whose ships brought over oil seeds from the Far East and were so fortunate as not to suffer any loss from torpedo attack during the war. He had very influential friends both in London and Germany, but in Denmark it was he himself who was the fount of influence.

I had not availed myself of the many invitations with which I had been privileged to become personally acquainted with Mr. Andersen. To the neglect of such opportunities may possibly be due the profound ignorance in which I remained steeped throughout the war of the value of Danish agricultural produce as it affected the respective interests of England and Germany.

Mr. Andersen in 1915 proceeded to Petrograd in the cause of general peace, for which Germany at that time was negotiating. His disinterested services on the occasion of this delicate mission were referred to by the German Chancellor as endeavours made by a " highly-deserving man."

It is remarkable that, according to the evidence of the late General von Falkenhayn and the then Imperial Chancellor, the late Herr von Bethmann-Hollweg, Germany was also negotiating at this time for a *separate* peace with Russia. With these negotiations, however, Mr. Andersen was in no way connected, a fact to which the late German Chancellor himself has borne testimony. The incident is mentioned only because it is not thought to be generally known that two independent sets of negotiations for different types of peace were taking place simultaneously.

Mr. Andersen with other delegates visited London in the spring and summer of 1916, and was received by Lord Robert Cecil, the Minister of Blockade. The result of the discussions that took place led to a change favourable to Great Britain, as promised, in the distribution of the Danish produce : but this improvement during the summer of 1916 left matters in a most unsatisfactory state.

Denmark at this period was still receiving imports greater, in respect of many important items, than she had received before the war, and for the transport of which nearly all the coal and part of the tonnage was provided by Great Britain. This enormous access of wealth and trade had enabled her to expand her food industries and even to open up new ones. In the first seven months of 1916 the absolute quantity of agricultural produce, not including lard, horses or fish, that Denmark exported to Germany was close upon 117,000 tons. The meat export alone during this period, 62,561 tons, was sufficient to furnish about 1,000,000 meat rations per day throughout the seven months on the scale of the current German Army ration.

The Danish population suffered hardships, not from our blockade, but because the Danish farmers sold to Germany and the Danish Government was powerless even to retain sufficient supplies in the country for domestic consumption. Cows in calf were sent to Germany for slaughter until the Government prohibited this traffic. Three hundred butchers' shops were closed down in Copenhagen alone.

In reply to a memorandum which I wrote on this subject it was pointed out by the Foreign Office that the double difficulty of interfering with the sea-borne trade between Denmark and Germany on the one hand, and, on the other, of adequately safeguarding the carriage of produce to the United Kingdom on board Danish vessels appeared to have been disregarded.

The trade in agricultural produce between Denmark and Germany was partly across the land frontier and partly by sea. With regard to the sea-borne trade of Denmark, it would not only have been difficult but futile for the Navy to have attempted to stop it; moreover, Danish coastal traffic with

Germany could be carried on inside territorial waters. The only method of using naval forces for stopping Danish supplies to Germany was by preventing raw materials from reaching Denmark. No naval difficulties, however, stood in the way of seeing that faith was kept by the Danes respecting the conditions under which they received their goods.

As to the difficulty of safeguarding the carriage of produce to the United Kingdom, there was the alternative land route to Christiania, Bergen and Trondhjem. The Norwegian traffic was carried on by this route : it was used by Germany herself, and later it was in fact used for the carriage of Danish produce, which was shipped from the Norwegian ports under escort across the North Sea. There was also a possible route through Swedish and Norwegian territorial waters : this route, however, was not to be recommended.

In August, 1916, the thread of negotiations was taken up by the new Minister, Sir Ralph Paget, with whom I discussed the whole question of the Danish exports to Germany.

The war had now been in progress for two years. Supplies were still pouring into Germany, and the result of the efforts of two years to get them stopped had proved to be unavailing.

I again visited Copenhagen in the autumn and urged upon the Minister the necessity of recommending the adoption of measures which had formed the subject of my official, semi-official and private correspondence during the war. The principal points upon which I had always laid stress were : that the 1913 basis of rationing was unsound; that our imports were indirectly feeding the Germans, and that the principle of " releases " should be carefully scrutinised with a view to the adoption of measures for the prevention of the obvious and glaring abuses to which they were open; that a German invasion of Denmark was improbable and in any case not a matter to be feared; that no action of ours, however drastic, was likely to provoke Germany to take retaliatory measures by interfering with the Danish produce boats to England; and, even if it should do so, that there existed alternative protected routes.

With regard to the threatened invasion of Denmark (colloquially referred to in Scandinavia as the " invasion bogey "), this fear was of a periodic character, synchronising as a rule with great scarcity in Denmark : it was a sure draw, and the invasion was only to be averted by plenty of replenishments from the United Kingdom.

These matters formed the subject of very lengthy and detailed discussion between us. I succeeded ultimately in gaining the support of the British Minister, who finally accepted my views and expressed his approval of them in unequivocal terms which left me in no doubt of the sincerity of his beliefs.

It then became necessary to take steps for forestalling the resistance with which these novel proposals would be met when they became known to the Danish delegates. To this end Mr. Andersen was forthwith warned by the Minister of a probable impending change in our blockade policy and of its nature. A Dane, like other sensible people, will always submit philosophically to circumstances that cannot be avoided. It is only fair to the Danes to say that hitherto no attempt had been made to impose our will upon them, and that, as Danes, they were perfectly justified in sending their goods to the best market. Mr. Andersen on receiving warning would not be slow to make up his mind as to the best course to be pursued; and the classical case of the Danish Mr. Hobson in circumstances resembling so closely those with which Mr. Andersen was now confronted would doubtless commend itself to him as a precedent which it would be wise to accept as a guide.

That Mr. Andersen did adopt some such line of reasoning was soon made abundantly clear by the conciliatory spirit shown at the next meeting, when the question of the revision of the existing agreement was discussed by Danish and British representatives. Up to this time, December, 1916, the opinion had been held—or rather it had been tendered—that any reduction of exports of agricultural produce to Germany would be both difficult and dangerous : and then difficulty and danger disappeared as if by magic.

But when negotiations were again resumed with a view to the embodiment of new and amended terms in the Danish agreement, trouble again arose. Discussion hinged largely upon the meaning of " Danish *bonâ fide* home requirements "; by which the Danes took it to be understood that so long as imports were not re-exported there could be no objection to their receiving supplies without limitation, and irrespective of the quantity of home-grown produce that was released for export : that is to say that the Danish policy was to continue to trade with Germany and to resist the imposition of any restrictions that interfered with it; whereas the only *raison d'être* of the agreement was to restrict supplies to Germany through Denmark, on which account the rationing of imports should take into consideration Danish exports to belligerent countries similar to, if not identical in kind with, the article rationed. The Danes expected us to acquiesce in a suggestion which entailed supply-ing " bunkers," the result of British labour, and in allowing Danish exporters to do a profitable trade with Germany at our expense. They expected us to view with favour the employment of valuable shipping, which Germany was destroying, to carry these unnecessary commodities to Denmark.

Negotiations continued : but time slipped away. A contributory cause to the change in the Danish view above recorded, and one which caused the British Minister more astonishment than it caused me, was the electrifying news carried on the wings of ubiquitous rumour that Sir Edward Carson (now Lord Carson) was to take the place of Viscount Grey at the Foreign Office. None better knew than the Head of the Danish delegation what that change would have portended. But when this report proved to be false, courage returned; the Dane again became his old original self and resisted the proposed terms of the new Agreement.

So matters went on until the early part of 1917, when a set of circumstances arose which placed the whole situation in a new light.

On 1st February, 1917, Germany's campaign of unrestricted submarine warfare was opened. In the words of the Kaiser : " I command that unrestricted U-boat warfare shall be instituted with the utmost energy on 1st February."

There seems to have been a tacit understanding between Denmark and Germany that the Danish ships trading with England should not be molested provided they did not carry cattle or fish, and that fodder and fertilisers were allowed to pass through our blockade. Germany, as compensation for the immunity from interference that the Danish shipping obtained, received the meat, lard and miscellaneous imports, in addition to a heavy and disproportionate percentage of dairy produce.

As the war progressed England began to feel the shortage of food which she had enabled Denmark to supply to Germany : she became dependent in an increasing degree, accentuated by the heavy losses to shipping, upon Danish supplies : the economic advantage which she had held in the early stages of the war had to a great extent been dissipated; and she was unable to foil either the Danes or the Germans in their attempts to turn the changed circumstances of the situation to their own account unless, accepting all risks, she declined to be a party to further negotiations.

The effect of cutting off fodder and fertilisers at any time would have been the necessary slaughter of cattle and pigs that could no longer be fed : this would immediately have led to an increased supply to Germany, lasting, according to the Danish delegates, for about three months.

It was thoroughly realised at home that at this time, February, 1917, the coming three or four months were to be a very critical period for Germany. The U-boat campaign for the moment settled automatically the question of Scandinavian supplies : but Germany now viewed with good hope the possibility of obtaining a decision before being overtaken by starvation.

Germany had seen the situation slowly but surely change to our disadvantage : she had seen the havoc that her submarines had wrought on our shipping and imports : and to us her warfare had brought home our dependence upon the sea for our supplies. Shortage was felt in England and losses could not be made good : the position had become an anxious

L

one; and Germany reckoned that, were she to devote all her energies to the sinking of ships bound for our shores, she would in from six to nine months be able to compel our surrender.

When the U-boat warfare was proclaimed consternation reigned in shipping circles. The first effect of the campaign was to cause the Danes to stop their service of ships carrying produce to the United Kingdom, the Scandinavian traffic became precarious and uncertain, and in blockading us Germany had blockaded herself; for imports could now only reach Denmark at far greater risk than had previously been encountered.

In order to meet our pressing demands for produce negotiations took place between Denmark and Germany, and an arrangement was made by which, in return for British coal to Denmark, Germany would allow three boats with agricultural produce to leave Denmark once a week for Aberdeen and to return during the following week. This arrangement involved, it will be observed, a modification of the German blockade. In deciding upon her policy of unrestricted submarine warfare Germany had taken extraordinary risks; she had defied all recognised law and almost wantonly provoked America to hostility: but she had made careful calculations; she had measured the effect of her ordinary submarine activities on our shipping and supplies, and had reckoned that the new piratical submarine operations would enable her to achieve her object of starving us before she herself should be overtaken by starvation or by retributory measures which her unlawful action might provoke. She must starve us, but to do so she must act quickly. Yet we find Germany consenting to an arrangement imperilling the principal condition of success of her new submarine campaign. In sanctioning Danish supplies to England Germany was lengthening the limited period in which the successful accomplishment of her aim could be brought about; she was staking her chances of victory upon starving us, yet she was virtually sending us supplies.

Why?

The real truth would seem to have been that although Germany hoped, and many Germans thought, that the new U-boat warfare would reduce us to starvation, yet nobody could feel quite sure about it : it is known that grave misgivings on the subject were entertained in Germany; and since failure, were the extreme risk to be taken of having supplies of fodder and fertilisers to Denmark cut off, would spell disaster, it seems probable that more cautious counsels were allowed to prevail and that this risk was not accepted : Germany therefore allowed us some scraps from Denmark's larder as a premium on her life insurance.

Our own position amounted to this : that the housekeeper could not buy all she wanted. We had become inconvenienced by shortage and had been rationed : but England compared to Germany was a land of plenty. Denmark's food was important, but not vital to us as it was to Germany. The Board of Trade pressed for Danish supplies, and necessity had begun to define our policy. We were not free, as in the early days of the war, to ignore the existence of Denmark, for our economic weapon had become blunted. But the position that did not seem to be thoroughly appreciated was that Germany wished to make a bargain with us. To consent to the German proposal was to admit that Germany could dictate the terms to us on which we should receive supplies : nevertheless the proposal was accepted. Thus it had at last come about that by surrendering our maritime rights before the war and trading with the neighbours of our enemy during the war, and in rejecting proposals in which the present position was clearly foreshadowed and the principle of indiscriminate trading with Scandinavia was denounced, we had been brought to the inglorious position in which Germany, herself in the throes of starvation, could yet, after two and a half years of war, command the necessary replenishments for Denmark's soil and stock through our fleet, and could and did impose a definite limit upon the supplies that we received from Denmark. In 1917 we were reaping what we sowed in 1915 and 1916 when we were building up great food industries and establishing them at the gates of Germany.

The situation that had been created was truly extraordinary. Towards the end of February some thirty ships with cargoes of fodder for Denmark, which had been detained at home, were ordered to be released. It was very important at this critical juncture that Denmark should not have this fodder and that Germany, if possible, should be made to experience the effects of her new submarine campaign. Arising out of representations that I made to the British Minister at Copenhagen on this matter, telegraphic correspondence passed between the Legation and the Foreign Office, the latter being advised that if there was no objection to about 1,250,000 of cattle, pigs and horses going to Germany during the next few months fodder and fertilisers could be stopped altogether.

It will not be disputed that if Germany could have

obtained an early decision and could have been certain of obtaining it, and that if these supplies were necessary to her, it would have been wise to continue sending Denmark the raw materials necessary to prevent the slaughter of animals and their export to Germany. The military situation has been discussed in a previous chapter : it was reviewed at considerable length at this juncture during the war : this ground will not be re-traversed; the conclusions arrived at were that a descent upon Denmark became more and more improbable as the later stages of the war were reached, and that in no case could Germany have gained by such an operation; and further that at no time had Germany ever any reason for placing hopes upon an early and certain success.

As to the length of time that Denmark's capital would last, I have it on the authority of well-informed Danes that Danish supplies if Germany invaded Jutland would only bring a passing relief, estimated as likely to last only for three months : but conjecture on this point must give place to knowledge as derived from subsequent events; for when supplies were afterwards cut off, the Danish exports to Germany gradually dwindled away, and in 1918 up to the date of the Armistice they had become negligible.

Denmark pressed for fodder and fertilisers for certain ostensible reasons; but she knew that if her imports were stopped her pig industry must be smashed almost at once, and that her cattle industry must suffer seriously and could not long survive. The general effect would be to stop agricultural exports.

The large stocks in Denmark, it must be pointed out, had been made possible only by the continued supply of raw materials into this dangerous zone.

The official view is taken that the import of fodder and fertilisers into Denmark must be continued in order to prevent these stocks from reaching Germany. The position would thus seem to have been created that Denmark's agricultural industry must be kept going indefinitely simply because we dare not stop imports : our enemies must be supplied with food that they shall not ransack the larder that we ourselves have stocked. When, in 1914, the blockade could have been enforced and sure ruin brought to Germany, open trade was conducted with Scandinavia. In August, 1914, Germany could not be blockaded by reason of the attitude of America towards the subject of maritime rights; but in March, 1917, it would seem to have been the restive cattle and pigs of Denmark, which were held in leash by the British Minister, that stood in the way. It will be observed that the right and the power to stop the fodder to Denmark are left to be understood, America constituting no obstacle to the exercise of this power, the only consideration being a question of expediency.

The following unsolicited testimony from an unknown German friend was brought to the notice of the Foreign Secretary in support of the measures which I had proposed with regard to the Danish fodder ships.

A German submarine on 1st March, 1917, sank without warning in the North Sea the Norwegian ship " Gurre." She then turned her attention to an English ship, but was driven off by gun-fire, after which she captured and took into port as prize the Norwegian ship " Livingstone " with a cargo of saltpetre.

The submarine then approached the Danish ship

"Holthe" (Captain Hansen). On learning, however, that the "Holthe" was carrying a cargo of oil-cake to Denmark the commander of the submarine allowed her to continue her journey, informing her captain that "the oil-cake will benefit us just as much as you, and you can thank your lucky stars you have such a cargo." It was certainly sometimes difficult to distinguish friend from foe.

The telegram announcing the intention to release thirty ships with fodder and fertilisers followed close on the heels of grave disclosures concerning the conduct of officials responsible for carrying out the terms of agreement under which Danish pork was exported. Although the home markets in Denmark had been unable to obtain from the butchers the quantity of pork to which they were entitled, it was discovered that in December and January alone 36,000 carcasses of swine in excess of the quantity allowed by arrangement between the British and Danish Governments were exported to Germany. This gave a surplus income of 6,000,000 kroner (about £350,000) for division among private and co-operative butchers.

Adverting to the report of an inquiry which was held on this matter, a Danish paper, the *Extrabladet*, wrote as follows :—

The Commission's report does not present any satisfactory solution; but the most satisfactory feature, of which there is no word in the finding, is, we have reason to believe, that in spite of the affair our good relations with other countries, and not the least with England, have been preserved. As Lord Robert Cecil a few days ago explained in the House of Commons on the

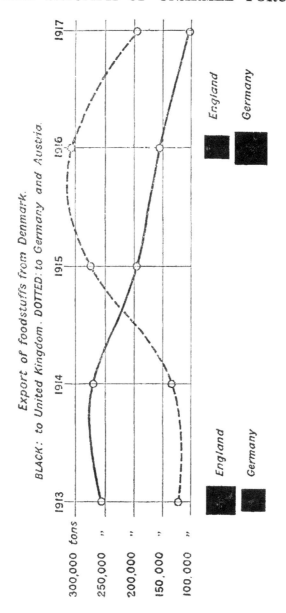

Export of foodstuffs from Denmark.
BLACK: to United Kingdom. DOTTED: to Germany and Austria.

part of the Government, he could express his full satisfaction with Denmark's conduct touching her obligations. This rolled away many a heavy stone from our hearts at home here.

That which stood behind this export affair like a heavy black threatening shower, was our constant anxiety that it would compromise our commercial position to an irreparable extent. From such a misfortune we escaped.

In September, 1917, I wrote as follows to the Minister of Blockade :—

DEAR LORD ROBERT CECIL,

I hope you will excuse the liberty I am taking in forwarding to you the enclosed report on Denmark.

It was given to me by an American diplomat and is written by a Mr. Conger, the representative in Denmark of the Associated Press.

I may mention that I have never met or corresponded with Mr. Conger, and for this reason the report appears to me to be of particular interest, containing as it does such striking confirmation of various reports written by me on the same subject during the last eighteen months.

Please believe me,
Yours very truly.

The report, slightly abridged, is to be found in the Appendix.

CHAPTER VI

THE fishing industry of Norway is by far the largest and most important of those in Northern Europe. In 1913 Norway's total export of fish was about 330,000 tons, as against 40,000 to 50,000 in the case of Sweden and Denmark.

Before the war a large quantity of this fish was taken by the Latin countries—Brazil, Cuba, Portugal, Spain, the Argentine and Italy—to meet the demands of fasting days and festivals; but on the outbreak of hostilities, owing to the special requirements for freight-space and to the general dislocation of trade, a large surplus of fish was thrown on the market. It was almost certain that Germany, to whom such large quantities of food and fish-oil would have been invaluable, would endeavour to obtain these surplus supplies; it would also have paid Norway to serve Germany at very remunerative rates, possessing, as she did, direct rail communication from her seaports to Germany.

Fish during the first two years of the war was the principal article of diet in German trains and restaurants; the fish-oil was very valuable on account of the glycerine—an explosive ingredient—which it contained; fish-guano and fish-meal were also produced.

The whole of the Scandinavian industries when war broke out felt themselves to be on a very precarious footing. Nobody knew what was going to happen; and in particular it was realised that if coal

154

was not forthcoming from us, it would not be obtainable elsewhere; and without coal the industries must collapse. But the fishing industries depended for their maintenance not only upon coal, but upon many other articles such as petroleum, tin, olive oil, tomato pulp and fishing gear, which, if not in every case an exclusive monopoly of Great Britain's, were mainly under her control.

Such, at any rate, was the view taken by the Norwegians and especially by the coastal population, which had a wholesome respect for our Navy, and would have hailed with relief any arrangements by which their livelihood could be ensured and the spectre of uncertainty removed. It is true that the high prices commanded in the German market offered a very alluring bait to the Norwegian fishermen; but the Norwegians recognised that before selling their fish to the Germans the formality of alluring the fish themselves out of the water would first have to be attended to; and that without the good-will and practical sympathy of Great Britain this would be no easy matter. The moment and the circumstances immediately following the outbreak of war could not have been more favourable for acquiring the Norwegian catch by purchase in return for a guaranteed supply of all fishing accessories.

In Christiania H.M. representatives kept themselves in close touch with the leaders of the fishing industry; they ascertained the prospects of success that might be expected to attend negotiations for purchase, and reported favourably.

It is believed that these sound proposals failed to gain the support of the Treasury; and, as in other cases, notably in those of cotton and copper, an opportunity was thrown away of saving millions of

money, and at the same time of cutting off a very
substantial part of Germany's food and oil, on the
supply of which her ability to continue the struggle
in a large measure depended.

In August, 1916, the proposals made two years previously were carried out, and a Fish Agreement was
concluded with Norway by which the greater part of
the Norwegian catch was obtained by purchase but
at three times the cost of the 1914 offer.

The result of the failure to conclude this Agreement
at an earlier date may be judged from the following
figures :—

EXPORTS TO GERMANY AND AUSTRIA FROM NORWAY (TONS)

1913	1914	1915[1]	1916[1]	1917
78,771	67,746	161,409	194,167	82,948

To have obtained the full benefit of the Fish Agreement with Norway it was necessary that the Danish
and Swedish fish industries should also have received
close attention, and that suitable pressure should have
been exerted to bring Denmark and Sweden into line
in the matter of the disposal of their fish.

Let us look into the figures.

The Swedish and Danish fish industries during the
war were very closely connected with each other :
they may therefore be considered together.

EXPORTS TO GERMANY AND AUSTRIA (TONS)

	1913	1914	1915	1916	1917
Sweden	30,303	43,298	53,406	51,113	7,820
Denmark	25,516	32,968	66,569	106,694	38,841
Total	55,819	76,266	119,975	157,807	46,661

The figures for the years 1914 and 1917 throughout
these statistics do not serve well for purposes of

[1] These include the diverted fish for Latin countries.

general illustration, 1914 being two-thirds a peace year, and 1917 two-thirds a year in which America was fighting on the side of the Allies.

A comparison of the totals for 1915 and 1916 with the total for 1913 would seem to obviate the necessity for entering into any explanation of the significance of these figures.

The exports of these countries to the United Kingdom were as follows :—

		1913	1914	1915	1916	1917
Sweden	. .	4,745	1,951	—	—	—
Denmark	. .	3,932	2,704	5,303	1,902	—
Total	. .	8,677	4,655	5,303	1,902	—

Comparing the total supplies during 1915, 1916 and 1917 with those of 1913 in the cases of the United Kingdom and Germany, we find that the United Kingdom's grand total for the three war years is 1,400 tons odd less than the quantity received in 1913 : Germany's grand total is 268,624 tons more. The figures are as follows :—

			1913	1915, 1916 and 1917.
United Kingdom	.	.	8,677	7,205
Germany	.	.	55,819	324,443

It is not suggested that the country that supplied the fishing gear should by right and without regard to other considerations receive all the fish; but it is suggested that such a country should have cared more for its own interests than to allow its enemies to receive forty-six times the amount received by itself. In addition to the whole of the cutch and blue vitriol—articles used for repairs and preservative purposes—we also supplied Denmark with practically all the fishing nets, yarn and rope.

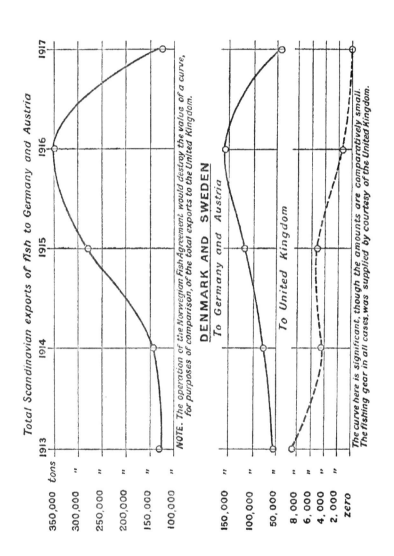

Total Scandinavian exports of fish to Germany and Austria

NOTE. The operation of the Norwegian Fish Agreement would destroy the value of a curve, for purposes of comparison, of the total exports to the United Kingdom.

DENMARK AND SWEDEN

To Germany and Austria

To United Kingdom

The curve here is significant, though the amounts are comparatively small. The fishing gear in all cases, was supplied by courtesy of the United Kingdom.

FISHING-NETS AND YARN FOR REPAIRS SUPPLIED TO DENMARK (TONS)

	1913	1914	1915	1916	1917
United Kingdom .	39	65	133	213	135
Germany . . .	78	72	—	—	10

In 1915 and 1916 a special effort, it will be observed, had to be made to meet the German requirements of 120,000 and 158,000 tons : hence our supplies of fishing-nets to Denmark in those two years, which were about 350 and 500 per cent. greater than in 1913.

Copenhagen is a city intersected with canals in which in normal times may be seen the tank boats containing the live fish for sale—fish being a staple article of diet among the Danes. Fish became the scarcer as the war progressed, until eventually it was practically unobtainable in Denmark. To secure supplies, especially for the poor, legislation was passed, but without effect; for the spirit of the regulations was evaded by technical loopholes to which unfortunately the regulations were open.

The radical cure was the stoppage of petroleum, the propellant used by the fishing boats. By an agreement which we had with the Danes a sufficient supply of petroleum was ensured them under guarantee that the fish should not be sent to Germany; but guarantees in the absence of supervision over the fish traffic were literally useless.

The scarcity of fish became so acute that the matter was taken up by the Danish Press; but neither the public exposure of this scandalous traffic nor personal protests availed to get it stopped. Any laxity in administration in one country was apt to exercise an evil influence upon the neighbouring States. The abuse by the Danes of their guarantees was made the subject of protest by the Norwegians. To know what was going on in any one of these Scandinavian countries it was only necessary to make inquiries in one of the others. Norway knew very well and very accurately what Denmark was receiving from us and what she was sending to Germany : she did not like this differentiation of treatment, which on the face of it was unjust, and by which she suffered in pocket. In the ordinary course of my work I interviewed very many Norwegian merchants, coal importers, shipping agents and others who would come to the Legation on the business of obtaining redress for alleged grievances, usually in connection with our coal, of which for the best of reasons they had been refused supplies. These men were all amenable to reason : they were very bitter on the subject of Denmark, who, they urged with equal truth and justice, obtained not only as much British coal as she wished, but was allowed to make use of it in mills and factories that worked in Germany's interests. The centre of disturbance according to these Norwegians was Aarhus, where we should be able to verify their statements and see Danish ships running goods to Germany on British coal.

I proceeded to Copenhagen, saw the Minister, and again urged the necessity for having some British officials sent to Denmark. This led to the appointment of a Vice-Consul, Mr. Thirsk, to Aarhus in April, 1916.

Mr. Thirsk was a shrewd man of business, and besides having an open mind he had also an independent one : his hobby was hard work; he had never before held any official post—I think he had been a journalist. He arrived on the scene of his labours filled with an insatiable curiosity and with the set determination to detect and expose abuses. We all have our faults :

the aptitude for acquiring facts together with the happy talent for recording them would have made Mr. Thirsk's selection for the post he occupied quite an ideal one but for a most improper prejudice which he seemed to entertain against our enemies.

Although it was the subject of coal that had brought Mr. Thirsk to Denmark, he soon found himself immersed in the business of fish, grain, oil, fatty acids, petroleum and guarantees. For the present we are concerned with the subject of fish only.

There was a Department with offices in London, whose special business it was to deal with the restriction of supplies to the enemy. Commander Leverton-Harris, R.N.V.R., the Head of this Department (R.E.S.D.), had arrived in Christiania in the summer of 1916 to conduct the negotiations for the conclusion of the Fish Agreement with Norway. We discussed together the subject of the Danish fish traffic with Germany. Commander Leverton-Harris was unaware of the flourishing state of this traffic, and of the injurious compromising effects it would have upon any economic measures that might be taken by the Department which he represented : the fact that the fishing industry depended in any way upon British or British-controlled supplies came, as he frankly confessed, as a great surprise to him. He asked me to communicate further and full particulars to him : this request I complied with, and I particularly asked that immediate action might be taken on his return for getting supplies of petroleum stopped.

On Commander Leverton-Harris's departure I again visited Copenhagen and requested that Mr. Thirsk might be directed to institute inquiries at certain fishing centres and to report. Mr. Thirsk visited several ports in Jutland, interviewed Danish fishermen,

M

agents and Customs officials, personally checked the quantities of fish in wagons bound for Germany and spared no pains in his efforts to arrive at facts, which he recorded in a series of reports of unusual interest and importance.

He found the fishing fraternity very reticent : they appeared to have something to conceal. Special fish trains ran regularly to Germany, and at times the resources of the railways could scarcely meet the requirements of the fish traffic.

With regard to petroleum, which was supplied to Denmark under guarantee that the fishermen should have only a limited supply, Mr. Thirsk tells us that these guarantees were not worth the paper on which they were printed, and that petroleum could be obtained in unlimited quantities. The Danes themselves recognised that the United Kingdom would be justified in safeguarding her own interests by preventing fish from reaching Germany; they admitted that the trade was dishonest in view of the guarantee they signed that petroleum should not be used to the advantage of the enemies of the Allies. Fishers acknowledged their indebtedness to Great Britain for the supply of petroleum and fishing gear and gave Mr. Thirsk the impression that were the petroleum stopped as a result of their breaking their bond, they would accept it as a just punishment. Mr. Thirsk recommended that the supply of petroleum to Danish fishermen should be stopped at once and discontinued until the Danish Fishers' Union arrived at some definite and satisfactory decision as to the control of the traffic.

Not only did Mr. Thirsk strongly advocate the adoption of any measures necessary for the restriction of fish supplies to Germany, but he pointed out that such measures, if successful, would be welcomed by the Danes themselves.

Mr. Thirsk's reports bring us to the end of 1916. Truth is certainly stranger than fiction. That we should be supplying the Danish fishermen with all necessaries; that the fishermen should be sending practically the whole of their catch to Germany; that the Danes themselves should not be able to obtain one of their principal articles of diet; that the fishermen should be able to obtain unlimited quantities of petroleum without hindrance from the British authorities, who could kill the industry if they felt so disposed without infringing international right or disregarding national moral obligations; that all this should be taking place without any serious effort to stop it, was both strange and true : but I confess that it came as a surprise to me to learn that it was with a heavy heart and an uneasy conscience that the fishermen plied their trade; that they disliked breaking their guarantees; and that they would really have been happier to have had their guilty souls shriven by H.M. Government by the cutting off of their petroleum supplies. A disinterested person might have been excused for thinking that British and Danish interests might perhaps have had something in common.

When Commander Leverton-Harris left Norway I kept him well posted in the latest fish news from Denmark, and, to guard against the possibility of the originals' miscarrying or being unavoidably delayed, I sent him copies of Mr. Thirsk's reports, for which he professed himself as being profoundly grateful. The letters of Commander Leverton-Harris, who was Lord Robert Cecil's (the Blockade Minister's) right-hand man, in the early stages of our correspondence

breathed hope in every line : the only defect to be
found in them was that they failed to stop the Danish
fish from continuing to reach Germany. The reports
were in his opinion " most interesting "; they were
" very admirable "; they had engaged his close attention, and he hoped the Foreign Office would follow
certain of my suggestions; Lord Robert was looking
into the matter, and so on. Presently, however, the
fire of enthusiasm began to burn down, and difficulties,
which had been smouldering, threatened to burst into
flames. The fish problem was found to be " one of
the most difficult to deal with "; the work of the
R.E.S.D. was daily becoming more exacting and
difficult : in short, it soon became clear that the
Danes were to be allowed to have their way in the
matter of the fish. With regard to coal pressure, on
which I had always laid great stress, arrangements
were already in contemplation for discussing this question, which might therefore be said to be approaching
its ante-penultimate stage.

More letters passed; and the order to stop supplying
petroleum to the Danish fishermen was at last given
by the Foreign Office on 30th November, 1916. (This
order was not carried out until some ten days later.)

Germany had in the meantime got into Roumania,
and although one of the finest pieces of individual
work performed during the war was the destruction
of the Roumanian oil wells, it is possible that it did
not prevent Germany from drawing off a quantity of
oil, which enabled her to send small supplies to
Denmark. This, however, is doubtful. As to Germany's ability to have supplied petroleum at an earlier
date and to have continued the supplies on an adequate
scale, there is good reason for supposing that she
could not have done so except at a sacrifice she could

ill afford to make, even for the fish of which she stood so much in need : to have compelled such a sacrifice would in itself have been well worth while; but if the order to stop petroleum, which could have been given at any time, had failed to achieve the desired result of stopping the fish traffic, economic pressure could have been exerted through fishing gear and coal.

Correspondence on the subject of Mr. Thirsk's reports will be found in the Appendix.

CHAPTER VII

OLEAGINOUS substances, which include many oil-seeds, nuts and beans, assumed a special importance during the war from their potential value as explosive substances, of which glycerine is the principal ingredient.

In former days, when the population in northern countries was much smaller, the agricultural and fishing industries were able to cover the requirements of the people in regard to oils and fats both for edible and technical purposes. As time went on and the populations increased, these industries were no longer able to supply the demand, and it became necessary to import vegetable and animal oils and fats from oversea. Oil-seeds and nuts, from which vegetable oils and fats are pressed, grow only in countries where there is an abundance of sun; that is to say, in tropical or sub-tropical countries such as the East Indies, Argentina, parts of the United States, Egypt and West Africa.

The bulk of the tallow imported into Europe comes from Australia, South America and the United States; America supplies most of the lard and other animal greases.

Parts of the British Empire, producing as they do large quantities of oil-seeds and nuts, tallow and fish-oils, play a very important part in the world's production as a whole. During the years previous to the war this trade had assumed enormous proportions, especially in England, which held the foremost position in the world in this industry; but Hamburg, Copenhagen and Rotterdam were also large centres; and it therefore became of great importance that a close watch should be kept over the imports of vegetable and animal oils and fats into Denmark and Holland, and that measures should be taken to prevent Germany from drawing upon these countries for supplies to meet the requirements of her lost markets.

These oils and fats, both vegetable and animal, are used in normal times principally for food, soap, candles, lubricants and fuel; but in war time their importance is much enhanced on account of the glycerine which they contain. Towards the end of 1915 the Germans discovered a process by which glycerine can be produced from sugar; this process, though exploited on a large scale in Germany, remained a secret until after the war. With this exception glycerine is produced entirely from vegetable and animal oils and fats. The importance attaching to this glycerine ingredient may be judged from the fact that during the war in the zone of the British Army all scraps of meat were carefully collected that the fat might be removed and used for the extraction of glycerine.

Most of the home-grown produce of Scandinavia and Holland consists of fatty substances. Before the war Germany obtained from these countries only very small quantities of oleaginous foods, such as butter, bacon, pork and fish-oils; but half her supply of butter came from the markets of Siberia, which were closed on the outbreak of war. England, on the other hand, obtained large quantities of these foods from Scandinavia and Holland : British markets had built up the Danish industries and England was Denmark's best

customer.   Any increase of Germany's supplies from
these countries would therefore be at our expense.

The situation, then, to be anticipated on the outbreak of war was that Germany would endeavour to
obtain maximum quantities of foodstuffs, and that
these foodstuffs should be charged with fat—that is to
say, with explosive ingredients; that Scandinavia and
Holland would, in the interests of their trade, increase
these home-grown supplies, with the special view to
their containing abundance of fats; and, to this end,
that the import of raw materials for agricultural
purposes would be based upon their suitability for
meeting the ultimate requirements of Germany for
explosives.

For nearly three years Germany and her neutral
neighbours succeeded in realising their wishes.   Denmark was supplied with vegetable oils and fats and
oil-cake from the British Empire far in excess of the
quantities she had obtained from us in peace time, and
which were urgently required in the United Kingdom
for increasing the productivity of the country and for
enabling the foodstuffs we had lost from Denmark to
be replaced.

During those fateful years, 1915 and 1916, it is
regretted that no protest should have been made by
the Legation in Copenhagen against the increased
traffic to Germany, which was justified on the ground
that the imports of fodder and fertilisers had shown
a yearly increase before the war.   But the important
fact was overlooked that this increase was due to the
steadily increasing demands of Denmark's largest
customer, England, for her agricultural produce; and
that since the outbreak of war a large part of the
produce properly belonging to us had been going to our
enemies.

In view of our policy towards neutrals, and particularly towards Denmark and Holland, it is not surprising that on 9th May, 1917, Herr von Batocki, the German Food Dictator, speaking in the Reichstag, should say : " Our reserves in fat, *regarding which we mostly depend on imports*, will last for a long time."

Dr. Helfferich, German Secretary of State for the Interior, is much more brutal :—

> In certain very important classes of goods our neighbouring neutrals were able to replace entirely the dropping out of the enemy countries and the neutral countries from which we were cut off, and even to increase our total supplies. This applies especially to the animal products trade, which was developed to a high efficiency in Holland and Denmark. . . . Naturally the neighbouring neutrals, whom we have to thank for these important contributions to our domestic economy, were not in the position to increase their output overnight in the degree necessary to furnish so material an extra supply for Germany. Some other customers, domestic or foreign, must have suffered for the benefit of Germany.
>
> So it was in fact. And the customer who went short was for the most part—ENGLAND ! !

Which is quite true : but how the Doctor does shout—and not a word of thanks. *R. n th.. r..o.... ! N onde.*

During the course of the war it became clear that Denmark was disposing of oils far in excess of the quantities credited to her in the British official statistics. In the beginning of 1917 it was impossible to reconcile reports received from various sources outside the British Legation in Denmark with the information given in our statistics. The position was thoroughly mystifying, and very disquieting, so much so that I went carefully through the whole of the entries relating to oils in the Danish Section of the British statistics for the years 1913 to 1916, but without finding any apparent reason for assuming that discrepancies existed.

In turning to the oil-seeds and nuts imports, however, the sought-for explanation was found. These seeds and nuts in the statistics were tabulated without there being given any oil values to them. Entering further into this question I obtained values of the various seeds, copra, earth-nuts, hemp-seed, linseed, palm kernels, rape, sessamum, soya-beans and others, in terms of oil and oil-cake (or fodder); and with this data translated the quantities of oil-seeds and nuts into their respective constituent values of oil and oil-cake, of which no mention was made in the statistics.

The following table will illustrate the position :—

SUMMARY OF VEGETABLE OIL IMPORTS TO DENMARK

	1913	1914	1915	1916
Edible oils .	14,839	9,288	10,844	8,586
Technical oils .	1,722	1,792	2,000	1,518
Totals shown by statistics .	16,561	11,080	12,844	10,104
[1] Oil values of imported oil-seeds not shown in British statistics .	31,648	39,821	58,805	60,975
Totals .	48,209	50,901	71,649	71,079
Increases over 1913 . .	. .	2,692	23,440	22,870

[1] These quantities, it will be observed, are in 1915 and 1916 about five times greater than the amounts with which Denmark is credited; that is to say, that Denmark was receiving a stated amount of oil, but in addition she obtained an unrecorded amount of five times as much.

Of the above the following came from the United Kingdom and British Empire :—

	1913	1914	1915	1916
Edible oils . . .	290	728	1,730	312
Technical oils . . .	146	588	1,369	986
Oil values of imported oil-seeds	5,459	9,736	17,547	12,239
Totals	5,895	11,052	20,646	13,537

The oil-cake or fodder values of the imported oil-seeds to Denmark, which had also been omitted from the official statistics,[1] are as follows :—

	1913	1914	1915	1916
Oil-cake from oil-seeds .	81,283	105,343	155,274	146,207
Of the above, the following came from the United Kingdom and British Empire	13,112	23,304	42,207	32,985

By importing their vegetable oils in the seed the Danes obtained large quantities of oil-cake for fattening cattle : an arrangement which suited them admirably. The export of cattle, thus fattened, which went on hoof from Denmark to Germany, attained the proportions shown as follows :—

1913	. . . . . .	152,357
1914	. . . . . .	187,438
1915	. . . . . .	250,843
1916	. . . . . .	305,031

Compare the import of soya-beans and copra to Denmark before and during the war :—

1915	Soya-beans	100,781 tons
	Copra	55,168 ,,
1916	Soya-beans	102,537 ,,
	Copra	42,342 ,,
2		300,828 ,,
Average 1915, 1916	. . . .	150,414 ,,
Average 1911, 1913	. . . .	68,208 ,,

[1] Resulting from a report which I made on this matter later tables of statistics showed the fodder value and the oil value of all oil-seeds.

It should be noted that the whole of the copra came from British colonies and the soya-beans from Manchuria.

It is little wonder that H.M. Government had difficulty in prevailing upon the Japanese Government to prohibit the export of soya-beans to neutrals engaged in supplying foodstuffs to our enemies when our own colonies were supplying these neutrals with copra.

Copra contains a large proportion of oil, and was a very dangerous commodity to allow into a country that was supplying our enemies with grease : yet in the years 1915 and 1916 Denmark imported 97,510 tons of copra. This means roughly 20,000 tons of oil and 70,000 tons of oil-cake.

In two years, therefore, the imports of one commodity alone from our own colonies released to our enemies 20,000 tons of grease, and in addition supplied 70,000 tons of fattening material for cattle exported to our enemies.

Further, it should be noted that a large part of these soya-beans and copra were brought from the Far East with British coal.

Lard is a substance from which glycerine is extracted. Under an agreement with the American packers we allowed the importation of a certain amount of American lard for the use of the Danish margarine factories. This lard, which was more suitable than the Danish for the manufacture of margarine, released Danish lard for export to Germany. " If it has been so arranged," wrote the British Minister at Copenhagen, referring to the contract, " we cannot now go back on our word and stop the import." This would seem to imply that there was some point of honour involved here. Setting aside the fact that the import of lard was eventually stopped, the parties to business contracts are protected by substantial legal penalties attaching to breach of contract : in the case of this lard it could with advantage have been bought by us; and, moreover, it was received by Denmark only on condition that it should not benefit our enemies.[1]

Another invaluable source of fat was offal. The offal of almost every beast killed in Denmark was exported to Germany. Factories had been established near the frontier for the extraction of grease and fat: yet Denmark was allowed to import large quantities of edible oils for her own use, while exporting at the same time large potential supplies of oils and fats available for home consumption.

Among the most important ingredients for the manufacture of explosives are :—

(a) Sulphuric acid,
(b) Nitric acid,
(c) By-products of coal,
(d) Glycerine.

(a), (b) and (c) Germany herself could supply, but glycerine is a product of the fishing and agricultural industries, and Germany depended upon Danish supplies for making good her deficiencies.

It was not cattle that Germany required, but *fat* cattle, and the Danes, that their cattle might come up to the German standard, spared no pains in the care they bestowed upon them, feeding them on the most fat-producing food procurable.

The growing of fodder depended upon the quantities of fertilisers imported and the amount of land available. The available fodder-producing land in

[1] For letter on this subject, see Appendix.

turn depended upon the amount of cereals imported. If sufficient cereals were imported for human food the whole of the land became available for pasture or the cultivation of fodder. During the war Denmark's imports of cereals decreased, thus reducing the amount of land available for growing fodder from the necessity of having to sow cereals 'on it; but the increased imports of fodder-stuffs more than compensated for this reduction in the fodder-growing area of the country.

Now the fodder-stuffs used in Denmark consisted of:—

    (a) Maize and meal,

    (b) Oil-cake and meal,

both of which possess great fattening value : also of

    (c) Bran, peas and beans,

which are much inferior to (a) and (b).

The import of (a) and (b) increased during the war; (c) decreased; but the total amount of fat-producing fodder imported into Denmark in 1916 was greatly in excess of the average in 1911–1913. The position was aggravated by the fact that the abnormal export of horses and cattle to Germany since the outbreak of war would allow the remaining stock to receive its normal ration on a total quantity of imported fodder-stuffs less than the pre-war quantity. It is estimated that 200,000 tons of fodder were economised in this way in 1916, and used for fattening stock to serve Germany's special purposes.

The imports of fodder to Denmark, as has been said, were steadily increasing before the war; but that was because the exports of agricultural produce to England were increasing. Nor could these increased imports be accounted for by the food requirements of the population; for the figures show that so far as human food is concerned the imports, with the exception of cereals, had increased; and imports as a whole, including fertilisers, had been well maintained : the productivity of the country had, therefore, been maintained on its pre-war basis.

We turn again to Mr. Thirsk's reports. During his rounds of the Danish ports he went, with characteristic thoroughness, into the movements of grain, oil and cattle-fattening products; the matters that came under his personal observation may be accepted as typical of the transactions that were taking place throughout Denmark. It must be remembered that the ostensible aim of our blockade policy was to prevent Scandinavia, and in particular Denmark, from importing more than she required for domestic consumption, and to restrict her trade with Germany.

Many Danish merchants and exporters faithfully carried out their obligations not to use imported goods for the benefit of the enemy; and Mr. Thirsk, in the spirit of impartiality with which he pursued his investigations, is careful to cite such cases as came under his observation : at the same time it has to be remembered that infringement of the regulations, if discovered, carried risks which would not lightly be incurred; and although the love of virtue may have moved many manufacturers to refuse tempting German offers, the fear of the consequences of a breach of guarantee would undeniably have tended to swell the ranks of the virtuous.

Mr. Thirsk's reports, as in the case of fish, are full of cold incontrovertible facts. All the grains with which he deals are found to be largely " in excess." The imports of maize and oil-cake for June, July and August, 1916, at Aarhus—to take a random selection—

are 19,616 tons in excess of the quarterly average for
the three years preceding the war. So huge were the
accumulated stocks in Danish ports that it was
common to see whole cargoes, which had been discharged on the vacant spaces near the docks, protected
from the weather by waterproofs lent by the Danish
State Railway for the purpose.

Mr. Thirsk was anxious to obtain the percentage of
dairy produce exported respectively to the United
Kingdom and Germany, but this was Denmark's
secret, and, as it was guarded by the substantial penalty
of 20,000 kroner for divulging it, it would seem to have
been something well worth keeping from us; at the
same time it gives a clue as to what was in the minds
of Sweden and Denmark at the conference which took
place at Malmo in December, 1914.

The impression created on Mr. Thirsk by all those
with whom he came in contact—importers, dealers,
farmers and dairymen—was that a period of unprecedented prosperity was being experienced. Although
grain and cattle-feeding products arrived under
guarantee not to be re-exported, and were, moreover,
further protected by the Danish export prohibition,
yet the traffic was ruled entirely by the high prices
obtainable in Germany: only an insignificant percentage of the products of these imports, i. e. of meat
and dairy produce, was sold in Denmark, the prices
having risen to the German figure, which to most
Danes was prohibitive. It was the popular conviction in Denmark that Great Britain was the cause of
these high prices, not by reason of any obstacle that
was put in the way of importing articles, but because
there was no prohibition on the export to Germany of
the finished product of the imports, i. e. of meat and
dairy produce.

Butter, bacon, eggs and even cattle were, in Mr. Thirsk's opinion, the finished product of the foodstuffs imported by Denmark. He properly regarded their export to Germany as being in contravention of the fodder and foodstuffs prohibition, and thought that the fodder and foodstuffs that reached Denmark were very excessive.

There were stocks of grain, fodder and cattle-fattening products warehoused at Aarhus sufficient to supply normal needs for some months. Such was the state of Denmark in 1916; and it may be concluded that Mr. Thirsk was not one of the " experienced officials " who were " of opinion that practically no commodities of military importance are now being imported in quantities appreciably above the amounts legitimately required for home consumption." [1]

Nearly all the chief towns in Jutland were visited by Mr. Thirsk, who found much the same conditions existing as at Aarhus. All convenient storehouses were filled to overflowing, and new and commodious warehouses had been erected to meet the increasing need for accommodation that had arisen since the outbreak of war. In short, all evidence pointed to the fact that the quantities of grain and fattening products allowed into Denmark, including immense amounts from the British Empire, were in excess of her proper and normal requirements and were being used for Germany's benefit. Mr. Thirsk obtained his information under difficulties : Danish official sources were denied him, and he was obliged to limit his investigations to such knowledge as could be gleaned from chance acquaintances, from Danish firms and from close personal observation. He was, I believe, at that time the only Englishman in Denmark outside

[1] Parliamentary Debates, No. 153, p. 3189.

N

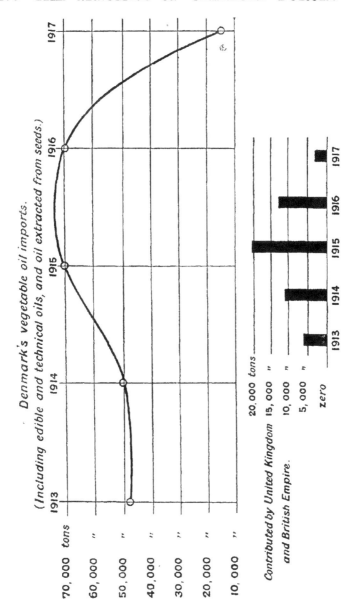

Denmark's vegetable oil imports.
(Including edible and technical oils, and oil extracted from seeds.)

Contributed by United Kingdom
and British Empire.

Copenhagen, and his opinions were, to the best of my belief, based entirely upon independent inquiry and observation.

Fats are synonymous with explosives. It is not possible to separate the fatty from the other ingredients of all the commodities containing fat that reached Germany. Nor is it possible diagrammatically to show the war value of fats : to Germany they were the breath of her life.

The graph on the opposite page is a fair example of the scale on which supplies reached Scandinavia in the early years of the war.

CHAPTER VIII

LUBRICANTS

To record all the rascality in which the transactions in lubricants were involved during the war would require a goodly-sized volume.

Lubricants were one of those indispensable commodities of which Germany at all times stood much in need, but especially in 1915 and 1916, when she found it so difficult to obtain them.

Mr. J. W. Gerrard, the American Ambassador in Berlin, recorded in his war diary in December, 1915 : " Probably the greatest need of Germany is lubricating oil for machines, etc."

Ludendorff makes frequent references to the difficulty of obtaining lubricants : " Lubricants presented us with some of our greatest problems. . . . Roumanian oil was of decisive importance," etc., etc.; all of which agrees with the evidence on the subject that was to be gathered in Scandinavia both from travellers returned from Germany and from official quarters. In 1915 Germany was offering 1,800 marks (about £90) for a barrel of oil whose market value in Denmark was 125 kroner (about £7).

The figures in the Scandinavian statistics (see Appendix) tell the same tale as the figures for most other commodities which we controlled during the war, and therefore require no special notice.

I had not been vastly interested in the matter of oil until the summer of 1915, when I received a communication from an anonymous correspondent, who signed himself " X Y," to the effect that a German steamer, which he named, was then lying alongside a jetty in the Free Harbour loading " Morris Fatbacks " and barrels with lard; and that a Swedish steamer was also there loading oil barrels. My correspondent reminded me of some of the previous history of this latter vessel and, with regard to the former, observed, " I wish you had a submarine." This was on a Friday morning.

The Free Harbour receives goods in transit only; goods, that is to say, which are not for consumption in Denmark and are not subject to tariff or customs duties.

In the afternoon I proceeded to the Free Harbour, where I saw barrels of vacuum oil, wagon oil and heavy engine oil being loaded on board these ships. These barrels bore the initials of a well-known firm in Stockholm, which was then importing oil in large quantities under guarantee that it should not reach Germany. It was this class of oils of which Germany stood greatly in need.

I reported the matter to the Legation, who communicated with the Danish Foreign Office and Ministry of Marine. A search was ordered to be carried out on board the German steamer, but since no precautions were taken until Sunday morning to guard against the possibility that the oil might be discharged on to the immense uncovered stock from which the barrels had been shipped, the report, which exonerated the ship, must be considered worthless.

Of the sincerity of the Danish high officials and of their desire to give all possible assistance there is no question : all were most sympathetic and courteous : nevertheless no oil was discovered and the ship left.

The Customs officials did not enter actively into the

matter until Saturday morning, the ship in the meantime remaining under the supervision of the Free Harbour authorities, who were responsible for the prevention of irregularities.

In reply to inquiries from the Foreign Office concerning the *bonâ fides* of the firm which was implicated in this business, it has been reported by the Legation that its connection was an innocent one. Inquiries on the same subject had, however, elicited the reply from the British Minister at Stockholm that since the outbreak of war the firm had assumed a German connection. This information was not mentioned in the telegram from Copenhagen.

Transactions similar to the above had been made the subject of official reports on more than one occasion, but to no effect.

The Swedish steamer mentioned by my anonymous correspondent was boarded by the Germans when fully laden with heavy lubricating oils belonging to the firm in question and taken to Swinemunde. It was afterwards stated in the Swedish papers that she had arrived in Stockholm and that her cargo had not been touched. Inquiries failed to trace this oil and, as happened also in the case of another ship, it is probable that the *barrels* were returned though the oil certainly was not.

Early in 1916 another Swedish steamer left the Free Harbour at Copenhagen bound for Gottenberg and other Swedish ports. This same firm had loaded her with some 2,200 barrels of the best lubricating oil, a fact which had been brought to the notice of the Legation authorities in plenty of time, it is thought, for inquiries to be made and steps taken to prevent what subsequently occurred. The steamer after clearing was promptly captured by the Germans and taken to Swinemunde. When questioned, and being uncertain as to how much was known to us about this deal, the firm's representative admitted to 1,200 barrels; he could not, of course, know that it would fall into German hands, and he assured us that the Germans would return it. The Danish newspapers made very light of such trivial incidents as this, a three-line reference to the effect that the S.S. " So-and-so " had been held up laden with a *general* cargo being deemed quite sufficient to meet the requirements of the case. Many papers suppressed all reference to these transactions.

As to the warning that was given to the Legation, this came from a certain person who stated that if any questions were raised he was prepared to swear an affidavit to the fact. Moreover, a report had been received from a Danish Government official that ships of the same line to which the steamer in question belonged, when on voyage between Copenhagen and Stockholm, were invariably taken into a German port by the patrol : yet the above firm was allowed to forward oil by this line.

Said a certain shipowner to me :—

> I shall never forget the first declaration I ever asked for, and which gave me a very good insight into the whole business. In 1914 one of my ships was bringing over a cargo of oil from the States to Copenhagen, and as I was getting a bit anxious about her I thought I would have a declaration from the consignee that the oil was not going to Germany. In reply to my inquiries he said he would sign anything I liked, and accordingly I sent him the declaration form, which he signed and returned. The ship arrived safely at Copenhagen and every drop of that oil was transhipped and sent straight on to Germany.

There were three ways available to firms for sending their oil over to Germany.

(1) By allowing German ships to go alongside their " heaps " in the Free Harbour at Copenhagen, where they would pick up the oil at moments when the vigilance of the " authorities " should be relaxed. From one or two of the specimens I saw of these authorities I did not gather that it would be a matter of insuperable difficulty to find such moments, or even the means of creating them artificially.

Concerning this trick a friend wrote :—

> A report has reached me that consignments of oil from New York consigned to —— are reaching Germany through the intermediation of Mr. —— residing in this town.
>
> The oil, which is in barrels, is marked " in transit at buyer's expense," and addressed Nykjebing, Gottenberg and other ports. The barrels are brought down to the wharf ostensibly for shipment on vessels sailing for neutral ports, but on the other side of these are moored vessels bound for Lubeck and other German ports. The barrels are merely passed across the decks of the vessels which are supposed to receive them, and placed on board the vessels bound for Germany.

(2) By sending it to Sweden and obtaining guarantees against its re-export from Swedish buyers.

It would be insulting to anybody's intelligence to credit him with the belief that such guarantees were of any earthly value : this is not to mention the fact that the guarantees were not legally binding in Sweden. At the beginning of August, 1915, we knew that large quantities of oil had gone to Germany viâ Malmo from Denmark.

(3) By sending it round to Stockholm to be intercepted by the Germans.

With regard to this artifice, Sweden, if she wished, could (and under protest from us did) institute Prize Court proceedings. I can, however, recall no case in which any oil was proved by us to have been returned by Germany. As before said, *barrels* were returned, but they were not broached by any Englishman.

As an example of this method some 7,000 barrels of machine oil arrived in Copenhagen early in 1916 from Philadelphia. They all bore the mark of the importing firm above referred to; 1,500 of them were distributed to various oil firms in Copenhagen, and 4,000 were loaded on board a Swedish steamer which left the Free Harbour a few days later for Stockholm. The casks were labelled variously : Malmo, Gottenberg, Stockholm, Christiania, Bergen and other ports. After being dumped at Stockholm, they would be transhipped and forwarded on the line of route of German destroyers.

The ship that had brought the oil then left for another cargo. All this oil came from an American company for which the same importing firm was agent.

The procedure adopted to get Swedish consignments of oil over to Germany was as follows : a consignment is proposed for a Swedish consignee, whom we will call Mr. X, a merchant residing in Gottenberg or any port on the *west* coast of Sweden. The Legation is asked by telegram if Mr. X is a reliable consignee : probably many other names are included in the telegram for other descriptions of merchandise. It was not possible that the Legation could, without efficient consular representation, report on the trustworthiness of individuals scattered about the country. In this case Mr. X may be a *bonâ fide* consignee : but if he can sell his oil to Germany and make a swinging profit, naturally he will do so. The oil is landed in Gottenberg. Part of it reaches Germany through the ordinary process of smuggling, and part leaves by special licence which the Government can grant for goods on the prohibited list of exports; but the bulk of the oil is disposed of by sending it round to Stockholm on the *east* coast. It is probably intercepted by the Germans during its passage; or if not it reaches Stockholm in safety. Mr. X has an agency at Stockholm whose sole business it is to re-tranship the oil and send it to sea to give the Germans further chances. The Customs authorities, having dealt with the oil at Gottenberg, are not interested in it at Stockholm or at other Swedish ports.

This third method was discovered independently by H.M. Government themselves. When war broke out a new Legation at Stockholm was being built. Hundreds of pounds worth of stores, chiefly very fine and up-to-date electric fittings for the new Legation, were being sent round by sea from Gottenberg to Stockholm. They were promptly captured by the Germans, placed in the Prize Court and condemned.

There was probably no commercial harbour of greater importance during the war than that of Copenhagen. It had a large trade of its own, which increased the difficulty of bringing to light cases of illicit trading. The main stream of goods to Germany passed through Danish ports and over Danish territory, and Copenhagen's part in the fight for our lives was the most important in Scandinavia. It is possible that the nature of all the transactions such as those recorded in this chapter were not brought to the knowledge of the Minister, but, however this may be, the measures taken for safeguarding our interests and checking abuses fell far short of legitimate expectations.

It had at one time been the custom to report all irregularities such as those that have here been recorded to the Legation; but this zeal unfortunately had died down. To detect abuses it was very necessary that the wharves should be visited; yet the Vice-Consul at Copenhagen had incurred official displeasure for performing this important duty and had been ordered not to frequent the wharves.

I visited Copenhagen periodically, but Germany could not be fought single-handed.

There was considerable delay in the publication of the Scandinavian statistics after the war. I had been looking forward with considerable interest to a quiet study of the accounts. Agricultural produce held first place in my curiosity; but lubricants ran it very close, the Danish exports to Germany being the first item to which I turned. I had drawn a blank : they were not given. I wondered what Denmark had to say about her re-exports to Norway and Sweden; I therefore next looked up these figures, which were confessed. I then compared Denmark's statements with those of Norway and Sweden as to what they had received from Denmark. The object in making these comparisons was to ascertain if Denmark had been charging Norway with oil which had been sent to Germany; in which case the Norwegian figures would be less than the Danish. The figures are :—

	1915	1916	1917	
Denmark re-exports to Norway	1,120	1,140	1,131	metric tons
Norway imports from Denmark	990	569	488	„ „

which would seem to suggest that Germany had friends in Denmark.

In the case of Denmark and Sweden glaring discrepancies would not be expected, because Sweden

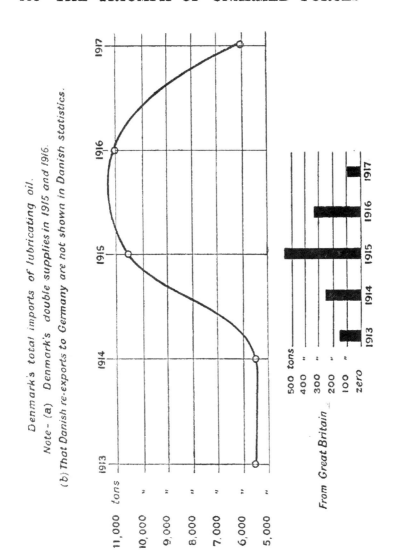

Denmark's total imports of lubricating oil.

Note - (a) Denmark's double supplies in 1915 and 1916.

(b) That Danish re-exports to Germany are not shown in Danish statistics.

herself sent all the oil she could to Germany. The figures are :—

	1915	1916	1917	
Denmark to Sweden . .	2,127	2,622	68	metric tons
Sweden from Denmark .	3,353	2,896	288	,, ,,

Re the 15,000 tons that passed in transit through the Free Harbour of Copenhagen, I can only say (confessing to the full the weakness of the line of argument) that I think some of it may have found its way to Germany.

To finish with this subject let me quote from a speech made by Lord Robert Cecil on 26th January, 1916 :—

> There was some criticism of what was going on in Denmark, and the Foreign Office was urged some weeks ago to deal with the matter. . . . We requested Sir Alexander Henderson (now Lord Faringdon) to go out, and he was asked to see whether there was any truth in the suggestions and charges made against the Legation. I am very glad to say that I have had several long talks with Lord Faringdon, and he assured me that there is not a word of truth in these allegations. On the contrary, the Government are remarkably well served by their Ministers. . . .[1]

The blind eye of Nelson was used on a certain historic occasion of glorious memory off Copenhagen. Another case of defective vision at the same place will be found recorded in another chapter with a view to its being assigned its proper place in history.

[1] Parliamentary Debates, No. 153, p. 3189

CHAPTER IX

METALS

COPPER

WHAT Wangenheim and the other Germans saw in the situation was that their stocks of wheat, cotton and copper were inadequate for a protracted struggle . . . " next time we shall store up enough copper and cotton to last for five years." [1]

The average of the world's total production of copper in 1914–1915 was about 1,250,000 tons. Of this America produced rather more than 250,000 and Germany about 40,000 tons, an amount quite inadequate for her requirements. Copper was of inestimable value to Germany : it is a metal that enters into every phase of naval and military warfare. Copper was not made contraband until 29th October, 1914; prior to that time Germany obtained immense supplies from America through Italy and Scandinavia.

Of the three Scandinavian countries, Norway was the only one that produced copper : her home production was comparatively unimportant in amount so far as export was affected and as compared with Sweden's export : Sweden, having no home production, depended upon her imports.

To get an idea of the nature of the copper transactions that were taking place in Scandinavia let us

[1] " Secrets of the Bosphorus," by H. Morgenthau, American Ambassador at Constantinople. Hutchinson.

have a look at some of the figures from the Scandinavian statistics. Take Sweden. The Swedish imports for 1913 and 1914 were (in tons) :—

1913	1914
9,559	12,455

Her exports to Germany and Austria were :—

1913	1914
1,215	3,960

It was not until towards the end of 1914 that the Scandinavian countries slammed the door to their statistics in our face.

The Swedish traffic in copper was common knowledge in Scandinavia, and the details of it in 1914 were known to H.M. Government. There were many possible effective retorts to the Malmo meeting, which was convened by Sweden at Germany's instigation; and if Sweden—in particular—thought it well to withhold from us information without which it was well-nigh impossible to gauge the effect of our measures for blockading Germany, then the duty of safeguarding our own interests became one of imperative necessity.

If it had been known that Sweden was not sending copper to Germany in excess of her pre-war consignments, there would have been no valid reason (on this account) to have withheld our own supplies. If there had been uncertainty about the Swedish transactions, British supplies should have been stopped. But if Sweden chose to send copper to Germany exceeding three times the amount she sent before the war—which she did—and if we knew of this—and we did know of it—to have stopped our own supplies to Sweden would of itself have been too insufficient a measure to meet the case; and Sweden should have been referred to Germany for her coal. But the British exports of copper to Sweden were doubled, as is seen by the following figures :—

BRITISH EXPORTS OF COPPER TO SWEDEN (TONS)

1913	1914	1915
517	710	1,085

No time was lost in Norway in endeavouring to bring the Norwegian copper supplies under our control. On 12th December, 1914, the export of copper, with the exception of the home production, was prohibited by the Norwegian Government; and on the same day proposals were made by the British Minister, for consideration by the Home authorities, for acquiring the Norwegian output by purchase. On 2nd January, 1915, these proposals were still under consideration, and remained so until 6th February, when it was requested that an expert in copper might be sent out as soon as possible with a view to arranging terms of purchase. As with the Norwegian fish, so with copper, the purchase fell through. No expert was sent out for many months, and the copper, which could have been bought at the price of about £50 a ton (the proof of this is to be found in the archives of the Legation), was fetching before the end of the war £150 a ton in the open market, which price H.M. Government paid for it.

Norwegian copper was of no especial value to us during the war : there were other sources open to us; but it was of vital importance to the fortunes of the Allied cause that Germany should not have it. Like all other commodities it had two values : the one being its own market value to us for our own use; and the other its value to Germany, *i. e.* the price that Germany was prepared to pay for it, and which it was therefore worth our while to pay to prevent Germany from obtaining it.

In the latter part of 1916 pressure was brought to bear upon Norway by which it was made possible for copper agreements to be drawn up with that country and with Sweden. Norway's copper in its native non-electrolytic form could not be consumed in the country, and electrolytic copper cable was urgently required for the country's development. Shipping facilities were refused by us for Norwegian consignments of copper cable until the Norwegian Government consented not to export copper except as agreeable to our wishes. These copper agreements undoubtedly struck a heavy blow at the enemy.

There are no serious faults to be found in the Norwegian figures : Norway's exports to Germany and Austria were :—

1913	1914	1915	1916	1917
685	406	1,573	1,229	18 tons

The inflated figures in 1915 and 1916 are accounted for by our failure to purchase Norwegian home products.

Denmark shows a clean sheet in her copper transactions. The destination of the 5,000 tons odd that passed in transit through the Free Port of Copenhagen has not been revealed. This is Denmark's secret (and Germany's).

ZINC

Before the war most of our supplies of zinc were obtained from Germany and Belgium, but when war broke out our requirements were covered mainly by America. America sent us refined zinc, but not quite

o

enough. To supply the deficiency zinc ore was obtained from Australia, and sent to Norway and Sweden for refining : it was then returned to us as refined zinc.

Zinc enters largely into the manufacture of munitions, and the Ministry of Munitions was a Department a call from which could not be disregarded : it can be conceived that considerable pressure could be brought to bear upon H.M. Government to keep all sources of supply open. Sweden was one such source : hence the anxiety to avoid trouble with Sweden and the tendency to overlook Sweden's anxiety to avoid trouble with Great Britain.

The refined zinc that Sweden sent to us was as follows :—

1915	1916	1917
747	4,113	2,365 tons

The other Scandinavian source, Norway, sent us :—

1915	1916	1917
4,373	12,765	7,600 tons

It will scarcely be denied that the combined efforts of America and Norway would have been able to rise so far to the occasion as to increase the output of zinc by the amount of Sweden's contribution and thus have removed one of the many sources of anxiety from the mind of the Foreign Secretary in his desire to retain the good-will of Sweden.

The transactions that took place in zinc with Germany furnish an admirable indication of the dearth of German man-power and the necessity for conserving it.

The total world's supply of zinc in 1913 was about 993,000 tons, of which :—

Germany produced	280,000 tons
Belgium ,,	195,000 ,,
U.S.A. ,,	315,000 ,,
British Empire produced	62,000 ,,

Germany and Belgium between them were before
the war the largest producers of zinc in the world :
they were also very large exporters.   Yet during
the war Germany imported large quantities of this
metal.   The want of man-power made itself felt in
all German industries : it prevented Germany from
supplying the needs of Scandinavia and Holland in
coal and cement (see Chap. XI); and it compelled
her to import large quantities of sulphite and sulphate
pulp (see under " Cotton " p. 221).   Germany would
take any manufactured article that was useful for
war purposes.   I have seen large quantities of sawn
timber going to Germany from Sweden during the
war, though Germany's forests could supply timber
in abundance.

Lord Devonport, who rendered conspicuous service
to the country by his searching and able criticisms
of our blockade policy. stated during the course of a
speech in the House of Lords on 22nd February,
1916,[1] that since the beginning of the year there had
gone direct from Rotterdam to Belgium 20,000 tons
of zinc ore.   The ore was sent to Liége, where there
was one of the biggest spelter-producing companies
on the continent.   This, of course, was under German
control, and, therefore, the zinc ore which we allowed
to go into Rotterdam went openly to a place where
it was converted into spelter and circulated all over
Germany.   The ore, too, was of that very quality
which Germany required in the preparation of
hydrogen gas for the inflation of her Zeppelins.

[1] See Parliamentary Debates, No. 3, pp. 118, 119.

NICKEL

The following extract is taken from the " Seventh Report from the Select Committee on National Expenditure " of 21st December, 1920 :—

Our Sub-Committee on the Board of Trade and other Offices have made prolonged investigation into the question of the dealings of His Majesty's Government with various Nickel Companies during and since the war. They have taken evidence on the subject from the Board of Trade and from the Secretary of the Mond Nickel Company, Limited. We beg to report as follows :—

Early in the war His Majesty's Government deemed it on military grounds advisable to enter into certain arrangements with the Kristiansand Nikkel Raffineringswerk and with at least one other Norwegian company. The total expenditure in this connection was £1,030,000. Into the military and diplomatic aspects of these transactions our Sub-Committee have not deemed it any part of their duty to inquire. They are, however, definitely of opinion that on purely commercial grounds the arrangements concluded and the payments consequently made cannot be defended.

The negotiations with the Kristiansand Nikkel Raffineringswerk have unfortunately involved His Majesty's Government not only in large immediate expenditure but in further liabilities which, unless they can be annulled, will entail a heavy loss to the Exchequer.

In order to facilitate these negotiations with

the Kristiansand Nikkel Raffineringswerk His
Majesty's Government concluded with the British
America Nickel Corporation a trading contract
under which His Majesty's Government agreed
to take nickel ore from that Corporation over a
period of ten years from 1917, the Corporation
having the right, if they wish to sell their nickel
to His Majesty's Government, to put 6,000 tons
a year to the Government at market prices in
deliveries of equal quantities per month. On
the other hand, the Government have under this
contract the right, in reduction of that put, to
call for the delivery of 1,000 tons of nickel a
year at a fixed price of £125 a ton. Irrespec-
tively of this contract, His Majesty's Government
subscribed in the year 1917 for 3,000,000 dollars
six per cent. First Mortgage Gold Bonds in the
British America Nickel Corporation at a cost
of £620,000. The Corporation undertook to pay
interest on this loan at the rate of six per cent.
per annum and to repay the principal in five
annual instalments from 1st January, 1920.

Up to the present time there has been no
delivery of nickel under the contract mentioned
in the preceding paragraph; and, as a fact, the
world-supply of nickel has been, and is at present,
in excess of the demand. No interest on the
loan of £620,000 has been paid, nor any instal-
ment of the redemption of the loan.

As the British America Nickel Corporation
have failed to carry out their agreement, we
recommend that an immediate effort be made
to recover as much of the capital as practicable,
and in particular that no further liability be
incurred in the matter.

The military, diplomatic and other aspects of these transactions will be briefly given here.

Nickel is a very hard metal of universal use in the manufacture of steel, and especially of steel armaments, to which it imparts strength : it is, moreover, a metal for which no substitute has yet been discovered.

The ore from which nickel is obtained is to be found in very few countries, and the only outside source from which Germany could obtain it during the war was Norway. Germany's own stocks of nickel were meagre, and during the war she called in nickel coins, nickel steel and manufactured nickel articles in general use : the Norwegian ore became indispensable to her.

There was only one factory in Norway that produced nickel in any important quantity, the Kristiansand Nikkel Raffineringswerk, known as the K.N.R. This company was under contract to supply Germany with a certain monthly quantity, which would appear to have been about 60 tons. Norway's total nickel exports, practically all of which went to Germany, were as follows :—

1913	1914	1915	1916	1917
594	696	760	722	442 tons

An agreement was drawn up by H.M. Government with the K.N.R. with the object of limiting the export of nickel to Germany. For this agreement H.M. Government paid the sum of £1,000,000. The particulars of the agreement are not accurately known; but the limit agreed upon as the maximum quantity to be exported was, there is good reason to suppose, about 80 tons a month. This limit appears to have been arrived at on information supplied to H.M.

Government that the K.N.R. could produce 1,500 tons of nickel a year. My own information on this point, taking the efficiency of production at the company's own estimate, was that 1,300 tons was a liberal allowance to make; but without supplies of nickel ore from New Caledonia, which ceased soon after the outbreak of war, the maximum production would be somewhere about 720 tons a year—possibly a little more.

Thus a million pounds was paid to prevent the K.N.R. from supplying Germany with nickel greatly in excess of the works' capacity : it was paid for a contract that bound us not to interfere with the supply of nickel to Germany. The negotiations with the K.N.R. were conducted by H.M. Government independently of the Legation, which, by suitable pressure, could have prevented the export of the larger part of the nickel to Germany, or could have stopped the production of the nickel itself.

This agreement led to H.M. Government's being involved in transactions with the British America Nickel Corporation; and the question that comes uppermost in the mind is, Who were the advisers of H.M. Government in these transactions, and why were the latter carried through without reference to the Legation in Christiania, which had been so successful in other directions in making Germany feel the pressure of our blockade ?

The representations that I made (officially) with the view of getting the nickel traffic stopped led to nothing; nevertheless on the 3rd May, 1917, the K.N.R. had sent almost its last consignment of nickel to Germany : it met its doom at the hands of the Norwegians themselves.

The indefensible sinkings of Norwegian ships by

German submarines, the loss of life they caused, and the sufferings endured by survivors in open boats created in Norway a deep and bitter feeling of enmity towards Germany. This feeling found expression in a petition by the Mates' Union to the Storthing for the cessation of all nickel exports to Germany, on the ground that nickel was the metal used in the construction of torpedoes; and soon afterwards, towards the end of April 1917, a very envenomed attack upon the K.N.R. was made by the Norwegian Press, including newspapers of all shades of political opinion.

In the fourth paragraph of the extract quoted on p. 197 from the Report on National Expenditure, allusion is made to the British America Nickel Corporation. This Corporation's interests were closely identified with those of the K.N.R. The managing director of the British America Nickel Corporation, Mr. James Hamet Dunn (now Sir James Dunn, Bart.), was then in Copenhagen. Conceiving it possible that Mr. Dunn might be interested in the attitude of the Norwegian Press towards the K.N.R., I forwarded to him without delay a cutting from one of the Norwegian papers, almost immediately on receipt of which Mr. Dunn proceeded to Christiania : but to no purpose; for soon after his arrival, in May 1917, the K.N.R. works were practically destroyed by fire.

This untoward event settled the question of nickel for the time. But when the incident had been forgotten the work of rebuilding the K.N.R. commenced at once; and the company stated that full production would again be possible in January 1918. A second agreement was drawn up by H.M. Government on much the same lines as the original agreement; but again the Norwegians came to our rescue :

for just before the new works were completed a
second Press campaign was launched, no less violent
than its predecessor of the spring. Bowing to
pressure of public opinion the Norwegian Government
intervened, and the K.N.R., instead of nickel, was
compelled to produce electrolytic copper, of which
Norway stood in need.

The effect of the fire at the K.N.R. works was to
reduce the export of nickel in 1917 to 442 tons.
Besides the benefit that Germany obtained from the
direct import of Norway's nickel, she profited extensively from the use that Sweden made of nickel in
her steel manufactories, which were worked in
Germany's interest. The Swedish statistics are as
follows :—

IMPORTS (METRIC TONS)

	1913	1914	1915	1916	1917
Total	150	136	504	125	40
United Kingdom and British Empire	27	60	328	78	16

EXPORTS (METRIC TONS).

Total	1	—	70	30	7
Germany and Austria . .	—	—	70	30	7

In 1915 the United Kingdom sent to Sweden more
than twice her pre-war imports; of Sweden's total
import of 504 tons in 1915, 70 tons were sent to
Germany. The greater part of this quantity was
virtually sent by us, the remaining 434 tons being
used in the country for Germany's benefit in the
manufacture of war materials. We sent Sweden twelve
times the amount of nickel in 1915 that we did in
1913.

When the first agreement was drawn up with the
K.N.R. a very large sum of money was paid for an
object which it did not achieve, and which could have

been effectively achieved by the resources at the command of the British Legation in Christiania. This agreement, however, was made in circumstances of stress when nickel was wanted, and when there was not time for the same careful financial and commercial scrutiny to be made before the transaction was concluded as there would have been in normal circumstances. But in the case of the second Agreement the circumstances were very different. There were no facts connected with the K.N.R. having either a military, a financial, a diplomatic or a doubtful bearing on the known and the suspected transactions in which the company was involved that were not brought by me to the notice of the proper authorities. This information included, in addition to what has been narrated here, such matter as must have made it clear that military and financial interests, that is to say the State interests and those of the private individual, were in conflict, and that the former were in danger. H.M. Government were well aware of the influence commanded in Norway by the British Legation, and of the beneficial results of the firm control that had been acquired and exercised over Norwegian private interests through the medium of British-controlled imports. Again, with greater pertinacity, the questions press themselves upon the mind : On whose advice was it that this consideration should have been overruled, and that, in the light of the knowledge in possession of H.M. Government, arrangements should have been made whereby Germany was assured of the greater part of Norway's output of nickel ? And that the nickel company should have been paid by H.M. Government for sending the nickel to Germany ?

The trucks that carried the nickel from the mines

to the factory were hauled by British coal : lubricating oil, canvas (for diaphragms) and food were all
controlled by us.   When the K.N.R. works were
destroyed by fire the work of reconstruction could
have been prevented or seriously impeded by " black-
listing " the firm, as it was the practice to do with
all other firms that worked against British interests.
In place, however, of such salutary action, a second
agreement was drawn up.   Let it be made clear that
the expenditure of a million pounds is not cavilled
at : it is the one bright feature in these transactions;
it was worth the expending for a fling at the enemy :
but everything else here recorded, and much, moreover, not recorded, is involved in very ugly obscurity.

TIN

Tin is a product of the British Empire, and is
found in large quantities in the Straits Settlements.
It is a commodity which enters into the manufacture
of cans for the preservation of foodstuffs, and on this
account is of great military importance.

In all the Scandinavian countries tin assumed vast
importance during the war.   In Norway it entered
essentially into the " canning " and the condensed
milk industries, of which the canning industry was
by far the more important.   When war broke out
there were in Norway large accumulated stocks of
the finished cans (the ordinary sardine tin is known
in the trade as a " can ") for packing fish, in addition
to stocks of tin plate; at first there was little that
could be done to prevent these stocks from being
made use of for packing the fish and enabling it to
be sent to Germany : this partly accounts for the
large Norwegian exports to Germany in 1915.   In the

packing of fish either olive oil or tomato pulp is used as a preservative, the oil itself being a fatty substance of high nutritive value : in some of the countries bordering on the Mediterranean it is extensively used with bread by the poorer classes as a staple article of diet. Pressure was gradually brought to bear on the " black canners "—a name given to those who worked in Germany's interest— by withholding supplies of tin, olive oil and tomato pulp. To circumvent these measures other means had to be devised for obtaining the fish : in this the Germans and the black canners were partly—but only partly—successful. Instead of tin, cases of enamelled iron were used : these were made in Germany and sent to Norway. The black canners had great difficulty in finding an efficient substitute for the olive oil and tomato pulp; they ultimately used a substance known as " fish bouillon," which, however, was of far less value than the oil and tomato pulp.

The effect on Germany of the control exercised by the Legation was two-fold : it stopped the supplies of tin and olive oil from reaching her—a result which alone was well worth the achieving; but it also made her work for her fish. Germany had to expend man-power in making the enamelled cases, which would not stand the same wear and tear as would the tin cans; she also lost the nourishment of the olive oil : in both cases she suffered a loss in military efficiency. It is to be noted that the canned goods exported by Norway to Germany included those which were packed in the German enamelled cans.

The great German purchasing agency, the Z.E.G., had its agents established throughout Norway. These agents had full knowledge of all measures

taken by the British authorities to prevent Norwegian
supplies from reaching Germany; it was no easy
work to make headway against the opposition of this
powerful and influential organisation, which had
unlimited funds at its disposal : nevertheless neither
the Z.E.G. nor the black canners were able successfully to withstand the pressure brought to bear for
defeating their ends. Though the black canners
searched every hole and corner in Norway, not an
ounce of tin was there to be found. Most of these
canners were brought round gradually to work in
the British interest, and those who did so were able
to ply their trade as in peace time.

It was the same in the condensed milk trade;
but here the traffic was stopped almost at once.
Norway's exports to Germany and Austria were as
follows (in tons) :—

1913	1914	1915	1916	1917
447	249	100	4	—

whereas our own supply was well maintained : it
was :—

1913	1914	1915	1916	1917
2,957	2,773	2,917	1,329	7,359

Most of the remainder of the condensed milk was
sent to our Allies.

Condensed milk has great military value : it will
keep well, is easily handled and is very nutritious.
When the condensed milk supply was cut off from
Germany by our control of tin, fresh milk was sent
to her in bottles. Fresh milk, being perishable, was
of far less military value than condensed milk : nevertheless it was a very important article of food and
it was not well that Germany should have it. Attention was therefore turned to the Norwegian glass

bottle-making factories, which depended for their working upon British coal : and coal was withheld from all firms that supplied bottles to milk exporters. The result was immediate and effective.

The figures for milk (sterilised, including cream) are as follows :—

NORWEGIAN EXPORTS (TONS)

	1913	1914	1915	1916	1917
To Germany and Austria	282	173	257	498	—
To the United Kingdom	427	1,310	1,685	1,469	1,261

The figures of the exports to Germany and Austria do not appear to reveal the effect of the coal pressure that was exerted; this effect would have been very apparent if pressure had not been applied, and the figures could then have been seen for the Norwegian exports. Germany obtained the above comparatively small quantities probably by sending her own bottles to Norway.

The bottle-makers were rather more difficult to deal with than the black canners : for whereas the canners had no case whatever, the bottle-makers could point, with considerable truth, to the injury to the community that would be caused by interference with the milk supply of Christiania and other towns. The health of the inhabitants, it was urged, was at stake and the importance of milk to children was paramount. Complaints poured in from all quarters, representatives of firms being sent to the Legation primed with every form of protest that reason could suggest. In some cases, it is to be feared, reason suggested very strong language, but on the whole a moderate tone prevailed, and in many cases it was only necessary to explain the cause of the trouble for these men to go away satisfied. They could have British coal, but it must not be used in the service of our enemies. Reason soon brought these men over to our side and no calamity overtook the women and children of Christiania. Many of these Norwegians enjoyed working in our service when they knew that our measures were directed against Germany and not against Norway.

Denmark's principal tin industry was concerned with the manufacture of tins for the export of butter to tropical climates. On the outbreak of war this trade in butter ceased, and Denmark's requirements of tin correspondingly decreased : but her supplies, which came almost entirely from the British Empire during the war, did not. The Danish imports were as follows :—

	1913	1914	1915	1916	1917
From all countries	329	379	339	471	240 tons
From the United Kingdom and British Empire	172	261	317	466	228 „

Her exports were practically nil.

The tin with which we so prodigally supplied Denmark was very largely used in the manufacture of cans for " Goulash " (known also under the more polite-sounding title of " Conserves "). Goulash was esteemed a great luxury in Germany : so much so that its export rose from 131 tons in 1913 to 16,000 tons in 1915 and 19,000 tons in 1916. It is due to the rapid growth of the trade in Goulash that the Goulash baron owes his title and renown.

Our tin was also used for making and maintaining in repair the milk cans that carried milk to Germany. The quantity of milk carried by these cans rose from 457 tons in 1913 to 3,000 and 8,000 tons respectively in 1916 and 1917 : so that on the whole Germany did not do so badly out of our tin trade.

Denmark, it is true, sent us considerable supplies of condensed milk; but these supplies were slightly below the pre-war round figure : and, moreover, it was to meet the requirements of this branch of the tin trade that a part of our pre-war supplies to Denmark was specially allocated. Seeing that Denmark's total requirements during the war would be the less from the loss of a large part of her oversea export trade, it follows that by continuing the import of pre-war quantities she had always a large balance available for other purposes : she had also accumulated stocks of tin and cans on hand when war broke out; and since Denmark did not export any of her tinned butter to her old customers she must have used it in the country for Germany's benefit.

Let us see what we were doing to help Germany in Sweden.

SWEDISH IMPORTS (METRIC TONS)

	1913	1914	1915	1916	1917
Total	1,082	1,481	4,189	996	308
From the United Kingdom and British Empire . . .	735	1,130	3,693	972	163

EXPORTS

Total	86	517	3,454	35	28
To Germany and Austria . .	2	306	3,180	35	28

Sweden was Germany's workshop, and what she did not send direct to Germany she used mainly in Germany's interests. And what did she send to Germany? Before the war nothing : in 1915 more than 3,000 tons, corresponding to the quantity she received from Great Britain in that year, and which was five times the amount she received from us before the war.

Tin serves as a good example of the potential war value as distinct from the ordinary commercial value

of commodities. Tin affected Germany's food supplies; copper, zinc and nickel affected chiefly her
munition supplies. The metals that we sent and
allowed to be sent to Scandinavia were food and
munitions for Germany. The transactions in metals
spoken of in this chapter are, I venture to think,
scarcely consistent with the accepted canons of
economic warfare in which our existence was at
stake. They militated against good results achieved
by economic pressure in other directions, and furnish
examples of the various contributory causes which
retarded the calamity that ultimately overtook the
German Empire after these un-warlike transactions
had been stopped.

P

CHAPTER X

TEA—COFFEE—COCOA

IN the debate in the House of Commons on 26th January, 1916, Commander Leverton Harris, R.N.V.R., in the course of a speech (described by Lord Grey as " most interesting and full of knowledge "), tells us that while we should keep out things they (the Germans) really needed—such as articles of military or economic value—by letting them have luxuries we were really doing them harm. It was interesting to find that while we were trying to keep certain classes of goods out of Germany the German Government was also trying to keep out the same goods. The difficulty lay in deciding exactly what goods Germany should be allowed to receive; whether, for example, tea and cocoa should be included, and he had changed his mind more than once about tea. All imports into Germany had to be paid for by exports or by gold.[1]

It is difficult to approach this curious thesis in serious vein except on the supposition that Germany possessed several years' stocks. It would have been interesting and instructive to obtain expert opinion as to the value of tea and cocoa from some of our own men, preferably from those who had just returned from the water-logged trenches of Flanders

[1] Parliamentary Debates, No. 153, pp. 3121, 3122, 26th January, 1916.

in winter time : I venture to think that their experience would have enabled them to form a tolerably correct opinion as to whether tea and cocoa had any military value.

Viewed from the rationing of neutrals' point of view, everything that is eaten or drunk, including alcohol, is produced from the land; and therefore all such imports into a neutral country release either some other form of food or drink—or land, which would yield other produce available for export. Let us suppose that all tea, coffee and cocoa were withheld from Denmark : some substitutes for these commodities would have to be found, and the Danes would be forced to consume more beer, milk or soups. More of these latter commodities would have to be produced : for beer more fodder, which is used in the brewing, would be required; an increase of milk would be obtainable only at the sacrifice of butter; and by consuming more soups there would be the less meat and vegetables for export, and therefore more land would have to be given up for the production of meat and the cultivation of vegetables.

We will look into the question of our trade in tea, about which the mind had changed more than once. The figures would seem to indicate that these processes of mental metamorphosis on the net balance inclined very strongly in favour of the trade in this superfluous luxury.

Exports from the United Kingdom (tons) to :—

	1913	1914	1915	1916	1917
Russia . . .	5,080	1,521	2,995	2,000	90
Sweden . . .	109	168	469	2,952	2
Norway . .	78	123	194	176	7
Denmark . .	370	1,970	4,528	1,602	105

(2,000 lbs = 1 ton except Russia = 2,240)

These figures at first sight would suggest that

Germany received through Denmark alone from the United Kingdom several thousands of tons of tea during 1914–1916, Denmark's total imports from all countries in 1913 being only 539 tons, which figure rose to 4,528 tons in 1915 from Great Britain alone. It cannot, of course, be asserted that all the surplus tea went to Germany, but it is certainly not easy to account for it in any other way; seeing that Sweden, Norway and Russia are charged separately with their consignments, and that Germany is the only possible remaining customer.

Lord Grey drew the attention of the United States to the fact that the dislocation of trade on the outbreak of war would cause diversion of traffic which would be reflected in abnormal trade figures shown in statistics. It is possible that the inflated figure of 4,528 tons in 1915 and other figures noticeable in the table may be attributable in part to some such cause. The British and the Scandinavian statistics on tea are so widely divergent that it is useless attempting to draw more than general conclusions from them; but an inference that can be drawn with certainty is that large quantities of unspecified amount reached Germany through Scandinavia, and principally through Denmark.

Denmark and Sweden acknowledge to the following receipts from all countries :—

	1913	1914	1915	1916	1917
Denmark	539	608	1,481	1,250	211
Sweden	233	212	250	496	96

The Danish exports were :—

	1913	1914	1915	1916	1917
To Germany	3	90	590	220	—
„ Sweden	17	27	33	142	—

and Sweden sent Germany 161 tons in 1916.

The facts of which we can be quite certain are these :
on Denmark's own admission she received from us
tea for her own use, *i. e.* tea not in transit, in 1915
and 1916 of an amount between two and three times
greater than that she received in 1913. She exported
to Germany very substantial quantities during the
war, whereas her pre-war export was negligible.
Great Britain sent to Scandinavia immense quantities
of tea whose ultimate destination cannot be traced,
but which probability strongly suggests reached
Germany. Indeed if the above quoted extract from
the speech of Commander Leverton Harris is to be
taken as seriously reflecting the considered views of
H.M. Government, there disappears any point to be
laboured in the discrepancies shown in the figures :
for the Foreign Secretary accepted the view that,
with regard to tea and cocoa, it was uncertain whether
Germany was not herself trying to prevent these
commodities from reaching her : in the case of tea,
at one time it was thought that she was; but at
another time that she was not : the conclusion to be
arrived at is that tea was being sent to Germany
against her will; and the deduction to be drawn
from the figures is that it was successful in reaching
her.

Another anonymous communication reached me one
day. I think it was from some honest Danish steve-
dore : (we had, fortunately, many friends, rich and
poor, among the Danes). If I wanted to know what
was going on would I come down to the wharves ?   I
went. This was during the height of the great tea
" ramp " in March, 1916. All the wharves in Copenhagen were choked with cases of tea, a large part of
which was from our colonies *en route* to Germany.
There was a good deal of China tea, but most of it

was from Ceylon. It was being piled up in cases mountains high by stevedores.

Exstruere hi montes ad sidera summa parabant.[1]

Some of my colleagues were on the scene, and the face of one of them was a very interesting study in sardonics.

On 4th April, 1916, I wrote as follows to the Admiralty :—

> Having put a check on cocoa and coffee, tea is now the game. All the wharves at Copenhagen are covered with very large quantities of tea. The Consul and I walked along the quays among thousands of cases. I must confess to a feeling of degradation when I see all this stuff, a large part of which comes from our own Colonies, *en route* to Germany. There is a very large quantity of China tea, but the greater part is Ceylon. Who is at the bottom of this business? To me it is quite incomprehensible. There is a shortage of tonnage and yet here we are allowing tea, a most bulky substance, to be shipped from the Far East in enormous quantities to comfort our enemies. Is it any wonder that we are called hypocrites?

As to sending tea to Germany for the purpose of extracting gold, if Norwegian fish, Danish agricultural produce and even Swedish iron ore failed to achieve this object it is not likely that an article of no military value would stand any better chances of success.

In an action that was brought against a firm of tea merchants for exporting large quantities of tea to Copenhagen without taking adequate measures to secure that it should not reach Germany, the Attorney-General for the Crown said (*Times*, 4th April, 1919) :—

[1] Ovid on teas, etc.

It would be shown that the total exports of
the firm to Denmark about the time, *i. e.* from
6th November, 1915, to 8th January, 1916, of
tea were 703 tons, and of that 514 tons were
sent to Caroe alone. On the other hand, the
pre-war consumption of tea for the whole of
Denmark *for the year* was only 491 tons. The
defendants, therefore, exported to Denmark in
two months to one consignee alone one and a
half times a whole year's pre-war supply. . . .
The defendants sent to Caroe for further forms of
guarantee; at the same time they said that they
were under the impression that Caroe was reviving
a connection with Russia.

On the point of law raised in the case the defendants
succeeded and a subsequent appeal made by the Crown
failed. In the course of the final proceedings Lord
Justice Scrutton made the following observations :—

It was clear that the goods consigned to Caroe
did go to Germany, and it was also clear that
the defendants suspected that goods were going
to Germany. The course which they adopted
was (1) to tell the Government the names of
their customers and to ask whether any of them
were suspicious. But they did not tell the
Government what they knew : and the Government did not necessarily know how large their
shipments to Caroe were as compared with the
previous shipments to him and their shipments
to other customers; (2) they took declarations
from Caroe. The form of declaration which Caroe
usually gave was either that the tea was " for
home trade only " or " will not be re-exported

by me." Both of these forms left the obvious loophole that Caroe should make a sale in Denmark to someone who would then re-export, and Caroe did not seem anxious to extend his declaration, nor were the defendants pressing to see that he did so extend it.

If the appeal had succeeded it would not have brought back the tea from Germany. The case is quoted here as illustrating the simplicity of trading with the enemy. The responsibility for allowing tea to leave the country in any quantity rested with tea merchants, not with the Government. The guarantee against re-export was appraised as to its worth not by the Government or the British Legation, but by the tea merchants. The only deterrent to trading in this and in other merchandise was a penalty in case of proof that regulations had been infringed. The regulations were of so lax a character that trade could be carried on with an immunity from risk in most cases that made it quite worth while to accept the risk in all cases. When Germany wanted goods she had merely to signify her pleasure to Denmark, and to leave it to that country to furnish the means of providing them, which caused her no trouble whatever.

The quantity of cocoa that Germany received was so prodigious that she converted it into sweets and sold them to the Scandinavian countries.

In 1915 Sweden alone imported 15,880 tons of cocoa as against 1,668 tons in 1913. Of this 15,880 tons (from British statistics) it is not possible to trace the quantities that went to Germany.

According to British statistics Denmark received in 1915 21,387 tons of cocoa, of which 4,719 came from the United Kingdom; we sent her more than twice her pre-war import.

The difference in the total imports to Scandinavia as charged in the Scandinavian statistics and the British statistics is partly accountable to the fact that Scandinavian countries did not give credit to supplies in transit. The ultimate destination of the immense supplies that were sent to Scandinavia must remain a matter for conjecture, in which Germany cannot be ignored.

Coffee is the universal and favourite beverage in Sweden. When shiploads of coffee were to be seen in the docks en route to Germany, not a peck of it at one time could be obtained in the Swedish cafés.

The coffee exports from the United Kingdom were as follows :—

	1913	1914	1915	1916	1917
To Sweden . .	922	1,266	2,137	1,063	20
,, Norway . .	337	847	2,029	2,522	1,868
,, Denmark . .	234	925	3,149	3,204	1,740

With which record we will leave the subject of these useless beverages, and pass on to Beer.

BEER

The following appeared in German orders in the early summer of 1917 :—

Strict orders

Regarding the representations which have been made on the part of the breweries that they were not able to fulfil their remaining obligations up to time in respect of deliveries to the army in the field on account of the lack of barrels, coal, rolling stock, workmen or other causes, the commissariat will naturally make every effort as far as possible to be of assistance; but it must be unconditionally insisted upon that the *full* quantities of beer guaranteed are forwarded to the termini arranged by the commissariat. This unconditional demand is made because the deliveries of beer to the troops in the field have already been restricted to the utmost, and it is of first importance that the fighting troops must in all cases be supplied with beer even though in restricted quantities.

The breweries were further warned that necessary measures would be taken to meet cases of negligence, and that such breweries would not be allowed to share in the approaching harvest.

Germany was in a bad way at that time, and there was extreme shortage in tea, coffee, cocoa, bouillon and milk. It need hardly be said that Denmark threw herself most gallantly into the breach, and sent Germany some additional 5,000 or 6,000 tons of beer in 1916 and 1917. The exports are as follows :—

	1913	1914	1915	1916	1917
Total . . .	4,779	5,328	7,070	9,859	6,729 tons
Germany . .	51	30	841	6,146	5,673 ,,
United Kingdom .	2,580	2,710	1,441	552	4 ,,

To enable her to do this she had to stop our supplies, which therefore became scarcer : beer at home had already begun to show a tendency to increase in price, and a rather more pronounced one to disguise its identity. For the brewing of beer, malt or malt substitutes are required, *i. e.* corn, rice, or maize, or, generally, fodder materials. These came through our blockade and were under our control : Denmark's breweries were worked with our coal, which Germany herself was unable to supply. Shortly it came to this : that the German troops were badly in need of beer; in order to meet the demand of the German troops we adulterated our own beer, raised its price, and reduced its quantity : we honoured Denmark's demand for fodder and, Germany herself being unable to meet the Danish requirements for coal, we ourselves supplied her with that commodity *ad lib.*

In 1917 we were quite satisfied with 4 tons of beer instead of 2,600 : Germany received about 6,000 instead of 50 tons.

COTTON

In an obituary notice, which appeared in *Nature*, it was said of the late Mr. Bertram Blount that " he appeared to be exhausted by his successful struggle in 1915 to bring cotton within the list of contraband goods."

The late Sir William Ramsay, who was untiring in his efforts to get an embargo on cotton, in a letter to a friend of mine, written in July, 1915, said : " We are still struggling to get cotton declared contraband."

When war broke out Germany concentrated her efforts—especially as she anticipated (wrongly) being cut off from jute, a product of our Indian Empire—on obtaining all the cotton she could. The success that she achieved may be judged from one or two figures from the Scandinavian and the British statistics.

Sweden's total imports of cotton (raw, carded and waste) rose from 24,800 tons in 1913 to 123,200 tons in 1915. Of this the supply from the United Kingdom and the British Empire, which was 1,940 tons in 1913, rose to 10,300 in 1915 (we were doing our best), and

Sweden's export to Germany and Austria increased from 236 tons in 1913 to 76,000 tons in 1915. British statistics place the Swedish imports at even a higher figure. In the case of Norway our pre-war supplies of 460 tons in 1913 increased to 6,600 in 1915; and Denmark, who received only 14 tons in 1913, was supplied with 3,000 tons in 1915 and 6,000 tons in 1916. The total quantities (in tons) of cotton waste, raw cotton and yarn that were supplied by us to Norway, Sweden and Denmark from 1913 to 1917 were as follows :—

1913	1914	1915	1916	1917
6,195	7,431	33,374	18,560	7,534

None of the above figures include piece goods, which are given below (for convenience) in millions of yards, and represent the supplies from the United Kingdom and the British Empire :—

PIECE GOODS

	1913	1914	1915	1916	1917
To Sweden	13	11	12	21	20
,, Norway	17	16	22	37	27
,, Denmark	16	22	32	46	41

Denmark in 1916 received in piece goods alone a quantity equivalent to over 16 yards per head of her population.

(Holland received over 100,000 tons more cotton in 1915 than in 1913.)

The effect of declaring cotton contraband (8th August, 1915) can be seen most clearly from the Swedish statistics, which show a fall in her total imports of 123,000 tons in 1915 to 29,000 in 1916 : the Swedish exports to Germany and Austria in 1915 were 76,000 tons; in 1916 they had vanished to zero; and there they remained.

Up to the time of the recent war nitrocellulose was invariably made of cotton; and although experiments were carried out by Germany with the view of finding a possible substitute, they were not successful.

When Germany was cut off from cotton she was obliged to fall back upon a pulp made from wood fibre, and known as sulphite pulp.   There is a sulphite pulp and a sulphate pulp.   The sulphite pulp was used for the manufacture of explosives, and the sulphate pulp for sandbags and for general military and commercial purposes for replacing cotton.   The effect of declaring cotton contraband is seen in the figures of Sweden's exports of these two classes of pulps to Germany :—

	1915	1916	1917
Sulphite	33,600	60,000	90,500 tons
Sulphate	21,600	88,400	91,700 ,,

Most of the largest pulp mills of Sweden are fitted with " mechanical stokers " adapted specially for the burning of British coal; and it was British coal to a large extent that was used by the Swedish mills : further, for every 18 tons of these pulps that were produced about 15 tons of coal had to be used. Although Germany is a great manufacturer of wood pulps, yet during the war she was unable to develop these industries—perhaps it would be more correct to say that it was with difficulty she could keep them going—because, although she had large forests, the felling of timber and the carrying of it to the mills was a drain upon her man-power beyond her resources : nor was there the man-power for mining the coal necessary for working the mills. Every ton of imported cotton or imported pulp was a saving of man-power to Germany, where cotton was most strictly rationed : nothing in the cotton line was to be bought or sold in the shops without authority. When the great demand for cotton arose not an ounce of chemical pulp was obtained from Norway's mills, which also depended upon British coal.

Our cotton transactions during the war are not inconsistent with the Foreign Secretary's expressed wishes before the war that the " contraband list should be made as small as possible " : nor with the views of the humane part of the population of these islands (that is to say, of the part that was engaged in trade) that war should be confined to the armed forces and that trade should go so as usual with everybody else.

For further particulars the reader is referred to the frontispiece of this book.

BINDER TWINE

Binder twine is a strong cordage used with reaping and binding machines. To an agricultural country like Denmark, which was dependent for her twine upon supplies from oversea, it was one of the most important of all commodities, and particularly so because reaping and binding machines are labour-saving devices. Before the war the Danes imported every year at harvest time a very large quantity of cheap labour from Poland. This and all external sources of labour were cut off when war broke out: binder twine then assumed a greatly enhanced value. Again, so far as is known, it had not been found possible to use wood fibre instead of hemp as a basis in the manufacture of this twine, which must be of small diameter but capable of standing a heavy strain.

The figures for imports, taken from the British statistics, are as follows :—

	1916 Tons	1917 (Jan. to Sept.) Tons
From the British Empire .	1,135	156
„ foreign countries .	1,235	1,442, of which 1,403 were from U S.
Total	2,370	1,598
Average 1911–1913 . .	1,463	1,098

It will be noticed that during 1916, when the exports of agricultural produce from Denmark to Germany were continually increasing, the imports of binder-twine were allowed to exceed the pre-war average by 38 per cent. ; and practically half of the whole amount came from the British Empire.

One of the most influential and efficiently conducted concerns in the world is the American International Harvester Company. The agent of this company in Denmark would be fully alive to all our transactions in binder-twine : the nature of these transactions would therefore not be slow to reach Washington. Implicated, as we ourselves had been, in this traffic, we were not in a position at the end of 1916 to ask the United States to reduce their imports during 1917. It is not, therefore, surprising to find that although during the period January to September 1917 our own exports had been reduced to 156 tons those of America show a substantial increase, bringing the total imports to Denmark during 1917 to an amount largely in excess of the pre-war average.

That a demand for binder-twine during 1916 had not arisen by reason of any shortage of commodities of a similar nature is shown from the imports of " ropes, string and other cordages " for that year, which were as follows :—

	Tons
From the British Empire	1,281
„ foreign countries	432
Total	1,713
Average 1911–1913	1,154

These imports, it will be noticed, also exceeded the pre-war average : they were supplied almost entirely by the British Empire for the maintenance of the Danish fishing industry at a time when the whole of that industry was mobilised in the German service.

By our own trade in 1916, which had stimulated America to increase hers in 1917, we had forfeited any moral right to speak to America on the subject.

FLAX AND JUTE

Many trades at home were threatened with semi-extinction by the supplies of raw materials that were sent to neutrals. Mr. Ernest S. Brown in a letter to the *Morning Post* on 28th March, 1918, quotes the case of the Irish linen industry, which was so vital to our air offensive. The occupation of Belgium seriously affected the supplies of flax with which the linen industry is fed; and with the fall of Riga in September, 1917, practically the whole of the world's supply of flax became the monopoly of the enemy. The linen industry, in which 70,000 people in the north of Ireland alone were engaged, affected indirectly some two hundred other trades, as, for instance, book-binding, saddlery and boot-making; yet in spite of the shortage of flax and of the fact that the Irish flax crop of 1917 was the worst for ten years, huge consignments containing flax in the shape of yarns, piece goods and linen thread were allowed to leave the country. It was not until January, 1918, that the authorities awoke to the stern realities of the situation,

which had become so desperate that an Order in
Council was published forbidding all exports.

> "The inevitable panacea," says Mr. Brown, "to
> cover departmental blunders, in the shape of a
> Committee, has been appointed to investigate in
> all its bearings the question of increasing the
> supply of flax within the British Empire; but
> probably before the Committee has even reported
> the shortage will be so acute that it will be
> necessary for us to issue licences to trade with
> the enemy.   This ignominious device was resorted
> to by Mr. McKenna when we were destitute of
> dyes in 1915.   Quite apart from the commercial
> aspect, the shortage is more serious just now, as
> the supply of flax is almost as important as that
> of shells.   The German Press is jubilant over the
> acquisition of this vast supply of raw material,
> in the shape of flax from Courland, and states
> that 'it adds immensely to the wealth of Ger-
> many, and makes her more independent than ever
> before of foreign countries.' "

Speaking of jute Mr. Brown tells us that our exports
to Scandinavia during the war were so excessive as to
place the home trade in a very precarious position.

> "For the next six or seven years," he says,
> "when the British housewife deplores the loss of
> her napery she will have to console herself with
> the elevating thought that its absence is due to
> the 'humanitarian principles' upon which the
> blockade was run by Viscount Grey and his
> successor, Lord Robert Cecil."

Q

HIDES AND SKINS

During the war Denmark exported close on 1,000,000 head of live cattle to Germany. With the 200,000 tons of meat and fat for explosives represented by these exports we are not here concerned, but with the question of leather only. Hides and leather are the principal raw materials for boots and other articles of military equipment : boots were worn by German troops when marching as a protection for the feet : this discovery was made in 1917.

Hides and leather were to be obtained by Germany by importing either cattle on hoof or the raw hides and tanned leather : it is clear that the less we sent to Scandinavia the less would be available for re-export to Germany. By withholding hides, leather, boots and tanning materials from Denmark and Sweden, those countries would be compelled to use their own hides : but even so they could not make use of them for the purposes of leather without tanning materials.

During the war Great Britain supplied Denmark not only with very large quantities of hides, skins, leather and tanning materials, but also with boots and shoes, thus enabling Denmark not only to continue the export of cattle on hoof, which had commenced in the early days of the war, but also to send thousands of tons of the raw materials, and many hundreds of tons of leather, boots and shoes. One of the ingredients of tanning material is a substance known as Quebracho, of which we sent Denmark 400 tons in 1915 as against 100 tons in 1913. We further accommodated the Danes by sending them hair, glue and fats such as oleo and lard, all of which are component parts of the beasts that Denmark exported to Germany.

Except in respect of live cattle, the export of which was on a far smaller scale than Denmark's, Sweden's traffic in leather materials and goods was greatly facilitated by British importations. During 1915 and 1916 Sweden sent to Germany 3,470 and 2,664 tons respectively of boots and shoes : the boots were of military pattern and for the use of the German Army, and the above figures represent for these two years over 4,500,000 pairs. During the same period, in addition to the boots, Sweden sent to Germany and Austria nearly 50,000 head of cattle on hoof, 6,000 tons of hides and skins and more than 2,000 tons of tanning materials and tanning extracts. This traffic was assisted by 2,800 tons of hides and skins and 3,400 tons of tanning materials and extracts which Sweden received during 1915 and 1916 from the United Kingdom and the British Empire.

FERTILISERS

A word or two about Denmark's method of obtaining fertilisers.

Although the exports of agricultural produce from Denmark to the United Kingdom continually decreased and those to Germany increased, yet until 1916 the export of artificial manures (chiefly basic slag, sulphate of ammonia, superphosphates and Chile saltpetre) from the United Kingdom to Denmark steadily increased. The figures are as follows :—

1913	1914	1915	1916	1917
23,296	28,153	33,659	380	11 tons

When our supplies to Denmark were cut off in 1916 the Danes resorted to other methods of obtaining fertilisers from us.

Of the 33,659 tons we sent to Denmark in 1915,

24,650 consisted of the valuable fertiliser superphosphate, which is made by dissolving raw phosphatic
minerals in sulphuric acid. The phosphate rock in
1916 was obtained by Denmark from Algiers and
Tunis, and the sulphur ingredient from the Rio Tinto
mines in Spain. These mines are entirely under
British direction, the Rio Tinto Company being a
British company with head office in London. These
ingredients were converted into superphosphates in
the Danish Superphosphate Factory.

The following figures show how matters were
arranged :—

PHOSPHATE ROCK

Imports (Tons)

	1913	1914	1915	1916
From Germany	3,225	—	—	—
„ the United Kingdom . .	15,757	23,325	5,300	nil
„ Algiers and Tunis . .	55,875	49,301	58,238	*108,866*

Please note the figures in italics.

Pyrites (containing the sulphur ingredient) was
obtained from the Rio Tinto company in the following
amounts :—

1913	1914	1915	1916
12,193	17,937	28,933	18,253 tons

The phosphate rock appeared only in the French
statistics, and the pyrites in the Spanish statistics;
these transactions were therefore unlikely to become
known to those who were not privy to them. As for
our French compatriots-in-arms, they had themselves,
in emulation of our example, taken very kindly to
trading with Scandinavia (though on a much more
modest scale than we did); they would not be likely
to sever their connection as our compatriots-in-trade
without better reasons than we were in a position to
supply them with.

Professor Somerville, Sibthorpian Professor of Rural Economy, Oxford,[1] pointed out that the wheat area of the United Kingdom was not of sufficient extent to absorb our exports of sulphate of ammonia : our failure, he stated, to use this invaluable fertiliser on our land was equivalent to the loss of several hundred thousand tons of shipping. The state of our shipping during the war had reached a perilous stage; and several hundred thousands of tons of it was no trifle of an amount to lose the use of. By utilising supplies of ammonia not only would the strain on shipping have been greatly reduced, but a large part of our staple foodstuffs, thus produced at home, would have been freed from the risks to which all oversea supplies were exposed.

Yet in 1915 and 1916, 294,000 and 259,000 tons respectively of sulphate of ammonia was exported, part of it to countries from which we received no foodstuffs in return, and part to countries that were working mainly in the interests of our enemies.

The adoption of the Sibthorpian Professor's scheme would, as far as is known, have entailed no risk of compromising our relations with America.

Space forbids making mention of many other commodities, the transactions in which all tell the same tale. If the reader should care to study the summary of supplies in the Appendix he will find it to contain much information of melancholy interest. Suffice it to say that although the power of our unarmed forces was finally and fully vindicated, yet the curves of supplies to Germany, which are shown on the diagrams in this book, would have taken their downward direction at a very much earlier date had our

---

[1] This may be taken by the uninstructed reader to mean that the Professor knew what he was talking about.

forces been placed in harness on the outbreak of war.

A few words remain to be said about prohibited exports.

There was an impression widely prevalent in England that goods placed by the Scandinavian Governments on the list of prohibited exports were thereby prevented from leaving the country. This was not the case. Government licences were issued for a variety of reasons, chief among which were : political pressure; pressure brought to bear by trade combinations; in exchange for goods urgently required from Germany, such as aniline dyes, electrical machinery, steel angles and plates and medicines; and lastly through German diplomatic pressure.

These licences were dispensed with a free hand, and it is needless to say that they deprived the prohibition regulations of the Governments of practically all value. It was common to see in the advertisement columns of the Danish Press announcements by Danish importers of goods for sale ; these announcements, that intending purchasers should be relieved of all anxiety on the score of being unable to dispose of goods on the prohibited export list, were accompanied by the notification in bold type " EXPORT LICENSE ARRANGED."

I sent home a sheaf of Danish newspapers containing this unblushing evidence of the worthlessness of export prohibitions. Owing to representations which I made on this subject the accusing legends were soon afterwards withdrawn from the advertisement columns of the newspapers.

Stocks of goods, which had been proscribed by Government export-prohibition regulations, would in most cases have been sent to Germany before the date on which the regulations came into force, the date, if necessary, being advanced to meet the convenience of exporters. Prior to such date Germany would have organised successively regular drives in tea, coffee, soap, lard, copper, oil and other commodities. The neutral felt justified in assuming that at the worst, when the country had been denuded of a particular commodity and our attention had been directed to the matter, he would not appeal in vain for supplies necessary for his own needs.

Prohibited exports were regarded by the smuggler in a peculiar sense as his lawful game.

Smuggling was rife in Denmark throughout the war, especially in rubber : here the smuggler proved a real friend in need to Germany.

The Danish smugglers worked in connection with a gigantic smuggling centre in Helsingborg, a town on the Swedish side of the northern approach to Copenhagen. One captured smuggler admitted to 10,000 cycle tubes to his credit in a short space of time; and another had earned a round half million kroner (about £28,000) during six months. A cycle tube which in Denmark cost from four to five kroner was sold for fifteen kroner on the Swedish side of the Sound, and the cost of automobile tyre covers increased from 300 to 2,000 kroner.

All surplus rubber was passed along to Germany by the smuggler. Our trade in rubber (and not in rubber alone) gave rise to what may be described as an undesirable though quite natural feeling of commercial jealousy on the part of the French; it provoked rivalry : French motor-tyre makers conceived that they were not getting their proper share of the Scandinavian rubber trade : this was true; and it was unpleasant that it should be true.

CHAPTER XI

In 1917 British cement in very large quantities was shipped to Holland. In October of that year the matter was thrust upon the public notice by a report to the effect that this cement was re-exported from Holland to Belgium, where it was used in the construction of German defences. This report appeared to receive reliable confirmation from the front in a letter to *The Times* from an officer of the R.F.A. containing the following extract :—

> Having just read the protest of the members of the Baltic Shipping Exchange against the shipment of cement to Holland, I have no doubt that it will interest them and others to know that the pill-box in which I now write, and which was built by the enemy, is made of British cement. This I know by a small tin label which was dislodged from the middle of a thick wall by a shell; the label was embossed in English.

Public indignation was aroused by this report, questions were asked in the House of Commons, and meetings were held in the City to demand the stoppage of the cement traffic.

On 20th November, 1917, Lord Robert Cecil, Minister of Blockade, appointed a Committee, under the presidency of Admiral of the Fleet, the Honourable Sir Hedworth Meux, " to inquire whether it is desirable that the export of cement from this country to Holland should be resumed when the general embargo on exports to Holland is raised, and if so, on what conditions."

The export of cement to Holland had been prohibited on the 8th October except under licence, for reasons, we are told, in no way connected with the agitation. The case, as stated by the Committee, is as follows :—

> Two theories appear to have been put forward to support the contention that the export of cement from the United Kingdom to Holland is dangerous and undesirable. One was that British cement was re-exported from Holland to Belgium, and there utilised for the construction of German defences. The other theory, advanced by Mr. A. R. Miles, of A. R. Miles and Company, ship and insurance brokers, and a member of the Baltic Exchange, was that the cement exported to Holland from the United Kingdom relieved Germany of the necessity of supplying equivalent quantities, and therefore enabled her to send proportionately more to the front. These theories are not on the face of them incompatible; indeed, the arguments in favour of the former have been used by advocates of the latter, even though they attach no credence to the alternative.[1]

With regard to the first theory it was proved conclusively both from the legends on the tin label and from chemical analysis of the cement that the latter was not British : this theory was therefore rejected.

We pass to the second theory, viz., " that by permitting these exports from this country, the Foreign Office was releasing equivalent quantities of cement

[1] Cd. 9023.

in Germany, for utilisation in military works, which must otherwise have been sent to Holland."

Mr. Miles had already been in communication with the Foreign Office, whose views are quoted by the Committee. They are :—

(a) That there was a surplus of cement in Germany which, in order to maintain her trade and support her exchange, Germany was able and eager to export to contiguous neutrals.

(b) That in any case the guarantees, under which alone cement may be exported to Holland from the United Kingdom, preclude the possibility of re-export to Germany or Belgium.

(c) That so long as Germany continues to export cement to neutrals, it is not conceivable that she should have insufficient for her own military purposes.

(d) And that, as in these circumstances the export of cement to Holland from the United Kingdom cannot benefit Germany in any way, it is desirable to continue such export both in the very pressing interest of our own exchange, and also in order to increase economic pressure on Germany by lowering through competition the prices obtainable for German cement.

With regard to (d) the conclusion that is drawn is, of course, correct if the assumption on which it is based is correct; that is to say if the views contained in (a), (b) and (c) are correct. Of these (b) refers to the possibility of direct re-export to Germany which was rejected by the Committee. The implicit faith of the Foreign Office in guarantees is not justified by any security which our goods in Scandinavia were supposed to receive under this form of safeguard.

The Committee, speaking of the Netherlands Oversea Trust (N.O.T.), say : " It seems to the Committee highly improbable that such a commodity as cement, which to be of any value must be obtained in considerable quantities, should escape discovery while other goods of a more elusive character are detected and stopped." Nevertheless, 36,000 carcases of swine, whose coefficient of elusiveness is probably not higher than that of cement, managed successfully to evade the vigilance of the Danish authorities.[1] With this reservation (b) may be eliminated, which leaves (a) and (c) only to examine. These points are taken up by the Committee.

The Committee tell us that the main feature of Mr. Miles's argument was that Germany, in order to obtain Holland's produce, was under a definite necessity of keeping Holland supplied with cement, which was necessary for maintaining her dykes and drainage system in repair to prevent the incursion of the sea.

It is properly pointed out that Mr. Miles's argument would only have weight when Germany's ability to supply Holland, after meeting her own needs, fell short of Holland's indispensable requirements.

This being the case it is only necessary to know :—

(1) What was Germany's cement-producing capacity during the war ?

(2) What were Germany's military requirements ?

With regard to (1) the Committee point to the fact that Germany is the largest European producer of cement for export, and that during the war she had continued to export certainly to Holland and Denmark, perhaps also to Norway.

[1] See p. 151.

The facts are that Germany sent to Norway far more cement than to Denmark and Sweden. Both Sweden and Denmark before the war produced and exported large quantities of cement : Norway produced none : she obtained her supplies from Germany and Denmark.

The impetus given to trade after the outbreak of war was the cause of considerable industrial development in Scandinavia, necessitating the building of new and enlargement of old workshops and warehouses, in the construction of which large quantities of cement were required. As the war progressed, a shortage of coal in Sweden and Denmark, but especially in Denmark, seriously crippled the cement industry and reduced the normal output of cement. But the Scandinavian requirements continued to rise. The result was that the Swedish and Danish cement manufacturers were unable to fulfil their forward contracts, especially in South America; exports from Denmark to Norway fell away almost to nothing; and the comparatively small amounts that the Scandinavian countries had been accustomed to import from Germany became of considerable importance, especially to Norway.

In the case of Norway it is seen that her imports of cement from Germany were far in excess of the pre-war figures.

But Norway's case was exceptional : she was the only Scandinavian country from which nickel could be obtained, and nickel was, as Dr. Helfferich tells us, vital to Germany. The increase in the German exports to Norway are also partly to be accounted for by the loss of the Danish supplies during the war. The Committee make no reference to these facts. They go on to say :—

Of her (Germany's) pre-war exports of cement, amounting in 1913 to over 1,100,000 metric tons, less than 250,000 metric tons were taken by countries to which she can still send it. Thus to meet her military requirements she has a large excess balance on her normal output, while in addition to this she has the extensive resources of Belgium upon which to draw.

These figures leave it to be supposed that Germany had a surplus of, say, something like 1,000,000 tons of cement (including the Belgian output) to meet her military requirements, assuming her output to have come up to the pre-war figure. But the output of cement was, as pointed out by the Committee, affected by three main factors during the war : labour, transport facilities, and coal. These factors are disposed of by the Committee as follows :—

As regards labour, the Committee are advised that the manufacture of cement requires mainly a low grade of labour, and is unlikely to be very seriously curtailed by the lack of man-power in Germany. Transport difficulties are certainly great in Germany at present, and no doubt coal shortage would tend to diminish the production of cement if there were more pressing or more lucrative employment for the coal. The Committee have, however, been unable to obtain any evidence that any of these difficulties have reached a pitch at which supplies to neutrals have had to be drastically reduced. On the contrary, a report recently received shows that Germany is able to maintain her export of cement to Denmark. . . . The Committee are satisfied that the curtailment of output, though realised

to some extent, is still far from the point at which
Germany would be compelled to draw on external
sources of supply (apart from Belgium) to meet
her military requirements.

These matters are taken more seriously in other
quarters; Ludendorff, for instance, tells us that man-
power caused him the gravest anxiety, especially
during 1916 and afterwards :—

> As early as September, 1916, the Chancellor
> received the first demands of G.H.Q. for the ruth-
> less requisition of all our man-power. We in-
> sisted emphatically on the point of view that in
> war the powers of every citizen are at the disposal
> of the State, and that accordingly every German
> from fifteen to sixty should.be under an obliga-
> tion to serve, an obligation which, with certain
> limitations, lay on women too.

The low grade of labour required in the manufacture
of cement was a grade of labour which Germany's
military commanders were straining every effort, but
unsuccessfully, to obtain. The lowest grade of labour
is sufficient to direct a bayonet, fire a gun or hurl a
hand-grenade, but it was not to be had.

Coal in Germany could not be obtained for want
of man-power. Three tons of coal at least are required in the production of ten tons of cement. Fifty
thousand men in the later stages of the war had to
be withdrawn from the fighting line to work in the
coal mines. The loss of this man-power, according
to General Ludendorff, was the direct cause of the
ultimate collapse of Germany.

There was no question of Germany's capacity for

producing cement : there was raw material enough for an output to meet her requirements; there was enough coal in the mines of Westphalia to supply all Scandinavia : but neither coal nor cement would produce and transport itself, and man-power and transport had to be provided.

Man-power was indispensable; coal was indispensable; cement was indispensable; but Holland's food was also indispensable. Germany could not get goods from Scandinavia for nothing; she had to maintain her export trade as best she could. Man-power governed her exports; and man-power, scarce as it was, had to be produced for this purpose. The difficulties that Germany must have experienced in complying with the demands for cement from Scandinavia and Holland will be realised by a scrutiny of the figures showing her exports of potash manures. These manures, which require no treatment before export, and from which Germany ultimately obtained considerable benefit in the shape of food, fell from 127,078 tons in 1913 to 73,988 tons in 1917.

The decline in the German export trade at the end of 1916 (on which subject H.M. Government were kept fully informed), of which the marked shrinkage in the export of potash manures here given is an example, is at least strongly suggestive evidence of Germany's inability, in view of other urgent calls upon her man-power, to supply Holland with her full requirements of cement; and the coincidence of the decrease of Germany's exports of all commodities to all neutral countries at the same time that the demand in Holland for British cement arose gives very strong colour to the supposition that the Dutch were told by Germany that they must obtain their cement elsewhere. As things stood the benefits that

Germany was receiving from Holland far outweighed those that we were obtaining.

The export of cement from the United Kingdom to Holland was as follows :—

1913	1914	1915	1916	1917
4,916	20,838	4,118	1,304	48,930 metric tons

All these matters are overlooked in the report of the Committee.

We pass on to (2) : What were Germany's military requirements ?

There are two official publications dealing with the transit traffic across Holland of materials, especially sand and gravel, susceptible of employment as military supplies (Cd. 8693 and 8915). A few words on the subject of this correspondence may be of interest.

Cement is one of the essential ingredients in the production of concrete, which the Germans used in immense quantities for the construction of fortifications in Flanders. Other ingredients are sand and gravel, which were brought down the Rhine in barges from Germany to Belgium, passing through the Dutch inland waterways *en route.*

The Netherlands Government admitted the traffic to be illegal if the cargoes were intended to be used for military purposes, but not otherwise. The Dutch determined this point by the simple expedient of requiring Germany to issue " certificates of peaceful usage " for each cargo, a formality with which Germany readily complied. The Dutch themselves made an estimate of the peaceful requirements for Belgium of sand and gravel, fixing it at 75,000 tons a month. The Dutch accounts were audited by a German expert and, as a result, the monthly quantity of sand and gravel allowed transit through Holland was changed from 75,000 tons a month for July and August (which the Dutch blandly informed us was a mistake), to 420,000 tons, the latter figure being still considerably below the German estimate.

It may here be mentioned incidentally that, in one case at any rate, a cargo covered by a German "certificate of peaceful usage" had been ascertained by the Netherlands Government, after it had succeeded in passing into Belgium, to consist of arms and ammunition concealed under gravel.

German and Dutch experts (at the invitation of the former) then proceeded in company on a tour of inspection of the Belgian ground in order to verify the basis on which the German calculations had been made. The Netherlands Government decided, on the strength of the report of their representative, that the German certificates of peaceful usage were quite genuine, and henceforth would no longer lie under the stigma of suspicion.

A French expert, M. Tur, Inspecteur général des Travaux Publics, examined the Netherlands report and found in it inaccuracies of figures and exaggerated bases of calculation. He made his own estimate of the annual requirements of Belgium, based upon statistics of her previous needs. M. Tur's conclusion was that "there was no justification for the Netherlands Government to allow a single ton of sand or gravel to pass into Belgium on the plea that it was required for works of a pacific character."

Although Germany's absolute requirements of cement are not to be accurately measured by the extent of the traffic in sand and gravel, this traffic may at least be accepted as furnishing trustworthy data for concluding that they were in excess of the output that Germany was capable of producing for

R

military purposes, taking into consideration the state of her man-power, coal and transport.

Between 1st January and 15th August, 1917, some 3,000,000 tons of sand and gravel passed from Holland into Belgium.

In an Enclosure to a Foreign Office despatch of 30th October, 1917 (Cd. 8693), it is stated :—

Next there is the certain knowledge that the German demands for these supplies for direct military objects, such as fortifications, is enormous, and there is the evidence that the concrete used for such fortifications is derived from material which comes from Germany.

The main ground taken by the Committee for drawing the conclusion that Germany's output of cement was in excess of her military requirements is the fact of her exportations to Scandinavia : but the circumstances of this trade receive no examination and, moreover, cause is confused with effect. Germany's export of cement did not necessarily or even probably argue a superabundance of that commodity for ordinary trading purposes, as the Committee would themselves seem to think; but, conversely, in our opinion, Germany's dearth of man-power, without which cement could not be produced, coupled with the known fact that her man-power was used for trading in cement in spite of its dearth, must be regarded as pointing to the logical conclusion that the resources of the Scandinavian States were one of the chief military necessities of Germany, for which a sacrifice of man-power in the production of cement had to be made.

On the last page of their report the Committee say :—

On the evidence, therefore, the Committee have no hesitation in recommending the immediate resumption of the export of cement to Holland when the political situation permits, and they see no reason for applying to it any more drastic conditions than those in force at the time when the export was suspended;

whereas on a previous page one of the " less obvious " though more important reasons for sending cement to Holland was advanced on the ground of its " political desirability."

Cement is the only commodity that formed the subject of inquiry on the general question of our trade during the war. The circumstances that gave rise to this inquiry were much the same as those that led to Lord Faringdon's being sent to Scandinavia in 1915. The Committee's conclusions appear to be at variance with the established fact that our trade was the very life-blood of Scandinavia and Germany. They are based upon false premises and are in disregard of a large mass of important evidence to which the Committee had access but which they did not make use of. Nor is it understood how, knowing the scarcity of labour and difficulties of transport in Germany, knowing also the intimate connection that the official correspondence on the traffic in sand and gravel bore to the subject into which the Committee had been appointed to inquire, H.M. Government—or their representative—could have accepted a report in which only perfunctory reference to these matters is made, and in which certain omitted facts tending strongly towards conclusions the reverse of those arrived at by the Committee were fully known to H.M. Government.

There is a vital fact which has been overlooked in this report. The cement that we sent to Holland cost us coal, shipping-space and labour. When this cement was landed in Holland, so long as Holland was using cement and her only alternative source of supply was Germany, the British cement released German man-power and substituted for it British man-power.

CHAPTER XII

THE export of goods from the United Kingdom and the British Empire has been justified on the two-fold ground that even if they reached our enemy either directly or indirectly they would draw gold from him; and further that they would, as in the ordinary nature of trade, effect an improvement in the exchange.

The following observations are confined mainly to the first of these suppositions, where it must be assumed that the goods in question were of no military value, and that the Germans themselves did not appreciate the necessity for conserving their gold reserves in war time.

There were, as has already been pointed out when speaking of tea, coffee and cocoa, scarcely any goods that did not possess military value during the war: the surest test of this value was their acceptance or rejection by Germany.

It became known very early in the war that the Germans were fully alive to the importance of conserving their gold. Our attention was sometimes directed to this matter by the efforts, frequently successful, which were made by Germany to obtain for herself gold balances held by some of the South American States in Scandinavia and Holland. Again, the large supplies of food and other commodities, which Scandinavia and Holland exported to Germany during the war, far exceeded in value the coal, dyes, chemicals, iron and other goods which Germany exported to Scandinavia and Holland. The Germans did not pay off the adverse balance in gold, the amount of gold exported by Germany to Scandinavia and Holland during the war being insignificant; but instead, German Government bonds were deposited with several banks in neutral countries. These banks then opened credits for the Germans for an amount equal to a certain proportion of the face value of the German bonds on deposit. Merchants, and especially ship-owners in neutral countries, were making large profits from their dealings with the Entente Powers and North and South American neutrals, all of which transactions were on a gold basis. There was thus a great influx of gold to Scandinavia and Holland, not from Germany but from the Entente Powers and particularly Great Britain; the Scandinavian and Dutch banks, finding themselves with large liquid assets, were therefore able to open credits for Germany. The amounts of these credits at the time of the Armistice were as follows :—

Denmark	.	.	.	.	154,000,000	kroner
Sweden .	.	.	.	.	193,000,000	,,
					(15,000,000 dollars)	
Norway .	.	.	.	.	72,000,000	kroner
Holland .	.	.	.	.	66,000,000	florins

At the rate of exchange current in 1918 this represented a sum of nearly 45 millions sterling.[1]

[1] These loans were all repaid by the end of 1921. In view of Germany's having defaulted in respect of her payments due to the Allied Powers under the terms of the Treaty of Versailles, these repayments do not appear to be consistent with a proper regard for the just claims of the Allied Powers. Allied interests have clearly been subordinated to those of States some of which showed a notoriously benevolent neutrality towards our late enemy, and to all of which the war brought prosperity. As

ERRATUM

Page 246—

Denmark	.	.	.	.	.	15
Sweden	.	.	.	.	.	19
					and	15
Norway	.	.	.	.	.	7
Holland	.	.	.	.	.	6

Throughout the war I made repeated efforts to get some sort of control established over the activities of neutral banks, but without success. Even after America's entry in April, 1917, financial pressure was withheld although combined action would have proved irresistible. It is thought that the Foreign Office in justification of their policy took the view that they had not the support of American opinion; and that pressure on neutral banks, according to financial authorities, would prejudice the chances of obtaining a loan in neutral countries.

There were, however, many British officials in Scandinavia, in addition to myself, who regarded this latter view as ill-founded, seeing that our enemies were not only continually obtaining credit from neutral banks, but even so late as 1918 had raised a loan in Norway. Moreover, certain neutral banks were known to have rendered enormous services to enemy countries in assisting the exportation of merchandise, well knowing that much of this merchandise had been imported under guarantee for consumption in a neutral country.

Some features connected with this question of finance were very disquieting. For instance, certain neutral financiers, who were known to be on the best of terms with our enemies, and who had amassed great wealth during the war by furnishing them with supplies, were throughout the war treated with marked favour when visiting England. One of these gentlemen, who, on account of his dealings with the Germans, became a pariah even in his own country,

far as is known these repayments have been made without protest from the Allied Reparations Commission and in disregard of Belgium's prior claim to re-imbursement by the Scandinavian States in respect of her stolen property—to wit her coal, to which reference has been made on pp. 114, 115.

would boast during the war of the kindness extended to him in England by British officials : among such tokens of kindness mentioned by him was a dinner which he had attended in London at the private residence of a British Under-Secretary of State.

Again, some of these neutral financiers were not only large shareholders in, but directors of a London bank, and conversely certain British financiers were interested in Scandinavian banks. British and Scandinavian private interests were thus united by a golden link, and in time of trouble Scandinavian financiers could rely with confidence upon their British *confrères* for all necessary support.

So secure was the banking business considered that some black-listed firms in Scandinavia reconstructed themselves as banks and insurance companies and, having done so, felt perfectly secure from any pressure.

The feeling of uneasiness referred to above was not relieved by certain financial transactions, which took place during the year 1918, between the United Kingdom and Scandinavia.

At that time the Germans were making great efforts to obtain large quantities of British and American paper money.

American officials in Scandinavia formed certain views with regard to the uses to which the Germans intended to put this British and American paper money. Although they did not consider the grounds upon which they based their opinions as conclusive, they were nevertheless unanimous in holding it a duty to prevent the Germans, if possible, from realising their desires; and, as on this account the export of American paper currency from America was strictly forbidden, it is clear that the American Government shared this view.

It may be presumed that H.M. Government took the other point of view, for large sums of money in British paper currency were allowed into Scandinavia and were actually carried by the British Foreign Office messengers; again it would appear that the American officials, at any rate in Scandinavia, were taken completely by surprise when they discovered that British paper currency was reaching Scandinavia. The profits from its sale to the Germans reached, I think, the colossal figure of 50 per cent., and some American firms requested the American War Trade Board to grant them facilities which would enable them to develop this business.   All requests were met with a flat refusal : moreover, applicants were informed that if they had anything to do with the business they would be reported to the United States Government.

The questions that naturally arise are the following :—

Whose money was the Foreign Office messenger carrying?

Who suggested this business to the Foreign Office?

Into whose pockets did the profits go?

The answers to these questions would be interesting. It would also be interesting to know why this matter was never referred to in the Weekly Bulletin of Information issued.

In November, 1917, I had discussed the question of bank control in neutral countries with Lord Robert Cecil, who appeared to share my views on the subject. Time slipped away : our enemies, buttressed by Scandinavian finance whose power we could have smashed, were enabled to command available supplies.

The following extract is from a letter I wrote to Lord Robert Cecil on 28th April, 1918 :—

As you were actively interesting yourself in the matter I naturally hoped that it would be dealt with promptly and effectively, and my hopes were raised still further when I found that the information necessary for the purpose was being collected under your instructions at this (Christiania) Legation at the beginning of this year.

It is with all the more regret, therefore, that I find that we are at the present still without any control at a time when the enemy is making great efforts to obtain large quantities of our own and the American paper currency.

As showing how helpless we are here to prevent our enemies from achieving their object, I may mention that this afternoon I met an American official who told me that one of the Norwegian banks held a considerable amount of American paper currency and he could not see how we could prevent them from selling this to the Germans.

I have, during the last year, frequently heard it stated that no Scandinavian bank could exist if its connections with Paris, London and New York were cut off. I have never heard statements of this sort seriously challenged. It would appear, therefore, as though we had a powerful weapon for use against our enemies which at present we are not using. This point of view appears to be confirmed by the fact that in every case so far in which we have taken coercive action against a bank in Sweden or Norway the result has been that our demands have been immediately complied with.

I am under the impression that Lord Robert Cecil

himself was strongly in favour of bringing pressure to bear against neutral banks and that as Minister of Blockade he exerted his influence to achieve that object. In spite of this, however, no such pressure was exerted and our enemies continued to obtain great financial support from all neutral countries up to the end of the war.

With regard to the subject of the Exchange, in war time this is not governed by the same factors that operate in peace time, when it largely depends upon the balance between exports and imports. In war time exchange depends largely upon prestige, and prestige depends upon many factors which in the aggregate represent, as it were, the moral and material strength and position of a country.

To the neutrals, living as they did in what may be called the zone of the economic war, the most important of these factors was the conduct of the blockade : any action therefore on our part that enabled our enemies to obtain goods of any sort weakened our prestige, and adversely affected our exchange.

It can safely be assumed that almost everything the neutrals obtained from the British Empire during the war benefited our enemies either directly or indirectly : in other words, those goods increased the holding-out power of our enemies.

In conclusion it can be said with certainty that the export of goods directly or indirectly to enemy countries, or the export of goods to neutrals which benefit our enemies in any way, cannot be justified or excused on any grounds other than those of military expediency. On the contrary, this traffic, besides being grossly unfair to our Allies and our fighting forces, lowered our prestige in neutral countries, and gave hope and strength to our enemies.

Finance was indeed a rod to conjure with and tighten our economic grip over Germany. It was one of the most potent of our unarmed forces, and essentially a British weapon. But it had commenced to show signs of rust before being brought into use. Even then, however, as is instanced particularly in the case of the Norwegian copper and fish agreements, its work was good. It spurred our enemy into paroxysms of impotent wrath. Can there be any doubt but that a bold Treasury policy by which many of the supplies that reached Germany through Scandinavia could have been acquired by purchase would have helped materially to precipitate the end, besides saving untold millions to the exchequer?

CHAPTER XIII

TOWARDS the end of 1915 a Member of Parliament, Sir Alexander Henderson, visited Scandinavia and Holland in order to make independent inquiries on behalf of H.M. Government on the subject of the supplies that were reaching Germany through those countries.

The general feeling of exhilaration experienced on receipt of this news was much as what might have been expected on receiving tidings of a great victory. The war was felt already to have been shortened : but as the matter was talked over wood was touched as a precautionary measure against unpleasant surprises, which are so apt to follow on the heels of brilliant expectations. Whether it was that our expectations had been oversanguine, or that the wood was of poor quality, or that the touches had been given with too light a hand that was the cause of our precautionary measures' miscarrying, the charm in any case did not work successfully.

The cause of this inquiry was the growing feeling of alarm that had sprung up at home, and was reflected in the columns of the Press, in public meetings and in questions in the Houses of Parliament, that proper use was not being made of our naval power.

Sir Alexander Henderson came, saw and reported, and became Lord Faringdon, under which title he will now be referred to.

As to what Lord Faringdon saw and heard, enough has already been said of what was taking place in Scandinavia, and especially in Denmark, for enabling a fair idea to be formed of what should be the probable result of inquiries directed to the detection of abuses.

Lord Faringdon's report, on which the future and especially 1916 so much hinged, did not represent the facts as reported to Lord Faringdon by myself, or as reported by me officially through the British Legation to the Foreign Office; or as disclosed by official statistics published after the war : all of which showed that the Scandinavian trade with Germany at the time of Lord Faringdon's visit was on an unprecedented scale. Referring to this visit Lord Faringdon stated in the House of Lords on 23rd February, 1916, that with regard to contraband he was convinced that but little was passing and that neutrals were doing their best to regard their obligations.[1] To this statement I must strongly demur, being convinced that they were disregarding them; the Danish fishermen themselves told us that they were doing so, and almost went so far as to ask us to see that they were made to regard their obligations. By others breaches of faith were regarded as " good sport."

In Denmark, we are told, the organisations at work were under thoroughly responsible and honest men. Nobody will doubt that there are as many honest men in Denmark as in any other country, but this assurance does not satisfactorily dispose of the subject under immediate discussion, which had to do with hundreds of thousands of tons of foodstuffs and merchandise thought to have been passing through neutral countries into the territory of our enemies and for

[1] Parliamentary Debates, No. 4, p. 155, 23rd February, 1916.

which facts and figures were both available. This traffic together with the news of successive reverses had caused a feeling of consternation to come over the country. Goods placed on the prohibited list of exports, to which reference is made, found themselves on a very slippery inclined plane with elevated end in Denmark and foot in Germany, the releasing mechanism being worked by the smugglers.

Lord Faringdon considered that the Government were to be congratulated on the way they had dealt with many difficulties, and they deserved encouraging support. H.M. Government appeared to be of the same opinion.

Lord Grey thought on the whole that the report was very satisfactory. Lord Robert Cecil was encouraged not only by the reports from Germany, but by the fact that Lord Faringdon had said that not much was going through neutral countries.[1] Lord Faringdon quotes the figures for butter we received from Denmark in 1915 as an instance of the loyal disposition many neutrals were showing to Great Britain.[2]

As to this, compared with 1913, we *lost* from Scandinavia and Holland, butter :—

In 1915	.	.	.	33,238 tons
„ 1916	.	.	.	51,795 „
„ 1917	.	.	.	75,915 „

160,948 tons

though in margarine we gained from Holland 105,726 tons during the same period. (Our margarine from Scandinavia was an unimportant quantity.) The net loss to England in butter and margarine was over 50,000 tons, whereas Germany gained in butter alone 140,000 tons.

[1] Parliamentary Debates, No. 153, p. 3194, 26th January, 1916.
[2] *Ibid.*, No. 4, p. 155, 23rd February, 1916.

However, the true state of the disposition of each of the Scandinavian neutrals at that time (adopting a similar unit of measurement to Lord Faringdon's) can now be shown exactly.

NORWAY'S DISPOSITION

As expressed in metric tons of food sent

	1913	1915	1916
To the United Kingdom	61,464	69,512	35,701
To Germany and Austria	81,538	182,630	215,593

DENMARK'S DISPOSITION

To the United Kingdom	256,754	197,398	156,100
To Germany and Austria	123,547	274,401	314,328

SWEDEN'S DISPOSITION

To the United Kingdom	26,567	8,563	115
To Germany and Austria	37,043	104,203	90,835

The above figures are from the countries' own official statistics : they include meat, fish, dairy produce, eggs, lard and margarine : they do not include vegetable oils, beer, fish oil, tea, coffee, cocoa, horses, fruit and vegetables. If these latter items were included the situation would show up much worse. Live cattle have been reckoned as running to 200 kilos. or about 441 lb. per head; whereas the Danish fat cattle would be nearer 250 kilos., which would make a difference of over 12,000 tons in 1915 and more in 1916.

Take the above figures for Denmark for 1915. They show that by comparison with 1913 we lost 59,356 tons of food, whereas Germany gained 150,854. Here is a batch of figures which show what was going on at the time that Lord Faringdon was making his investigations. The figures for 1916 are given in order that the claimed improvements towards the end of 1915 may be correctly appraised. They should be compared with 1913.

EXPORTS FROM DENMARK TO GERMANY (METRIC TONS)

(From Danish official statistics)

	1913	1915	1916
Fish	25,516	66,569	106,694
Meat conserves	131	16,022	19,758
Cheese	57	3,886	4,344
Eggs	1,160	12,466	20,422
Fats	72	6,474	6,794
Butter	11,317	37,455	36,891

The export of purely Danish butter to Germany was in 1913 less than 2,000 tons. The figure 11,317 includes re-exports of Swedish and Russian butter, of which there was a considerable transit across Denmark before the war.

	1913	1915	1916
Fish oil	1,631	3,017	1,518
Bone fat	1,080	2,529	2,165
Coffee	81	2,339	1,574

Denmark, be it noted, was able to send these amounts to Germany after satisfying her own requirements.

	1913	1915	1916
Tea	3	590	220
Cocoa	—	764	106

The above figures are exclusive of the goods which passed through the free port of Copenhagen.[1] Being Danish figures they may be regarded in all cases as safe minimums; and since no smuggled goods are included, the 1915 and 1916 figures probably fall short in their aggregate total by 40 or 50 per cent. of the traffic they stand for.

[1] See Appendix, p. 315.

S

With regard to Holland Dr. Helfferich gives a few figures which are of interest :—

> The export from Holland to Germany and England in one or two commodities for which the two countries competed during the war developed as follows :—

BUTTER
(All in metric tons)

					1913	1915	1916
England	.	.	.	.	7,900	2,500	2,200
Germany	.	.	.	.	19,000	36,700	31,500

CHEESE

England	.	.	.	.	19,100	8,400	6,800
Germany	.	.	.	.	16,100	63,300	76,200

PORK AND BACON

England	.	.	.	.	34,000	7,600	10,300
Germany	.	.	.	.	11,000	55,100	24,100

EGGS

England	.	.	.	.	5,800	7,800	800
Germany	.	.	.	.	15,300	25,200	36,400

SUMMARY

England	.	.	.	.	66,800	26,300	20,100
Germany	.	.	.	.	61,400	180,300 (a)[1]	169,200(b)[1]
England lost	.	.	.	40,500		46,700	
Germany gained	.	.	.	118,900		107,800	

Germany was thus able substantially to increase her importation from the Netherlands of these commodities so important for the feeding of the people and the supplying of the army, while at the same time England had to be content with a largely reduced supply.

Although the above figures were not known to Lord Faringdon at the time of his visit to Scandinavia, yet the evidence in support of the facts that they stand

[1] Reference to (a) and (b) is made on p. 266.

for was so abundant that it could not but obtrude
itself upon the notice of any casual observer, nor
fail to carry conviction where there was a desire to
be convinced. The one and only object of the Malmo
meeting was to prevent the figures for the Scandinavian trade from becoming known.

I was privileged when Lord Faringdon was in
Christiania to give him my own views. I placed him
in possession of certain information of a confidential
character which only the importance of his mission
and the war justified my doing; he knew in what
quarter to go to obtain reliable information and he
also knew where and why a certain discount should
be allowed. With regard to the traffic with Germany
I gave him the results of my personal observation
and the reports of foreign Legations. I referred him
to the congested state of the railways and ferries and
brought the Malmo meeting and its meaning to his
knowledge. I cannot but regard it as exceedingly
unfortunate that the situation as it really existed
should have failed to reveal itself to the distinguished
politician appointed by H.M. Government to report
upon it to them.

In February, 1916, important debates concerning
the conduct of the blockade took place in the Houses
of Parliament. Replies to criticisms of the Government policy appeared to show that the supplies which
were reaching Germany were far less than was supposed, that they were being effectively arrested, and
that there was no power in the hands of the Government of which full use was not being made. That
there was inevitable leakage was admitted, nor was it
possible to prevent it. Special attention was invited
to the position of neutrals and the question of neutral
rights, to which a very indulgent recognition was

extended. With regard to the bulk of the importations into Scandinavia and Holland, certain commodities were selected, and figures were given which would appear to show that the measures taken for arresting the main stream of the traffic from neutral countries to Germany had been successful: public confidence was further strengthened by a frank admission of past errors and by the hopeful view that was presented of future prospects.

First, as to neutrals.

Europe was ablaze. Tucked away in the north-west corner were three or four small neutral States, untouched by the general conflagration but in whose flames they were threatened to become enveloped. The danger of getting singed or burned came not from England but from Germany: of this these States were only too well aware; Belgium had already been consigned to the flames and not so much as a word of protest had been heard from Scandinavia and Holland. Neutral States situated as were these, in the sense of their having either the hope of preserving or the power of enforcing the same relationship towards Germany that existed in the normal circumstances of peace, could not expect to stand in the same relationship as in peace time with the Powers that were at war with Germany: for neutrality has no meaning if it is partial; and in the case at least of Denmark and Sweden both these States were the tools of Germany, the one the passive or unresisting and the other the willing one. Their relationship with Germany was one of benevolent neutrality; and in the same measure that Germany had gained by a partial surrender of the neutral rights of these States we had lost by it. Although we held these neutral States in the palms of our hands, yet until the year 1917 the lawful pressure that was brought to bear against them was insignificant.

There is a dignity in the eloquence of some of the tributes that were paid to these neutrals and a chivalrous regard for the susceptibilities of a weaker State, which is felt to be peculiarly appropriate as coming from the greatest maritime Power; and but for the war it would certainly have been in the very worst taste to have set to work deliberately to endeavour to destroy the good effect that such words must have upon all right-minded people. With all that has been said as applying to that part of the community of neutral States which suffered innocently from the calamity of war there can be no dispute that everybody must find himself in whole-hearted agreement. This solicitude for neutrals in theory was admirable, though cynics have been heard to say that it may have sprung from a desire to advertise a high moral standard. Be this as it may, it was a luxury that could not be afforded in war time. These neutrals, moreover, showed scant regard for our belligerent rights, though they showed a very nice appreciation of their own neutral rights : nor could they complain that they had been altogether left out in the cold, for America had voluntarily taken over the duties of championship on their behalf, and it was to America that any complaints should properly have been addressed. We entered into this conflict in vindication of Belgium's rights : Belgium was the representative of these northern European neutrals. We fought Germany for these neutrals' cause. There was no single instance of a sign of gratitude having been shown for our disinterested and fateful action, nor any instance where the moral obligations under which these neutrals were placed were found to have been held superior to self-interest.

The neutrals did not by any means regard themselves as proper objects for pity; nor, truth to tell, did I, who was for four years living amongst them; nor did any member known to me of the Allied Legations. Denmark sent her most astute men to England for the express purpose of depicting the country as suffering from the harsh effects of our blockade and fear of German invasion; and by such misrepresentations to extort a pittance from our compassion. In this she succeeded beyond the hopes probably of her wildest dreams.

It is impossible not to note the hyper-sensitive feeling for neutrals' rights which is expressed by the Government during these debates, and to compare it with the historic statement to which reference has already been made that "it was not intended that our measures should be entangled in a network of juridical niceties." The sentiments here expressed are in direct opposition to each other : but they were very convenient each to its own occasion.

Neutral susceptibilities, which were spoken of at Westminster, though having their seat formally established in the neutral heart, were not completely cut off from all means of communication with the neutral pocket; to which, indeed, there would seem to have been a convenient and not unfamiliar route. Looking at this matter from the " powerful State " point of view, it is a little puzzling to know what are the particular advantages of being in the position of a powerful State, if the weaker State is never to feel this power except as an increment to its own; and when and where the power is to be made use of, if not on perfectly lawful occasions in war time, and where it can best be made felt. Let it also be remarked, to finish with these parentheses, that while these neutrals

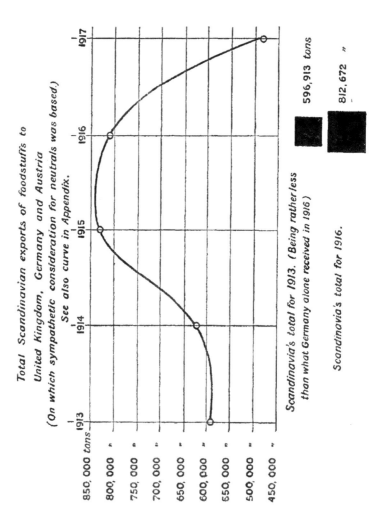

Total Scandinavian exports of foodstuffs to
United Kingdom, Germany and Austria
(On which sympathetic consideration for neutrals was based.)
See also curve in Appendix.

Scandinavia's total for 1913. (Being rather less
than what Germany alone received in 1916)

Scandinavia's total for 1916.

596,913 tons

812,672 „

264 THE TRIUMPH OF UNARMED FORCES

fought for wealth and obtained it from us, we were fighting for and sacrificing our lives.

Turning now to facts and figures, the Marquess of Lansdowne in his speech in the House of Lords on 22nd February, 1916, sets out to illustrate the manner in which progress is being made as precautionary measures begin to operate. Cotton is selected.

Take the import of cotton to Scandinavia and Holland. The figure for 1913 is 73,000 tons. The figure for 1915 is 310,000 tons. That is a very alarming figure—an increase nearly fourfold. But if you make the comparison as I conceive it ought to be made, and compare the year, not as a whole, but month by month, you will find —I put it in this way for convenience sake— that in the last six months the figure for 1915 was 52,000 tons and for 1913 was 49,000 tons.[1]

That is certainly one way of looking at this matter. Let us put down these figures and make them clear:—

	1913	Tons
Total		= 73,000
Last six months		= 49,000
Therefore first six months		= 24,000

	1915	Tons
Total		= 310,000
Last six months		= 52,000
Therefore first six months		= 258,000

All these figures, it was stated, required extremely careful scrutiny before any conclusions were based upon them. Subject to this reservation there is another conclusion to be based upon the above figures : for by making a comparison of the first six months of 1915 with the same period for 1913 the result is not

[1] Parliamentary Debates, No. 3, p. 98, 22nd February, 1916.

as 52,000 to 49,000 but as 258,000 to 24,000; and the conclusion to be drawn from these latter figures is that the situation stood in need of improvement. On a fair balance of the lessons to be learned from these two sets of figures it would seem that the 310,000 tons, which it was sought to show was not an alarming figure for 1915, was in reality more alarming than was supposed. Lard and other commodities are also dealt with on the same lines.

If you are to make a fair comparison in regard to these figures it is quite obvious that you ought not to compare the figures for the whole of the year 1915 with the whole of the year 1913, but that you should take the figures month by month during the year and see how the matter was progressing as our precautionary measures began to operate.

The figures for the commodities which were selected for the purpose of illustrating this method of judging the effect of the Government blockade measures showed the improvements which were sought to be shown : and, taking the figures generally for the year 1916, they show an improvement on those for 1915, though not in all cases. But is the decrease of the 1915 figures rightly to be regarded as an improvement having regard to the magnitude itself of the 1916 figures ? Is any set of figures to be viewed favourably because it shows an improvement on a preceding set ?

Take Dr. Helfferich's figures on p. 258.

Looking at what England lost and Germany gained, the figures, it must be confessed, make the position look rather blue and do not show up as well as they might for our blockade. But if we compare the total food that Holland sent to Germany in 1915 with the total for 1916 in order to see how matters were progressing as our precautionary measures began to operate, these figures may be examined with a considerable feeling of satisfaction at the progress indicated. Thus (*b*) tells us of great all-round improvements in 1916 over (*a*) in 1915 : but it is important in looking at these figures that the eye should not be allowed to wander over to the left : a downwards movement would be fatal.

The importations into Scandinavia during 1915 were on a scale generally of unparalleled dimensions, and our blockade to establish its pretensions to any real meaning could not but have brought about a decrease in 1916 of these importations. But such decrease is in itself far from showing that the improvement is not erroneously so claimed, comparisons with 1913 being the only criterion by which the effectiveness of the blockade is to be judged. Such comparisons are unfavourable in the case of a large number of commodities, excluding most foodstuffs.

But the supreme test of the blockade of Germany lay in the quantity of foodstuffs which she was prevented from obtaining; and the worst feature of our trading with Scandinavia was the assistance she derived from it in enabling food to be produced and exported. When our entry into the war appeared to be probable, Germany at once turned her attention to the question of her food supplies.

On August 2nd, 1914, Geheimrat Frisch, who afterwards became the director of the Zentral-Einkaufs-Gesellschaft (Central Purchasing Corporation), came to Hamburg, in order to inform Ballin, at the request of the Ministry of the Interior, that the latter felt very anxious in regard to the quantity of food actually to be found in Germany, which, it was feared, would be very small, and that it was expected that a great shortage would arise after a very brief period. He therefore asked him to use his best endeavours in order to secure supplies from abroad. A Hamburg firm was immediately requested to find out how much food was actually available in the country, and although the figures obtained were not quite so bad as was expected, steps were taken at once to remedy the deficiencies by importing food from neutral countries.[1]

The year 1916 was the most critical year of the war in that Germany had begun to feel the pinch of starvation; and it required comparatively little pressure, which it was well within our power to apply, to precipitate disaster.

Germany had hoped to have brought about a separate peace with Russia by the end of 1915, and had reckoned upon the success of her negotiations for ameliorating her food situation. Her efforts came to nothing: but she had taken other steps to meet the dark menace of famine by building up and elaborating a vast organisation whereby she acquired foodstuffs from overseas (including, be it said, ourselves) through the agency of certain prominent Scandinavian and Dutch profiteers; it was solely due to the success of these arrangements and our neglect to frustrate them that she was able to continue the struggle. At the beginning of 1916 we were about to enter the period in which the greatest risk was justified in any measures necessary for stopping supplies to Germany, more especially in view of the impending new submarine menace which ultimately brought America into the war.

[1] From " Albert Ballin," by Bernhard Huldermann. Cassell & Co.

The supplies that reached Germany in 1915 helped her through 1916; but the 1916 supplies were far more important to her. Constant references are made by Ludendorff to the famished condition of Germany, which was critical in the pre-harvest periods of 1916 and 1917. It is clear that but for the supplies obtained from Roumania after the invasion of that country, Germany would have been brought to her knees; in 1917 she was again saved by supplies from the Ukraine. In 1916 there was just sufficient food and munitions to enable Germany to continue the struggle; but there was no margin. An effective blockade in combination with an embargo on British exports in 1915 and 1916 could not have failed to have brought about Germany's collapse before Russia's and before Roumania had taken the field.

> " A *three* years' war was only possible," says Ludendorff, " because we had in Germany abundant coal, and so much iron and food that *together with* what we could obtain from occupied territory and neutral countries, we could, by practising the most rigid economy, manage to exist in spite of the hostile blockade. . . . The importance in war of coal, iron and food was known before this war; but how absolutely decisive they would become was only demonstrated to all the world as hostilities proceeded."

Copious examples are also given of the physical and moral effect on the German people of the strangling hunger-blockade and enemy propaganda " and of the " inconceivable hardships suffered and endured in the four long years of war." But the most significant of all the admissions made by German writers is, perhaps, that during the great German advance on the Western Front in April, 1918, certain divisions had failed to show any inclination to attack; the troops would stop round captured food supplies, while individuals stayed behind to search houses and farms for food.

"The 'silent pressure of sea-power' gives one to think," says von Tirpitz; who adds, "As Herr von Hydebrand said in 1911 in the Reichstag, 'England is the enemy.'"

The effect of our blockade, inadequate as it was, caused such widespread distress throughout Germany that it was not possible for Germany to conceal it. The physical and moral deterioration that set in among the German people from want of food was proclaimed publicly in the columns of the neutral Press, and by authentic accounts from the pens of neutral travellers : it is confirmed and authenticated now by German writers. Although it is not known by what margin Germany escaped early destruction, the margin was small; and it was the additional supplies that she received through us that kept this margin continually open and destroyed all hopes of an early peace.

The foodstuffs (not including certain oils, beer, tea, coffee, cocoa, horses and several other articles of diet) received from Norway, Sweden and Denmark by Great Britain and Germany are as follows :—

			Great Britain	Germany
			Tons	Tons
1913	.	. .	344,785	252,128
1915	.	. .	275,473	561,234
1916	.	. .	191,916	620,756

Germany also received immense quantities from Holland, in addition to substantial quantities of smuggled goods.

The following statement was handed in to Lord Milner by me at an interview which he was so good as to accord me in November 1917 :—

AN EXAMPLE OF SEA POWER AS APPLIED TO DENMARK

STATEMENT OF THE NUMBER OF TONS OF FOOD LOST AND GAINED BY ENGLAND AND GERMANY WHEN COMPARED WITH THE AVERAGES OF 1911, 1912 AND 1913

					Lost by England Tons	Gained by Germany Tons
Butter	1915	.	.	.	16,499	20,981
,,	1916	.	.	.	23,359	22,826
Eggs	1915	.	.	.	7,455	11,216
,,	1916	.	.	.	16,330	19,253
Bacon	1915	.	.	.	17,031	31,231
,,	1916	.	.	.	36,541	16,194
Meat	1915	.	.	.	463	26,990
,,	1916	.	.	.	491	25,393
Fish	1915	.	.	.	—	23,000
,,	1916	.	.	.	—	77,000
Sheep	1915	.	.	.	—	1,511
,,	1916	.	.	.	—	803
					118,169	276,398

This statement shows that during 1915 and 1916 Germany had therefore obtained nearly 300,000 tons of food from Denmark, mostly of a greasy nature, in excess of her pre-war amounts. During the same period we had lost over 100,000 tons, the whole of which was taken by Germany. The real situation, therefore, shows a *gain* to Germany during the two years of 400,000 tons of food from Denmark alone.

Lard is not included in the above statement. In 1916 Germany obtained from Denmark about 7,000 tons : Great Britain nil.

" Returns "—to quote from one of the Government speeches—" have sometimes been compiled with an obvious inability to grapple with the arithmetic of the case."

There are no arithmetical faults in the above figures

that would lessen the significance of their meaning, which is : that whatever favourable inferences are to be drawn from figures quoted by H.M. Government in the case of certain commodities, such inferences are not to be applied to the bulk of the general merchandise which passed through our fleet into Scandinavia : that in respect of foodstuffs which reached Germany— and they could only reach Germany through importations into Scandinavia of raw and other materials— there is no *real* improvement to be pointed to as our precautionary measures operated : on the contrary the 1915 total is more than double that of 1913, and the 1916 exceeds even the 1915 total. Their further meaning is that these excessive supplies to Germany together with those that passed through Holland were in all probability more than enough, had they been withheld, to have sounded Germany's death knell at an early date, having regard to the views expressed by the highest German authorities on the critical condition of their country at successive stages of the war.

The above figures are, I think, the best test by which are to be judged the results achieved by the greatest maritime Power in the world at a time when, in the zenith of her naval strength and efficiency, she was engaged in a deadly economic struggle against an almost defenceless enemy.

Our miserable and inglorious trade prolonged the war : a stricken world, for now over four years, has been pursued by its nemesis; which still derides the efforts of puny humanity to restore in its ranks the order so wantonly committed to the forces of disruption.

It is profitless to dwell upon the past. It is difficult, however, altogether to obliterate the sad thought of the prosperity that this country would now be enjoying had victory been assured early in the war by the timely application of those forces whose latent power has perhaps been thrown into even stronger relief by the grim difficulties over which they ultimately triumphed.

CHAPTER XIV

FINAL

AMERICA took the field in April, 1917. The Government proposals as to America's blockade policy were contained in instructions to Mr. Balfour (now Earl Balfour), who proceeded to the U.S.A. to discuss the question of combined action. These proposals, so far as I am aware, were not communicated by H.M. Government to the Legations in Scandinavia : according to the statements of Americans, Norway was to be mulct of many of her importations from the United States, including cereals, metals and important commodities necessary to her industries, unless she made very serious reductions in her normal export trade with Germany.

The only burden to be imposed upon Denmark was that the supply of fodder should be regulated with a view to obtaining pre-war percentages and amounts in respect of the distribution of Danish agricultural produce to Great Britain and Germany.

Suitable pressure was to be brought to bear upon Sweden by the restriction of supplies from the United States with a view to the question of Russian transit compensation and the Anglo-Swedish draft agreements being placed on a satisfactory footing. Swedish food exports to Germany had to be reduced, and a reasonable proportion of Swedish shipping placed at the disposal of the Allies.

The proposals with regard to Denmark, bearing in mind the prosperity that the war had brought to that

T   273 country at our expense, were the least, surely, that should have been adopted in August, 1914. They were admitted by the Danes themselves in 1916 to be reasonable. Compare them with the treatment to be meted out to Norway, who befriended us throughout the war. The best comment upon these proposals is to be found in the attitude of America herself, who, after some months, instituted a strict embargo on all unnecessary commodities to Scandinavia and Holland. We followed America; and an uninstructed observer might be excused for supposing that the blockade of Germany was undertaken by England at America's suggestion. Supplies to Germany gradually fell away, until in 1918 they dried up. The blockade was two and a half years late.

Summing up what has been said in the foregoing chapters, the effect of British trade was to stimulate the Scandinavian industries. Broadly, it was the Scandinavian native produce that reached Germany, and the supplies from oversea, whether British or British-controlled, that either released Scandinavian supplies or made it possible for them to be produced. Thus, it was the Danish agricultural produce, the fish and the fats that reached Germany, but it was the fodder and fertilisers, the fishing gear and the petro-leum, and the oil-seeds from oversea that enabled these commodities to be obtained.

British coal was a vital cog in the Scandinavian industrial machine. It was not so much a commodity as a source of irresistible power. It was dispensed with a lavish hand and with but little regard for its war value. It was our prime source of economic pressure, and it was used to good purpose in Norway and by H.M. Government, when necessary, against neutral shipowners. It was not, however, made to serve the ends of diplomacy in our negotiations with Sweden, nor was it used for bargaining purposes during the protracted and sterile parleys that formed so conspicuous and sorry a feature in our policy towards Denmark.

Fish was a product of Scandinavia. In the case of the Danish fish the quantity of British fishing accessories that reached Denmark was comparatively small, but the amount of Danish fish that they enabled Denmark to send to Germany was immense.

The policy of trading, which was justified on the two-fold ground of the benefit to the exchange and our obligations to neutrals, would not seem to have been fairly balanced against the succour that it brought to our enemies. This country was rich and could afford to make sacrifices. Yet when the war had been in progress for nearly three years and our finances were becoming unstable, trade was stopped and the question of the "improvement of the exchange" was put to one side. As to our obligations to neutrals, there were also obligations to ourselves to be considered. Neutrals were protected by international law. No Scandinavian neutral has successfully challenged the legality or, I think, even the propriety of any belligerent action of ours.

Perhaps the strongest indictment of our blockade policy and of our administration in Denmark is to be found in Mr. Thirsk's reports. We made trading agreements with neutrals under, professedly, appropriate safeguards. But no provision was made by the appointment of consular officers for supervising and reporting upon the working of arrangements so vital to the success of the objects that they had in view : nor were the necessary measures taken locally for the detection of abuses or the observance of guarantees.

Reference to this subject has been made (with some reluctance) under " Lubricants " which, together with " Nickel " and " Finance," possess certain features that distinguished them from the remainder of the commodities that have been dealt with.

I reported fully and repeatedly upon the supplies that were reaching Germany and upon the necessity of far greater stringency in the granting of trade licences. The matters touched upon in this book form a small part only of the subjects of my correspondence. In the summer of 1917, when in England, I waited upon the Minister of Blockade, Lord Robert Cecil. One of the subjects to which I drew particular attention was binder-twine (see page 222). The other was the importation of oil-seeds into Denmark. On my return to Scandinavia I learnt that the further import of soya-beans had been stopped by telegram. My written reports had dealt fully with both these subjects; I must own, therefore, to feeling more astonished than flattered that so very important a war measure should have been withheld until chance opportunity had made it possible to represent verbally what already had been reported through the ordinary official channel.

The Permanent Secretary to the Foreign Office at this time, and probably its most gifted member, was Sir Eyre Crowe, with whom also I discussed the blockade. The Foreign Secretary is the titular and responsible Head of his Department, but his appointment is political : he changes with a change of Government, whereas the Permanent Secretary remains. The titular Head is known to the public, but the presiding genius is never heard of. The Foreign Secretary speaks, but his gifted subordinate prompts. The Permanent Secretary must have seen a good many of my despatches; but the potential value of certain commodities—the particular ones to which I refer being greasy substances—and their intimate relation to the man-power of Germany were at that time unsuspected by him.

On the first page of the Scandinavian statistics we find that Scandinavia's total exportation of foodstuffs in 1915 was 239,794 tons more than in 1913 : that, whereas before the war Great Britain received 92,657 tons more than Germany and Austria, this excess was changed to a deficit of 285,761 tons in 1915, and 428,840 tons in 1916. In these figures several items of foodstuffs, including immense quantities of vegetables, are not included.

In the French war against China in 1885, foodstuffs (rice) were declared by the French Foreign Minister to be contraband. Prince Bismarck himself endorsed the French action, and in 1892 Count von Caprivi gave his support to the view that it was legal to capture foodstuffs and raw materials indispensable for the enemy's industries. And, lest there be any lingering doubts in the reader's mind of the wisdom of these obscure authorities, let us hasten to inform him (with the full weight of the plural number) that this is precisely the view that we ourselves take.

The difficulties with which H.M. Government and those burdened with the responsibility of conducting the blockade of Germany were surrounded were without doubt very great. But from first to last no effort was spared to ascertain the exact particulars of all transactions by which the Scandinavian countries were enabled to supply our enemies, and to press upon the authorities the adoption of measures by which this traffic could be kept within the limits to which ultimately it was confined.

I must be pardoned, therefore, if, having given examples of the transactions referred to and having, I trust with fairness, examined the grounds on which H.M. Government justified their policy, I have conceived it proper to regard these matters as of public interest. Although we had a resourceful and determined foe to contend with and could not have it all our own way during the economic struggle in which we were engaged, and although in the conduct of the blockade there were certain features which—as the title of this book seeks to indicate—it would serve no useful purpose now to recall, yet the failure to prevent supplies from reaching our enemies on a less immoderate scale than that recorded stands, I think, in need of fuller explanation than has yet been given.

Copies of all my official and semi-official reports in addition to *précis* of conversations on the subject of the blockade were sent to the Admiralty, who gave the full weight of their support to the views which I expressed throughout the war in circumstances, sometimes, of considerable difficulty.

This book has been written to but little purpose if it has failed to make clear that the unarmed forces with which it deals rest, for their power of being applied, upon naval and air supremacy; and that there is no security for the sea-borne supplies upon which we mainly depend for our existence except in our Navy and its sister Service, the Royal Air Force.

APPENDIX

I. From the Declaration of London

Article 30.—Absolute contraband is liable to capture if it is shown to be destined to territory belonging to or occupied by the enemy, or to the armed forces of the enemy. It is immaterial whether the carriage of the goods is direct or entails transhipment or a subsequent transport by land.

Article 31.—Proof of the destination specified in Article 30 is complete in the following cases :—

(1) When the goods are documented for discharge in an enemy port, or for delivery to the armed forces of the enemy.

(2) When the vessel is to call at enemy ports only, or when she is to touch at an enemy port or meet the armed forces of the enemy before reaching the neutral port for which the goods in question are documented.

Article 32.—Where a vessel is carrying absolute contraband, her papers are conclusive proof as to the voyage on which she is engaged, unless she is found clearly out of the course indicated by her papers and unable to give adequate reasons to justify such deviation.

Article 33.—Conditional contraband is liable to capture if it is shown to be destined for the use of the armed forces or of a government department of the enemy State, unless in this latter case the circumstances show that the goods cannot in fact be used for the purposes of the war in progress. This latter exception does not apply to a consignment coming under Article 24 (4).

Article 34.—The destination referred to in Article 33 is presumed to exist if the goods are consigned to enemy authorities, or to a contractor established in the enemy country who, as a matter of common knowledge, supplies articles of this kind to the enemy. A similar presumption arises if the goods are consigned to a fortified place belonging to the enemy, or other place serving as a base for the armed forces of the enemy. No such presumption, however, arises in the case of a merchant vessel bound for one of these places if it is sought to prove that she herself is contraband.

In cases where the above presumptions do not arise, the destination is presumed to be innocent.

The presumptions set up by this Article may be rebutted.

Article 35.—Conditional contraband is not liable to capture, except when found on board a vessel bound for territory belonging to or occupied by the enemy, or for the armed forces of the enemy, and when it is not to be discharged in an intervening neutral port.

The ship's papers are conclusive proof both as to the voyage on which the vessel is engaged and as to the port of discharge of the goods, unless she is found clearly out of the course indicated by her papers, and unable to give adequate reasons to justify such deviation.

II. The Principal Articles of the " Reprisals Order " are as Follows :—

I. No merchant vessel which sailed from her port of departure after the 1st March, 1915, shall be allowed to proceed on her voyage to any German port.

II. No merchant vessel which sailed from any German port after the 1st March, 1915, shall be allowed to proceed on her voyage with any goods on board laden at such port.

III. Every merchant vessel which sailed from her

port of departure after the 1st March, 1915, on her way to a port other than a German port, carrying goods with an enemy destination, or which are enemy property, may be required to discharge such goods in a British or allied port.

IV. Every merchant vessel which sailed from a port other than a German port after the 1st March, 1915, having on board goods which are of enemy origin or are enemy property may be required to discharge such goods in a British or allied port.

III. An American Report upon Denmark

COPENHAGEN,
August 14th, 1917.

I beg to present the following report and conclusions on the question of Regulation of American Exports to Denmark.

Since the question of the regulation of American Exports to Denmark became acute I have been approached at various times with requests and suggestions to present to the American public through THE ASSOCIATED PRESS the Danish side of the case, viz. propaganda matter to show the desirability and necessity of a continuance of American exports to this country. I refrained from touching the subject, however, first because the Danish censorship prevented any impartial presentation of the matter and secondly because I believed that the Danish presentation of the case was not only incorrect and one-sided but was calculated, if published in the United States, to embarrass the policy of the American Government.

I ultimately learned that a systematic attempt was being made to put this purely Danish interpretation of the situation before the American public through other Press media, even after the general policy of the President had been decided upon, that articles were being launched in Danish papers as an indirect means of getting them into the American press and that the Danish commercial commission in the United States was being given opportunity to get its side of the situation before the Government and public unhampered by any counter-representation of facts in despatches from here. I therefore believed that the State Department might appreciate the information and conclusions of a correspondent who has had six months' opportunity to study the Danish export situation and, from a long residence in Germany during the war, to know how much that country is benefiting from imports received from Denmark and other contiguous neutral countries under the present conditions.

The arguments which the Danish Government seeks to use to obtain a modification of American policy and on which the above-mentioned propaganda is based may be roughly classified as the " Starvation," " Economic Ruin " and " German Danger " pleas; viz. that

(a) the population of Denmark will go hungry unless the United States permits the export of food to Denmark;

(b) a cessation of imports of fodder and other raw materials for Denmark's meat and other industries will involve an unjust and unprincipled interference with Denmark's economic life and reduce the country to poverty; and

(c) a cessation of Denmark's present exports of meats, fats, fish, butter, eggs, etc., to Germany may bring about a German invasion of Denmark.

My opinion, based upon my knowledge of conditions in Denmark and Germany, was that all three conclusions were erroneous or fallacious.

Mr. Conger tells us that Denmark's home-grown supplies of food, if properly rationed, were sufficient for the needs of the population; and that her agricultural industry had become a " manufacturing industry for the conversion of imported materials into meat, fats and other agricultural products for export."

With regard to the Danish agreements Mr. Conger finds that all testimony is practically unanimous that the Danes loyally held to the *letter* (this word being underlined) of their arrangements with England. He adds, however, that there was no doubt that the Danes had been very clever in securing a form which would permit them to export to Germany the greatest possible quantities of the things desired by Germany; and that they had been very quick to take advantage of loopholes left in the agreements through carelessness or negligence. As an example he refers to the disposal of the slaughter-house offal, about which nothing is said in the agreements. From this refuse, rich in desired fats, Germany boasted of getting a large amount of neatsfoot oil, so indispensable for her torpedoes, in addition to large quantities of fat for commercial use.

" Smuggling prohibited exports out into Germany is one of the most flourishing industries in Denmark." Particulars are given.

Germany reaped immense benefit from the traffic that took place in fruit, and which received hardly any attention from us. Mr. Conger comments on the importance of this item in the German war dietary.

What I myself have described as the " invasion bogey " Mr. Conger refers to as the " German bugaboo." He says : " I am firmly convinced that the German authorities, up at least to the time of my departure from Germany, had utterly no desire to invade Denmark or to extend the theatre of war if this could possibly be avoided."

Mr. Conger's views are summed up as follows :—

(A) All exports of fodder-stuffs, such as maize, oil-cake, etc., to Denmark should be stopped.

(B) Denmark can and should be required to subsist her own population, imports only of such articles of foreign origin as tea, coffee, etc., as cannot be produced or substituted in the country being permitted and then only in rigidly limited quantities. (C) Fuel oil, kerosene, gasoline and other articles used in the industries should only be supplied in rigidly limited quantities for indispensable purposes and under rigid guarantees that no materials thus supplied should be used in industries such as fishing, the product of which results to the benefit of Germany. (D) Ingredients for chemical fertilisers should be supplied only in so far as Denmark applies her agricultural products to home consumption.

IV. EXPORTS OF AGRICULTURAL PRODUCTS FROM DENMARK TO GREAT BRITAIN

FROM 1ST OCTOBER, 1914, TO 30TH SEPTEMBER, 1915, COMPARED WITH CORRESPONDING PERIOD 1913-1914

(Returns after 30th September, 1915, are not yet available)

Article.	1st Oct., 1914, to 30th Sept., 1915.	Previous Year.	Amount of Decrease.
Butter (casks) . .	1,483,719	1,760,724	277,005
Butter (cases) . .	32,749	50,687	17,938
Pigs' heads (tierces) .	17,908	37,817	19,909
Feet (cwt.) . . .	36,828	45,268	8,440
Lard (cwt.) . . .	1,358	28,178	26,820
Other offal (cwt.) .	46,214	56,237	10,013
Mild cured heads (cwt.) .	7,133	12,140	5,007
Bacon (bales) . .	1,191,581	1,203,393	11,812

COMPARISON OF THE SAME EXPORTS
DURING THE PERIOD 1ST APRIL, 1915, TO 30TH SEPTEMBER, 1915

Article.	1st April, 1915, to 30th Sept., 1915.	Previous Year.	Amount of Decrease.
Butter (casks) . .	689,952	910,797	220,845
Butter (cases) . .	19,344	25,630	6,286
Pigs heads (tierces) .	2,085	23,347	21,262
Feet (cwt.) . . .	16,975	25,229	8,254
Lard (cwt.) . . .	—	13,824	13,824
Other offals (cwt.) .	16,856	28,421	11,565
Mild cured heads (cwt.) .	2,484	6,331	3,847
Bacon (bales) . .	427,091	636,056	208,965

V. EXTRACTS FROM CORRESPONDENCE

1. *Naval Attaché to H.M. Minister, Stockholm.*

The following extract is from a letter I wrote in December, 1918, to Sir Esme Howard, British Minister at Stockholm :—

It may not be generally known in official circles, but it is nevertheless a fact that among a large section of American business men very bitter feeling exists against England because they believe that during 1915–16–17 while interfering with American exports to Scandinavia and Holland we were ourselves exporting to these countries similar goods which either reached the enemy directly or indirectly. For instance they say that, while we refused to allow the International Harvester Company to supply Denmark with agricultural machinery, British agricultural machinery was reaching Denmark and in some cases was being discharged from ships straight into German railway trucks for transit to Germany. They also considered that we had no right to interfere with their exports of oil-seeds and the products of these seeds, seeing that during a period of two years our imports of copra to Denmark from British Colonies were three times greater than the pre-war average. Again, in view of the fact that British coal was being used in Danish dairies working for Germany, the Americans do not consider that we were justified in any way in interfering with the imports of oil for internal combustion engines required for Danish fishing craft, especially as the export of fish from Denmark to Germany was a pre-war trade, whilst the export of Danish butter to Germany was entirely a war venture.

I could quote many other instances to show that the Americans have very substantial reasons on account of our blockade policy during 1915–17 for treating us with suspicion. Unfortunately the bad feeling then engendered was revived quite recently

for two reasons. In the first case the representative of the American Singer Co. in Norway found out
that although, on account of various difficulties and
formalities put in the way—letters of assurance,
etc.—it was impossible for the firm to carry on their
business with Scandinavia, yet sewing-machines
were being exported from England to Scandinavia
subject to no restrictions whatever. It is curious
and also very regrettable that we should have come
up against the International Harvester Company
and the Singer Company, two of the most powerful
and well-organised concerns in America. The second
case is far the more serious one and is known to have
made a very bad impression amongst members of
the War Trade Board, who are all business men.

The particulars of this case, which refers to traffic
in paper currency, will be found in the Chapter on
Finance in Part II.

The military operations of the war were common
to America and our Allies, but the blockade was
particularly our own, and for this reason it was of
the greatest importance that, in order to set a good
example, our own hands should have been absolutely clean. Unfortunately it was well known to all
our Allies and to the Americans in Scandinavia that
we were ourselves competing with neutrals in
supplying the enemy. It is obvious therefore that
we were never in a position to approach even our
Allies with a view to restricting imports to Germany
—far less America when she was a neutral—without
causing friction. If the statistics of imports to
Denmark for the year 1917 are carefully studied any
uninstructed person would be tempted to assume
that we had started the blockade at America's
suggestion.

2. *Naval Attaché to H.M. Minister, Copenhagen.*

The following letter on the subject of lard is referied to in Chapter VII, p. 173.

BRITISH LEGATION,
CHRISTIANIA,
November 21st, 1916.

DEAR SIR RALPH,

I'm afraid we look at this matter—lard—from quite a different point of view.

I have never advocated the reduction of the imports but their complete and immediate cessation. The large amounts which came in last year are surely no justification for 1,000 tons coming in this year up to the end of September. On the contrary I should have thought this was an excellent reason why it should have been stopped months ago.

You say Germany *only* gets 40 per cent. of Denmark's total production. I think if we were in the trenches or in the North Sea we should consider this a lot.

Ten parts of lard yield approximately 1 part of glycerine by weight. The 1,000 tons we have already allowed into Denmark, in order to release a similar amount to our enemies, means therefore that the Germans have obtained 100 tons of glycerine. From one part of glycerine, two parts of nitroglycerine are obtainable. As the German propulsive powder for heavy ordnance contains one-third of nitroglycerine our benevolence has furnished our enemies this year, under one heading alone, with 600 tons of gun ammunition.

It seems to me unnecessary to follow this further, but I will only say once more that this traffic is by no means insignificant to our fighting forces.

Yours sincerely,
(Signed) M. W. P. CONSETT.

U

3. *Naval Attaché on Mr. Thirsk's reports.*

In December, 1916, a communication from one of H.M. Ministers reached me, in which my action in forwarding copies of Mr. Thirsk's reports to Commander Leverton Harris, the Director of the Department of Restriction of Enemy Supplies, was adversely criticised.

The grounds upon which I justified my action were set forth in a letter of which the substance of some of the extracts is as follows :—

As I told you during my last visit I have sent copies of all Mr. Consul Thirsk's reports on the fishing industry not only to Commander Leverton Harris but to Admiral De Chair, the Naval Assistant to the Minister of Blockade, and also to the Admiralty.

My reason for doing this was because I wished to stop the large and *increasing* supply of food to our enemies, and I feared that these valuable reports might be delayed in transmission or possibly might not be forwarded at all. Moreover, I was certainly under the impression that in war time no harm could possibly arise if reports such as these fell—without delay—into the hands of officials such as I have named above.

When Commander Leverton Harris came to Christiania in July, I urged him to take up the question of the export of fish from Denmark to Germany. He then told me he had been under the impression that the amount being exported was unimportant. At that time, and during the first nine months of the year, the fish exports to Germany were continually increasing and averaged the large amount of 8,000 tons per month, and, although Great Britain was supplying the materials without which the fishing industry could not have prospered, the Director of one of the Government

Departments charged with the duty of restricting supplies reaching the enemy was actually unaware of these important facts, although we had been at war almost two years.

Under these circumstances I considered it my duty to leave no stone unturned in order to ensure that this valuable information should become as widely and quickly known as possible in various Government Departments.

I wish to make it quite clear that I have never communicated directly or indirectly with Mr. Consul Thirsk, either officially or privately, nor have I ever spoken to him, nor have I ever even seen him.

It would be interesting to know the dates on which all of Mr. Consul Thirsk's reports, not only those on fish, have reached His Majesty's Legation and the dates on which they reached the Foreign Office. I am sure that some of the reports forwarded by me reached London some weeks before the same reports forwarded by the Legation. I am also under the impression that one or more of Mr. Consul Thirsk's reports written months ago have not yet reached the Foreign Office.

Before closing this despatch I would like to mention that not long before the war I spent, in company with three other Englishmen, several days amongst the fishing craft based on Skagen both at sea and in harbour, and was able to get a very good idea of the industry in all its details at the principal fishing port in Denmark. The things that struck me most were :—

1. That most of the boats at Skagen were Swedish.

2. That a large amount of fish was landed at Skagen which went direct to Germany by train.

3. That all the boats were dependent to a large extent on petroleum, even their winches being worked off the main motor.

4. That the boats were exceedingly well found in gear of all sorts.

All this information was given—not once but many times, especially during the first months of 1916—to H.M. Legation, but I could get no interest taken in the matter.

On July 18th and other days, during conversations with Commander Leverton Harris at Christiania, I gave him full details about the fishing at Skagen and begged him to use his influence to have oil and other requisites cut off from fishermen whose catch went to Germany.

Petroleum allowed into Denmark, in accordance with an agreement drawn up between His Majesty's Government and Danish oil merchants, was not cut off from fishermen in Danish waters until December 12th, although the whole of the catch had been going for months to Germany in increasing quantities. Between July 18th and December 12th I estimate that at least 40,000 tons of fish reached Germany viâ Denmark, of which probably 20,000 to 30,000 tons might have been stopped if action had been taken in July. Nor is this all. A fish agreement was drawn up in 1916 between His Majesty's Government and the Swedish Government, but as there was no stipulation therein that the Swedish boats should land their catch in Sweden it is obviously not worth the paper it is written on.

It should be observed that during 1916 the fish rations to the German Army had been gradually increased.

I requested that a copy of my despatch might be forwarded to His Majesty's Principal Secretary of State so that it might be clearly understood that my action, although perhaps technically wrong, was dictated solely with a view to preventing supplies from reaching the enemy.

It was not until December that any notice was taken of my technical irregularities, although it was in August that I forwarded the first of Mr. Thirsk's

despatches for which the Head of the R.E.S.D. pro-
fusely thanked me. The irregularity would seem
to have been discovered towards the latter stages of
my correspondence with this Department : when, that
the correspondence should not prove to be the sterile
one it promised and a mere record of polite words, I
wrote in such terms as seemed best calculated to attain
this end : not without some measure of success, I trust,
seeing that the petroleum was stopped.

4. Naval Attaché to Admiralty.

The following extract is from a memorandum which
I drew up on the day of my arrival in England in May,
1917, before leaving the Admiralty :—

To those who have not lived, as the writer has
lived during the last five years, in Scandinavia, I
would ask, What is the impression likely to be created
on the minds of thoughtful Scandinavians and
especially Staff Officers who have studied the science
of war and have seen immense quantities of goods
reaching Scandinavia through our blockade, knowing that Scandinavia herself has been exporting
similar goods, or the products of the goods to our
enemies ? So far as I am able to judge, the impression created is that we are not taking the war
seriously, and may ourselves be finally defeated.

Various Government Departments have warned
us from time to time that they must have certain
commodities from Scandinavia—the Board of Trade,
food; Munitions Department, cryolite, steel of
various sorts, refined zinc, etc., etc., and this has
been advanced as a reason for not putting pressure
on these countries; but during the whole duration
of the war German munitions have been obtaining
far greater benefits from Scandinavia than British
munitions; we have, in fact, kept the Scandinavian
machine running greatly to Germany's advantage.

No doubt it is satisfactory to be able to pose as the champion of small nations, but in order to champion any cause it is necessary to maintain one's own life, and so far as Scandinavia is concerned the very people whom we are supposed to be championing have throughout been assisting our enemies in an endeavour to defeat us.

The blockade, emanating as it does from sea-power, is essentially a naval question, and I submit that Naval and Military attachés, who alone, among the members of the British Legations, have made a study of war, are particularly qualified to express an opinion on this subject. I have therefore considered it to be my duty to write reports from time to time dealing entirely with the blockade question.

In the autumn of 1916 Sir Ralph Paget assumed the duties of British Minister at Copenhagen. Early in October we discussed the blockade together at great length, and Sir Ralph Paget then asked me if I would put my views on paper in the shape of a memorandum. This I did, and on reading it through Sir Ralph Paget asked me if he might alter some of the wording in order to make it more palatable in official circles. To this I consented : several passages were altered by Sir Ralph Paget himself and can be seen to-day on the draft in his own handwriting. This memorandum did not meet with the approval of the Foreign Office.

At various times subsequently I have forwarded despatches dealing with the blockade question, all of which have met with the approval of the Head of the Mission.

I consider that, as Germany is still at the present time obtaining more supplies of all sorts from Scandinavia than we are, the time has now arrived when a full inquiry should be held into the question of the blockade, and that all the documents connected therewith, including private letters referring to the Naval Attaché, may be produced.

5. *Miscellaneous*.

The following short extracts are culled from some very interesting letters written in October, 1917, by a member who occupied a high position in a Government department in London and had throughout the war revolved in the orbit of maritime rights and international law.

I readily admit embargoes on Denmark appear to be panning out exactly as you predicted and that, except for a continued export of cattle of second and third grade and of fish to Germany, all exports to Germany of home produce should be stopped this winter and next year.

This Department became convinced last winter that, provided the war was not to end in the summer 1917, the stoppage of imports would have the effect you predicted, and would be wise from the purely blockade point of view. We did not get hold of this view, I frankly admit, as soon as you did.

I do not defend the policy of the Board of Trade which, in order to push British trade and keep up the Exchanges, refused to put a large number of articles on our prohibition list in spite of our repeated requests—the only method of giving the Government control over the profit-making instincts of private traders. It was this that led to the unfortunate forwarding of British goods to Germany which you saw on the Copenhagen docks.

The following is from a Danish naval officer :—

I cannot help saying to you how much we Danish naval officers sympathise with you in having to live as you do amongst these people who are making fortunes in supplying your enemies with food when the officers and men of the Navy to which you belong are risking their lives in trying to blockade your enemies. We know also as naval officers that your views on these matters are sound from the war point of view.

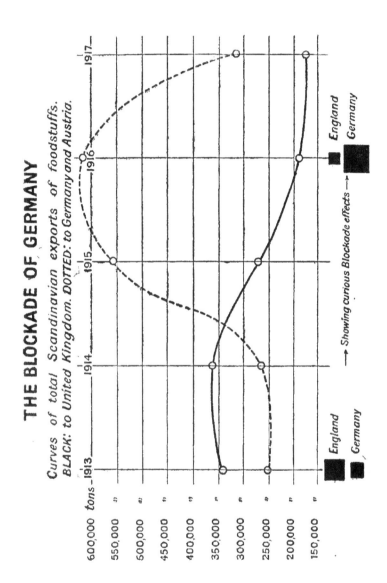

THE BLOCKADE OF GERMANY

Curves of total Scandinavian exports of foodstuffs.
BLACK: to United Kingdom. DOTTED: to Germany and Austria.

VI. SUMMARY OF SUPPLIES

The figures in the following tables have been taken from the official Scandinavian statistics.

The dislocation of trade owing to the war in many cases vitiates the value of figures for the purposes of comparison. It is to be noted, however, that goods in transit, that is to say goods that were not used for domestic consumption, were not credited in the Scandinavian accounts. A comparison, therefore, of the *total* imports before the war with the *total* imports during any subsequent year will stand good.

The statistics show generally the immense quantities of merchandise that passed into Scandinavia in the critical years 1915 and 1916 : in many cases these quantities exceeded the pre-war amounts. The year 1917 shows at a glance in nearly all cases the effect of the blockade after it had been rigidly enforced.

Compare in many cases the total importations from the United Kingdom in 1913 with those in 1915 and 1916. Compare also the Scandinavian exports to Germany and Austria for the same periods.

There are several discrepancies between :—

(a) The official figures of the Scandinavian countries,

(b) The figures compiled by the British Custom House as to exports from the United Kingdom, and

(c) The figures compiled by the War Trade Statistical Department.

Frequently the total imports from all sources in the importing country's returns fall short of the exports from England alone to those particular countries, as recorded either by the Customs Department or the W.T.S.D. This has probably arisen from the rule under the Customs regulations of the Scandinavian countries by which a consignment of imported goods may *on arrival* be declared to be " in transit." Again the delay in clearing consignments of imported goods out of bond, in some cases running into a matter of several months, has caused wide discrepancies to appear in the statistical accounts respectively of the exporting and importing country.

GRAND SUMMARY

METRIC TONS OF FOOD

From	To the United Kingdom.		To Germany and Austria		Total
Norway	61,464		81,538		
1913. Sweden	26,567	344,785	37,043	252,128	596,913
Denmark	256,754		123,547		
Norway	53,715		71,586		
1914. Sweden	28,526	359,820	56,685	262,376	622,196
Denmark	277,579		134,105		
Norway	69,512		182,630		
1915. Sweden	8,563	275,473	104,203	561,234	836,707
Denmark	197,398		274,401		
Norway	35,701		215,593		
1916. Sweden	115	191,916	90,835	620,756	812,672
Denmark	156,100		314,328		
Norway	69,680		101,847		
1917. Sweden	—	172,103	16,451	315,205	487,308
Denmark	102,423		196,907		

In this table the following are included : Meat of all sorts, fish, dairy produce, eggs, lard, margarine.

It does not include : Vegetable oils, beer, fish oil, bone fat, coffee, tea, cocoa, horses, syrup and glucose, fruit, vegetables.

DENMARK

TABLE SHOWING THE EXPORT OF FOOD FROM DENMARK TO THE UNITED KINGDOM AND GERMANY AND AUSTRIA DURING THE YEARS 1913-17

	To the United Kingdom	To Germany and Austria
	Tons	Tons
1913 . . .	256,754	123,547
1914 . . .	277,579	134,105
1915 . . .	197,398	274,401
1916 . . .	156,100	314,328
1917 . . .	102,423	196,907

N.B.—The foodstuffs included in above table are the same as shown on next page.

EXPORTS FROM DENMARK TO THE UNITED KINGDOM AND GERMANY AND AUSTRIA
(In metric tons)

	1913		1914		1915		1916		1917	
	Germany	U.K.	Germany	U.K.	Germany	U.K.	Germany	U.K.	Germany	U.K.
Meat	50,804	124,511	61,558	143,486	119,578	101,750	99,704	84,812	83,786	58,845
Tripe, pigs' heads and feet and offal	5,484	10,200	5,918	12,552	9,690	4,216	10,820	43	14,279	—
Fish	25,516	3,932	32,968	2,704	66,569	5,303	106,694	1,902	38,841	—
Meat conserves	131	88	6,676	72	16,022	66	19,758	110	10,587	18
Extract of meat	—	—	—	1	15	2	2,635	13	2,209	23
Milk (all sorts)	487	2,749	553	1,826	1,082	2,650	3,600	2,441	6,503	817
Cream	28,517	—	15,313	—	674	—	2,530	—	125	—
Butter [1]	11,317	87,272	9,430	88,932	37,455	65,402	36,891	57,041	21,594	31,295
Cheese	57	2	316	6	3,886	9	4,344	—	5,332	—
Eggs and egg-albumen	1,162	28,000	1,315	28,000	12,956	18,000	20,558	9,738	13,483	11,425
Fats	72	—	58	—	6,474	—	6,794	—	2,168	—
Total	123,547	256,754	134,105	277,579	274,401	197,308	314,328	156,100	196,907	102,423

[1] The export of purely Danish butter to Germany was in 1913 less than 2,000 tons. The figures 11,317 tons in the above table include re-exports of Swedish and Russian butter, of which a considerable amount went in transit through Denmark. This ceased on the outbreak of war.

TABLE SHOWING THE NUMBER OF TONS OF FOOD **Lost by England** AND **Gained by Germany** FROM DENMARK DURING **THE YEARS** 1915, 1916 AND 1917 WHEN COMPARED WITH 1913

	Lost by England	Gained by Germany
1915 . . .	59,356	150,854
1916 . . .	100,654	190,781
1917 . . .	154,331	73,360
Total . . .	**314,341**	**414,995**

In the above table the following are included : Meat; tripe; pigs' head and feet; slaughter-house offal; fish; meat conserves; extract of meat; milk (condensed, skimmed, sweet and dried); cream; butter; cheese; eggs and egg albumen; fats (including lard, margarine, oleo-margarine and premierjus).

N.B.—Live cattle are included in meat at 200 kilos. per head.

DANISH STATISTICS
Export of live cattle (number of head)

	1913	1914	1915	1916	1917
Germany and Austria .	152,080	187,438	250,839	305,026	300,339
Tons of meat .	30,416	37,488	50,168	61,005	60,068
All other countries .	284	46	4	5	4

Exports of other live animals are insignificant.
Live cattle may be taken at 200 kilos. of meat per head.

MEAT (all kinds except fish, game and conserves, excluding tripe, casings, pigs' heads and feet and offal)

Exports (including re-exports) : tons

	1913	1914	1915	1916	1917
Germany and Austria .	20,388	24,070	69,410	38,699	23,718
United Kingdom .	124,511	143,486	101,750	84,812	58,845

Imports

	1913	1914	1915	1916	1917
United Kingdom .	194	176	1,107	175	9
Iceland	2,740	2,313	2,486	1,104	—

TRIPE, CASINGS, PIGS' HEAD AND FEET AND SLAUGHTER-HOUSE OFFAL
Exports (including re-exports) : tons

	1913	1914	1915	1916	1917
Germany and Austria .	5,484	5,918	9,690	10,820	14,279
United Kingdom .	10,200	12,552	4,216	43	—

HIDES AND SKINS (all kinds—untanned)
Imports : tons

	1913	1914	1915	1916	1917
All countries . . .	9,810	8,310	5,459	4,158	1,891
United Kingdom and British Empire .	519	413	289	276	217

Exports (including re-exports)

	1913	1914	1915	1916	1917
Germany and Austria .	9,754	9,262	4,815	4,167	1,776
Norway and Sweden .	1,703	1,937	1,237	528	503
In transit Free Port .	—	8,800	2,650	1,016	19

LEATHER (all kinds)
Imports · tons

	1913	1914	1915	1916	1917
All countries . . .	1,458	1,284	1,481	1,540	734
United Kingdom and British Empire . .	70	74	94	142	31

Exports (including re-exports)

Germany and Austria .	47	289	21	4	1
Norway and Sweden .	390	348	300	229	95
In transit Free Port .	—	269	850	44	4

BOOTS AND SHOES
Imports : tons

All countries . . .	295	260	230	180	84
United Kingdom and British Empire . .	22	34	56	66	49

Exports (including re-exports)

Germany and Austria .	—	97	496	209	—
Norway and Sweden .	11	12	29	11	1
In transit Free Port .	—	73	100	44	2

HAIR (horse, cattle and pigs)
Imports · tons

All countries . . .	498	385	584	373	47
United Kingdom and British Empire . .	6	5	43	31	—

Exports ·

Germany and Austria	536	427	454	721	229
Norway and Sweden .	54	62	86	60	136
In transit Free Port (all kinds) . . .	—	220	160	53	—

GLUE AND GELATINE (all kinds)
Imports : tons

All countries . . .	483	480	634	666	231
United Kingdom and British Empire . .	4	9	20	239	130

Exports :

Germany and Austria .	11	3	9	24	—
Norway and Sweden .	6	29	20	23	5
In transit Free Port .	—	260	110	73	1

FISH (all kinds, excepting conserves)
Imports : tons

Norway and Sweden .	8,239	10,542	28,433	36,483	7,252
All others . . .	16,636	20,511	19,782	8,939	6,734

Exports (including re-exports) : tons

	1913	1914	1915	1916	1917
Germany and Austria	25,516	32,968	66,569	106,694	38,841
United Kingdom	3,932	2,704	5,303	1,902	—

CONSERVES (except milk and extract of meat)

Exports (including re-exports) : tons

Germany and Austria	131	6,676	16,022	19,758	10,587
United Kingdom	88	72	66	110	18

EXTRACT OF MEAT (Bouillon cubes)

Exports : tons

Germany and Austria	—	—	15	2,635	2,209
United Kingdom	—	1	2	13	23

✗ MILK (condensed and dried)

Exports : tons

Germany and Austria	30	183	601	625	1,426
United Kingdom	2,749	1,826	2,650	2,441	817

CREAM

Exports : tons

Germany and Austria	28,517	15,313	674	2,530	125
United Kingdom	—	—	—	—	—

MILK (sweet and skimmed)

Exports : tons

Germany	457	370	481	2,975	5,077
United Kingdom	—	—	—	—	—

BUTTER

Exports (including re-exports) : tons

Germany and Austria	11,317	9,430	37,455	36,891	21,594
United Kingdom	87,272	88,932	65,402	57,041	31,295

Imports : tons

Total all countries	14,104	9,676	3,735	221	—

CHEESE

Exports (including re-exports) : tons

Germany and Austria	57	316	3,886	4,344	5,332
United Kingdom	2	6	9	—	—

Imports : tons

All countries	679	486	394	145	17

EGGS

Exports (including re-exports) : tons

	1913	1914	1915	1916	1917
Germany and Austria .	1,160	1,308	12,466	20,422	13,482
United Kingdom . .	28,000	28,000	18,000	9,738	11,425

Imports : tons

All countries . . .	2,606	2,350	1,418	344	—

EGG-ALBUMEN

Imports : tons

United Kingdom . .	—	14	472	114	—
All other countries .	286	195	794	320	37

Exports (including re-exports) : tons

Germany and Austria .	2	7	490 [1]	136	1

FATS (including lard, neutral lard, margarine, oleo-margarine and premierjus)

Imports : tons

All countries . . .	7,766	9,178	15,016	6,806	1,478
Imports from the United Kingdom . .	532	451	1,155	427	159

Exports (including re-exports): tons

Germany and Austria .	72	58	6,474	6,794	2,168
Sweden . . .	40	1,932	1,695	—	23

VEGETABLE OILS (all edible oils, including compound lard)

Imports : tons

From the United Kingdom	290	728	1,730	312	27
All countries . . .	14,839	9,288	10,844	8,586	2,039

Exports : tons

Germany and Austria .	960	1,260	1,237	—	—

VEGETABLE OILS (all technical kinds, including soya oil)

Imports tons

All countries . .	1,722	1,792	2,000	1,518	629
From the United Kingdom	146	588	1,369	986	410

Exports · tons

Germany and Austria .	357	1,518	6,847	902	—
Sweden . . .	1,666	3,091	5,558	315	90
United Kingdom . .	557	1,185	—	—	—

SOAP

Imports · tons

All countries . . .	216	193	293	317	179
From the United Kingdom	—	—	146	234	100

Exports tons

Germany and Austria .	2	1	7,988	112	—

[1] Chiefly re-export—probably of goods from the United Kingdom.

BEER (all sorts)

Exports : tons

	1913	1914	1915	1916	1917
Total export . . .	4,779	5,328	7,070	9,859	6,729
Germany . . .	51	30	841	6,146	5,673
United Kingdom . .	2,580	2,710	1,441	552	4

LINSEED

Imports : tons

	1913	1914	1915	1916	1917
Total all countries . .	19,979	23,627	33,267	37,147	6,529
From the United Kingdom and British Empire .	5,413	3,798	7,310	2,247	—

RAPE-SEED

Imports : tons

Total all countries . .	2,148	645	1,352	1,319	—
From the United Kingdom and British Empire .	—	92	842	113	—

SESSAMUM-SEED

Imports : tons

Total all countries . .	4,017	6,122	9,333	18,360	—
From the United Kingdom and British Empire .	—	1,223	2,983	850	—

HEMP-SEED

Imports : tons

Total all countries . .	752	1,220	1,139	64	71
From the United Kingdom and British Empire .	44	81	175	64	15

SOYA-BEANS

Imports : tons

Total all countries . .	48,068	74,643	104,747	98,996	31,095
From the United Kingdom and British Empire .	—	2,918	—	—	—

COPRA

Imports : tons

Total all countries . .	33,686	32,767	55,018	41,550	12,558
From the United Kingdom and British Empire .	13,095	22,473	46,835	41,550	12,449

PALM KERNELS

Imports : tons

Total all countries . .	595	1,832	—	—	—
From the United Kingdom and British Empire .	19	960	—	—	—

EARTH-NUTS

Imports : tons

	1913	1914	1915	1916	1917
Total all countries . .	3,665	4,308	9,223	9,746	—
From the United Kingdom and British Empire .	—	1,495	1,609	—	—

OATS

Imports : tons

Total all countries . .	61,805	54,839	3,160	119	975

BARLEY

Imports : tons

Total all countries . .	42,740	52,295	108,366	23,866	10,138

MAIZE

Imports · tons

Total all countries . .	404,875	266,405	692,813	450,164	240,822

OIL-CAKES (all kinds)

Imports tons

Total all countries . .	594,798	445,954	566,982	471,794	153,314

OTHER FODDERS (including bran, oil-cake meal, broken rice, etc., but not hay or straw)

Imports : tons

Total all countries . .	69,102	61,536	64,989	25,324	2,768

OIL VALUES OF IMPORTED OIL-SEEDS

Linseed (40 per cent.) : tons

All countries . . .	8,000	9,452	13,308	14,860	2,612
United Kingdom and British Empire . .	2,160	1,520	2,920	900	—

Rape-seed (43 per cent.) : tons

All countries . . .	920	279	580	567	—
United Kingdom and British Empire . .	—	38	361	47	—

Sesame (57 per cent.) : tons

All countries . . .	2,291	3,488	5,318	10,465	—
United Kingdom and British Empire . .	—	695	1,705	484	—

Hemp-seed (35 per cent.) : tons

All countries . . .	262	427	399	21	24
United Kingdom and British Empire . .	15	28	61	21	5

x

Soya-Beans (20 per cent.): tons

	1913	1914	1915	1916	1917
All countries . . .	9,620	14,920	20,940	19,800	6,220
United Kingdom and British Empire . .	—	600	—	—	—

N.B.—These beans came from Manchuria, which is under Japanese jurisdiction.

Copra (25 per cent.): tons

All countries . . .	8,425	8,200	13,750	10,387	3,150
United Kingdom and British Empire . .	3,275	5,625	11,700	10,387	3,112

N.B.—All the remainder came from Allied Colonies.

Palm Kernels (50 per cent.): tons

All countries . . .	300	900	—	—	—
United Kingdom and British Empire . .	9	480	—	—	—

Earth-nuts (50 per cent.): tons

All countries . . .	1,830	2,155	4,510	4,875	—
United Kingdom and British Empire . .	—	750	800	—	—

Totals

All countries . . .	31,648	39,821	58,805	60,975	12,006
United Kingdom and British Empire . .	5,459	9,736	17,547	12,239	3,117

SUMMARY OF VEGETABLE OIL IMPORTS

Edible oils . . .	14,839	9,288	10,844	8,586	2,039
Technical oils . .	1,722	1,792	2,000	1,518	629
	16,561	11,080	12,844	10,104	2,668
Oil values of imported oil oil seeds . . .	31,648	39,821	58,805	60,975	12,006
Totals	48,209	50,901	71,649	71,079	14,674 [1]
Increases over 1913			2,692	23,440	22,870

OF THE ABOVE THE FOLLOWING CAME FROM THE UNITED KINGDOM AND BRITISH EMPIRE

Edible oils . . .	290	728	1,730	312	27
Technical oils . .	146	588	1,369	986	410
Oil values of imported oil seeds	5,459	9,736	17,547	12,239	3,117
Totals	5,895	11,052	20,646	13,537	3,554

[1] Of this total, 1,300 tons only came from the U.S.A. The remainder, except 2,000 tons, all came from the United Kingdom and British Empire and Allied countries.

OIL-CAKE VALUES OF IMPORTED OIL SEEDS

Linseed (60 per cent.) : tons

	1913	1914	1915	1916	1917
All countries . . .	12,000	14,175	19,959	22,287	3,917
United Kingdom and British Empire . .	3,253	2,278	4,390	1,347	—

Rape-seed (57 per cent.) : tons

All countries . . .	1,228	366	772	752	—
United Kingdom and British Empire . .	—	54	481	66	—

Sesame (43 per cent.) : tons

All countries . . .	1,726	2,634	4,015	7,895	—
United Kingdom and British Empire . .	—	528	1,278	366	—

Hemp-seed (65 per cent.) : tons

All countries . .	490	793	740	43	47
United Kingdom and British Empire . .	29	53	114	43	10

Soya-Beans (80 per cent.) : tons

All countries . . .	38,448	59,723	83,807	79,196	24,875
United Kingdom and British Empire . .	—	2,318	—	—	—

Copra (75 per cent.) : tons

All countries . . .	25,261	24,567	41,268	31,163	9,408
United Kingdom and British Empire . .	9,820	16,848	35,135	31,163	9,337

Palm Kernels (50 per cent.) : tons

All countries . .	295	932	—	—	—
United Kingdom and British Empire . .	10	480	—	—	—

Earth-nuts (50 per cent.) : tons

All countries . . .	1,835	2,153	4,713	4,871	—
United Kingdom and British Empire . .	—	745	809	—	—

Totals

All countries . . .	81,283	105,343	155,274	146,207	38,247
United Kingdom and British Empire .	13,112	23,304	42,207	32,985	9,347

IMPORTS OF FODDER-STUFFS

Oats . .	61,805	54,839	3,160	119	975
Barley . . .	42,740	52,295	108,366	23,866	10,138
Maize . .	404,875	266,405	692,813	450,164	240,822
Oil-cake . .	594,798	445,954	566,982	471,794	153,314
Oil-cake from oil-seeds .	81,283	105,343	155,274	146,207	38,247
Various .	69,102	61,536	64,989	25,324	2,768
Total . .	1,254,603	986,372	1,591,584	1,117,474	446,264

TALLOW (raw and melted)

Imports : tons

	1913	1914	1915	1916	1917
Germany . . .	42	18	—	—	—
Total all countries . .	144	158	372	205	8

Exports : tons

Germany . . .	552	918	1,480	44	777

FISH OIL (including cod-liver oil)

Imports : tons

Germany . . .	22	5	—	—	—
Total all countries . .	3,400	3,031	3,433	2,149	1,148

Exports : tons

Germany and Austria .	1,631	2,247	3,017	1,518	336
Sweden . . .	409	399	29	178	235

BONE FAT (and other technical animal oils and fats)

Imports : tons

Germany . . .	126	79	1	—	—
Total all countries . .	208	950	1,053	145	3

Exports : tons

Germany and Austria .	1,080	1,375	2,529	2,165	2,673

COFFEE

Imports : tons

Total all countries . .	20,528	18,463	30,626	24,068	14,184
	—	—	*38,506*	*23,544*	*13,651*[1]

Re-exports : tons

Germany . . .	81	711	2,339	1,574	—
Sweden . . .	2,882	1,936	4,216	2,866	—
Total	4,179	3,963	9,793	6,251	141

TEA

Imports : tons

Total all countries . .	539	608	1,481	1,250	211
	—	—	*5,315*	*1,649*	*131* [1]

Re-exports : tons

Germany . . .	3	90	590	220	—
Sweden . . .	17	27	33	142	—
Total	73	187	803	773	20

[1] From British statistics.

COCOA BEANS

Imports : tons

	1913	1914	1915	1916	1917
Total all countries .	2,069	2,361	4,666	3,441	2,970
	—	—	*21,387*	*3,805*	*3,702* [1]

Re-exports tons

Germany	—	387	764	106	none shown
Sweden . . .	7	17	485	—	,,
Total	17	439	1,676	115	,,

FISHING-NETS AND YARN FOR FISHING-NETS

Imports : tons

Germany . . .	78	72	—	—	10
United Kingdom . .	39	65	133	213	135
Total all countries . .	159	218	142	214	146

PETROLEUM FOR LIGHTING AND POWER

Imports : tons

Germany . . .	10,513	4,340	—	—	6,697
United Kingdom . .	2,853	1,517	734	832	168
U.S.A. . . .	107,194	101,414	124,805	123,092	49,050
Total all countries .	134,536	128,929	127,954	124,014	56,010

Re-exports : tons

Neutral countries (total) .	31,307	22,381	21,745	13,241	199

EUROPEAN HEMP

Imports tons

All countries . . .	1,634	1,600	739	251	826 [2]
United Kingdom . .	76	139	262	—	—

INDIAN HEMP

Imports : tons

All countries . . .	1,274	970	2,049	2,215	193
United Kingdom and British Empire . .	762	777	1,760	2,212	177

MANILLA HEMP

Imports · tons

All countries . . .	340	342	875	1,189	57
United Kingdom and British Empire . .	816	159	684	1,102	57

YARN OF " LINEN AND THE LIKE " (? including thread)

Imports : tons

All countries . . .	486	413	249	231	94
United Kingdom and British Empire . .	10	88	152	197	79

---

[1] From British statistics.   [2] 726 from Russia,

YARN OF COCOA-NUT FIBRE (? including rope)

Imports : tons

	1913	1914	1915	1916	1917
All countries . . .	935	718	1,041	1,135	87
United Kingdom and British Empire . .	277	231	1,010	1,094	87

CUTCH

Imports : tons

All countries . . .	65	42	195	77	2
United Kingdom and British Empire . .	17	14	138	77	2

Exports (including re-exports): tons

Germany and Austria .	—	2	—	—	—
Norway and Sweden .	—	—	1	—	—
Transit Free Port . .	—	92	11	—	—

BLUE VITRIOL (Copper Sulphate)

Tons

All countries . . .	267	266	365	—	110
United Kingdom and British Empire . .	202	210	350	—	—

PYRITES

Imports : tons

All countries . . .	28,776	35,980	49,064	40,676	34,527
Spain	12,193	17,937	28,933	18,253	—

BURNT PYRITES

Exports : tons

Germany . . .	11,928	10,656	7,202	—	—
Sweden . . .	7,802	8,393	14,335	7,671	20,417

LUBRICATING OIL

Imports : metric tons

	1913	1914	1915	1916	1917
Germany . . .	1,200	886	37	7	14
United Kingdom .	145	238	550	326	92
U.S.A. . . .	2,217	3,236	9730	10,696	5,937
Total all countries .	5,557	5,360	10,490	11,045	6,067

Re-exports : metric tons

Norway . . .	—	—	1,120	1,140	1,131
Sweden . . .	—	—	2,127	2,622	68
Germany . . .	—	—	none shown		

BINDER TWINE

Imports : metric tons

	1913	1914	1915	1916	1917
Germany . . .	111	442	1	3	—
United Kingdom . .	581	984	792	936	138
U.S.A.	785	430	976	1,425	1,380
Total all countries . .	1,605	2,041	2,050	2,370	1,518

Re-exports : metric tons

Germany . . .	—	12	45	none shown	

HORSES AND FOALS

Imports : head

Germany and Austria .	2,788	2,351	30	82	44
Total all countries .	18,054	19,885	7,775	3,940	131

Exports : head

Germany and Austria .	27,276	95,338	257	16,077	34,155
Total all countries .	27,913	95,710	264	16,100	34,217

COAL (exports insignificant)

Imports · tons

Germany . . .	189,211	131,321	109,713	508,116	644,060
United Kingdom .	2,931,094	3,046,678	3,116,658	2,295,023	824,762
Total (all) . .	3,152,576	3,226,957	3,232,498	2,814,820	1,473,911

COKE

Imports . tons

Germany . . .	124,611	147,209	2,526,398	4,523,609	3,789,213
United Kingdom .	2,213,914	2,109,930	1,587,492	1,527,488	397,393
Total (all) . .	2,391,603	2,260,430	4,114,140	6,053,542	4,186,607

FERTILISERS

Phosphate Rock

Imports : tons

Germany . . .	3,225	—	—	—	—
United Kingdom and British Empire .	15,757	23,325	5,300	—	—[1]
Total all countries .	55,875	49,301	58,238	108,864 [1]	8,429 [2]

Superphosphate

Imports : tons

Germany . . .	45,923	62,804	—	—	—
United Kingdom and British Empire .	13,680	18,946	24,270	3	—
Total all countries .	110,155	142,883	83,060	19,461	10,420

---

[1] From Algiers and Tunis.
[2] French.

Basic Slag

Imports : tons

	1913	1914	1915	1916	1917
Germany . . .	59	45	—	—	—
United Kingdom and British Empire . .	8,754	11,031	—	—	—
Total all countries . .	8,955	11,077	—	—	—

Bone-meal

Imports : tons

Germany . . .	59	21	12	222	35
United Kingdom and British Empire . .	—	—	—	—	—
Total all countries . .	282	214	1,420	1,683	1,252

Artificial Nitrates

Imports : tons

Germany . . .	—	—	—	—	—
United Kingdom and British Empire . .	—	—	—	—	—
Total all countries . .	5,066	11,781	3,879	761	1,137

Re-exports : tons

Germany . . .	—	1,021	—	—	—

Chile Saltpetre

Imports : tons

Germany . . .	20,206	29,414	—	—	—
United Kingdom and British Empire . .	—	475	2,918	—	—
Total all countries . .	35,049	42,743	42,066	34,949	39,601

Sulphate of Ammonia

Imports : tons

Germany . . .	502	645	—	—	—
United Kingdom and British Empire . .	523	695	149	9	49

Exports : tons

Germany . . .	2,791	1,923	—	—	—

Potash Manures

Imports : tons

Germany . . .	26,084	23,617	24,264	51,909	20,989
United Kingdom and British Empire . .	—	—	—	—	—
Total all countries . .	26,100	23,674	24,267	51,961	20,989

Cryolite

Imports : metric tons

Greenland . . .	8,451	7,373	5,801	10,922	5,897

Exports : metric tons

	1913	1914	1915	1916	1917
Germany . . .	1,505	1,303	2,800	2,900	1,248
United Kingdom and British Empire . .	1,040	1,108	1,676	1,122	899
France	1,785	638	529	1,548	2,130
Norway and Sweden .	463	781	735	1,870	1,016

WOOL (all kinds except waste and shoddy)

Imports : tons

	1913	1914	1915	1916	1917
United Kingdom and British Empire . .	279	298	538	876	208
Faroes and Iceland .	805	830	871	3	26
Total all countries . .	1,465	1,408	3,256	1,475	401

Exports : (including re-exports) · tons

Germany and Austria .	105	533	493	217	—
Norway and Sweden .	225	228	398	176	40

COTTON (raw)

Imports : tons

United Kingdom and British Empire . .	14	100	3,463	6,059	914
Total all countries . .	6,009	4,820	7,205	8,191	2,934

Exports (including re-exports) : tons

Germany and Austria .	3	5	—	—	—
Norway and Sweden .	7	8	50	31	9

WOOLLEN YARN (all kinds)

Imports : tons

United Kingdom and British Empire . .	872	809	1,048	1,559	833
Total all countries . .	1,935	1,408	1,182	1,678	853

Exports (including re-exports) : tons

Germany and Austria .	3	11	1	1	1
Norway and Sweden .	8	5	7	3	1

COTTON YARN (all kinds except for fishing-nets)

Imports : tons

United Kingdom and British Empire . .	791	792	1,817	2,717	1,963
Total all countries . .	1,749	1,812	2,491	2,931	2,026

Exports to Germany and Austria : Nil

RUBBER

Imports : metric tons

All countries . . .	115	262	333	404	126
United Kingdom and British Empire . .	67	213	292	401	122

Exports (including re-exports) : metric tons

	1913	1914	1915	1916	1917
Germany and Austria .	69	203	8	3	—
Norway and Sweden .	86	126	210	284	493
From Free Port, going to foreign countries .	—	172	220	—	—

N.B.—Rubber includes " regenerated rubber " and guttapercha and balata.

MOTOR AND CYCLE TYRES AND TUBES

Imports : metric tons

All countries . . .	549	595	446	503	338
United Kingdom and British Empire . .	127	205	292	378	203

Exports (including re-exports) : metric tons

Germany and Austria .	—	—	—	—	—
Norway and Sweden .	56	56	70	5	—
From Free Port, going to foreign countries .	—	700	51	33	—

ROSIN

Imports : metric tons

All countries . . .	1,547	1,388	2,253	2,082	670
United Kingdom and British Empire . .	1	53	1,029	625	61

Exports (including re-exports) : metric tons

Germany and Austria .	—	2	—	—	—
Norway and Sweden .	3	5	—	—	—
From Free Port, going to foreign countries .	—	1,057	183	1,684	—

TIN

Imports : tons

All countries . . .	329	379	339	471	240
United Kingdom and British Empire . .	172	261	317	466	228

Exports (including re-exports) : metric tons

Germany and Austria .	—	—	—	—	—
Norway and Sweden .	23	33	—	—	—
In transit Free Port .	—	91	14	2	—

COPPER

Imports : tons

All countries . . .	3,267	2,873	3,271	3,480	2,519
British Empire . .	174	228	410	249	3

Exports (including re-exports) : tons

Germany and Austria .	—	2	23	25	2
Norway and Sweden .	299	78	125	72	40
In transit Free Port .	—	4,762	362	145	217

QUEBRACHO EXTRACT (liquid form)

Imports · tons

	1913	1914	1915	1916	1917
All countries . . .	2.307	1,762	745	174	15
United Kingdom and British Empire . .	108	268	417	10	12

Exports : tons

Germany and Austria .	—	—	—	—	—
Norway and Sweden .	—	57	—	—	—
In transit Free Port .	—	2,360	1,660	26	19

OTHER SOLID EXTRACTS (this includes quebracho and apparently all solid extracts from woods except Gambier and Cutch)

Imports : tons

All countries . . .	98	645	3,320	3,874	1,110
United Kingdom and British Empire . .	—	144	1,758	—	—

Exports (including re-exports) : Nil

FREE PORT TO COPENHAGEN (transit from foreign country to foreign country)

Tons

	1914	1915	1916	1917
Pork and bacon . . .	4,050	11,800	398	—
Other meat . . .	700	2,160	201	—
Casings	1,600	3,200	46	—
Butter	1,530	986	—	—
Eggs	2,470	430	21	—
Fat	8,800	12,120	741	—
Oleo-margarine and premier jus	1,730	5,100	181	10
Margarine	450	560	16	—
Fish (all kinds except conserves)	9,004	7,107	791	1,874
Coffee	2,800	19,500	5,500	—
Tea	800	1,650	952	—
Cocoa beans	2,350	26,150	1,320	27
Wool	700	380	11	7
Cotton	3,353	3,160	5	—
Binder twine and sail rope .	1,876	2	6	—
Hides and skins . . .	8.800	2,650	1,001	18
Fish oil	2,490	4,000	—	12
Lubricating oil . . .	260	7,340	(8,160) [1]	380
" Unspecified " oils . .	16,000	5,200	1,688	172
Vegetable oils (specified) . .	707	2,376	809	300
Soap	64	140	99	50

[1] Not separately given : all kinds of mineral oil.

SWEDEN

	To the United Kingdom	To Germany and Austria
	Tons	Tons
1913 . . .	26,567	37,043
1914 . . .	28,526	56,685
1915 . . .	8,563	104,203
1916 . . .	115	90,835
1917 . . .	—	16,451

In the above table the following are included: cattle; fish; pork and
bacon; meat; meat conserves; milk; cheese; butter; eggs.

FROM SWEDEN TO THE UNITED KINGDOM

Exports : tons

	1913	1914	1915	1916	1917
Cattle	—	—	—	—	—
Fish	4,745	1,951	—	—	—
Pork and bacon . .	2,740	9,165	746	—	—
Meat	235	192	26	—	—
Meat conserves . .	20	20	11	4	—
Milk	167	118	19	—	—
Cheese	—	13	—	—	—
Butter	15,749	14,317	6,862	60	—
Eggs	2,911	2,750	899	51	—
Total . . .	26,567	28,526	8,563	115	—

FROM SWEDEN TO GERMANY AND AUSTRIA

Exports : tons

	1913	1914	1915	1916	1917
Cattle	3,180	5,474	4,761	2,665	528
Fish	30,303	43,298	53,406	51,113	7,820
Pork and bacon . .	703	2,160	16,936	14,093	4,760
Meat	2,306	3,015	8,954	3,905	2,641
Meat conserves . .	108	1,567	6,107	3,027	453
Milk	109	—	823	1,486	55
Cheese	—	15	276	—	—
Butter	310	1,083	9,730	12,823	—
Eggs	24	73	3,210	1,723	194
Total . . .	37,043	56,685	104,203	90,835	16,451

CATTLE (including calves)

Exports : metric tons

	1913	1914	1915	1916	1917
Total	8,451	16,034	7,298	2,720	535
Germany and Austria .	3,180	5,474	4,761	2,665	528
United Kingdom . .	—	—	—	—	—

SWEDISH STATISTICS 317

FISH

Exports : metric tons

	1913	1914	1915	1916	1917
Total . .	44,962	55,058	59,742	56,885	11,653
Germany and Austria .	30,303	43,298	53,406	51,113	7,820
United Kingdom . .	4,745	1,951	—	—	—

Imports : metric tons

Total	58,546	55,505	52,942	39,875	17,967
United Kingdom . .	2,270	3,383	721	—	—

PORK (including bacon)

Exports : metric tons

Total . . .	7,908	14,723	18,917	14,113	4,766
Germany and Austria .	703	2,160	16,936	14,093	4,760
United Kingdom . .	2,740	9,165	746	—	—

Imports . metric tons

Total . .	2,613	1,844	2,810	1,690	6,624
United Kingdom . .	—	—	10	25	—

MEAT (all other kinds except conserves)

Exports : metric tons

Total . . .	4,915	7,530	11,692	4,980	5,761
Germany and Austria .	2,306	3,015	8,954	3,905	2,641
United Kingdom .	235	192	26	—	—

Imports : metric tons

Total . . .	2,010	1,245	514	197	158
United Kingdom . .	181	203	199	—	—

MEAT CONSERVES (all kinds, including fish)

Exports : metric tons

Total	450	1,931	6,754	3,213	464
Germany and Austria	108	1,567	6,107	3,027	453
United Kingdom . .	20	20	11	4	—

Imports : metric tons

Total . . .	570	486	460	450	298
United Kingdom . .	87	113	75	12	—

MILK (including dried milk)

Exports · metric tons

Total	2,026	2,554	3,860	1,495	57
Germany and Austria .	109	—	823	1,486	55
United Kingdom . .	167	118	19	—	—

Imports . metric tons

Total	94	52	60	15	5
United Kingdom . .	—	—	—	—	—

CHEESE

Exports : metric tons

	1913	1914	1915	1916	1917
Total '	3	31	284	—	—
Germany and Austria .	—	15	276	—	—
United Kingdom . .	—	13	—	—	—

Imports : metric tons

Total	550	346	520	129	548
United Kingdom . .	—	—	—	—	—

BUTTER (including margarine)

Exports : metric tons

Total	19,670	19,032	18,850	13,020	—
Germany and Austria .	310	1,083	9,730	12,823	—
United Kingdom . .	15,749	14,317	6,862	60	—

Imports : metric tons

Total	563	826	1,035	308	7,149
United Kingdom . .	—	—	—	58	—

EGGS (and egg products)

Exports : metric tons

Total	3,227	3,282	4,974	2,042	194
Germany and Austria .	24	73	3,210	1,723	194
United Kingdom . .	2,911	2,750	899	51	—

Imports : metric tons

Total	2,847	1,669	4,154	614	1,863
United Kingdom . .	—	—	86	11	—

HORSES

Exports : No. of head

Total	6,837	12,631	12,725	22,357	11,246
Germany . . .	866	6,924	12,020	22,317	11,216
United Kingdom . .	—	—	—	—	—

ANIMAL OILS AND FATS (including stearin, tallow, olein)

Imports : metric tons

Total	7,326	8,449	8,966	7,656	1,083
United Kingdom and British Empire . .	1,023	1,138	2,131	2,104	273

Exports : metric tons

Total	1,194	1,494	1,352	879	696
Germany and Austria .	693	786	962	876	685
United Kingdom . .	34	28	39	—	—

VEGETABLE OILS AND FATS

Imports : metric tons

	1913	1914	1915	1916	1917
Total	28,053	27,934	38,807	19,478	801
United Kingdom and British Empire . .	4,738	5,745	8,475	1,808	283

Exports : metric tons

Total	181	876	2,334	2,099	50
Germany and Austria .	—	714	1,778	1,954	50
United Kingdom . .	—	—	—	—	—

SYRUP AND GLUCOSE

Imports : metric tons

Total	10,313	13,594	7,692	8,118	757
United Kingdom . .	7,449	9,549	3,791	929	—

Exports : metric tons

Total	—	2	1,796	12	—
Germany and Austria .	—	—	1,784	—	—

COFFEE (raw and roasted)

Imports : metric tons

Total	34,240	29,358	40,233	38,359	8,569
			94,051	*50,906*	*6,675* [1]
United Kingdom . .	1,318	1,212	1,027	223	556
			2,163	*1,121*	*29* [1]

Exports : metric tons

Total	13	431	3,943	3,524	—
Germany and Austria .	—	51	1,273	3,328	—

COCOA (beans and powder)

Imports : metric tons

Total . . .	1,668	1,940	4,568	3,401	646
			15,880	*2,726*	*188* [1]
United Kingdom . .	53	379	1,371	348	1
			5,992	*354*	*—* [1]

Exports : metric tons

Total	10	146	2,352	11	—
Germany and Austria .	—	112	2,265	6	—

TEA

Imports : metric tons

Total	233	212	250	496	96
			718	*3,022*	*—* [1]
United Kingdom and British Empire . .	126	167	198	433	40
			628	*3,018*	*—* [1]

[1] From British statistics.

Exports : metric tons

	1913	1914	1915	1916	1917
Total	—	2	2	161	—
Germany and Austria .	—	—	—	161	—

CRANBERRIES

Exports : metric tons

Total	3,174	3,084	3,571	1,844	723
Germany and Austria .	3,011	2,847	3,430	1,756	715

COTTON (raw, carded and waste)

Imports : metric tons

Total	24,886	25,480	123,185	28,862	7,093
United Kingdom and British Empire . .	1,940	2,807	10,297	552	176

Exports : metric tons

Total	831	6,032	78,178	55	7
Germany and Austria .	236	4,685	76,259	—	—

HEMP

Imports : metric tons

Total	4,004	4,081	5,899	3,290	1,788
United Kingdom and British Empire . .	529	640	1,154	585	5

Exports : metric tons

Total	3	80	479	382	—
Germany and Austria .	—	58	428	355	—

WOOL (all kinds, excluding waste)

Imports : metric tons

Total	5,944	4,459	4,952	7,236	1,342
United Kingdom and British Empire . .	3,205	2,576	917	1,541	1

Exports : metric tons

Total	74	32	686	29	—
Germany and Austria .	21	10	686	29	—

COTTON YARN

Imports : metric tons

Total	1,303	1,290	1,331	1,106	657
United Kingdom and British Empire . .	757	749	975	876	551

Exports : metric tons

Total	474	671	1,729	89	12
Germany and Austria .	1	202	1,201	40	—

SWEDISH STATISTICS 321

Hides and Skins (all kinds except furs)
Imports : metric tons

	1913	1914	1915	1916	1917
Total	14,130	10,713	14,420	7,725	1,150
United Kingdom and British Empire . .	688	865	2,725	75	—

Exports : metric tons

Total	10,811	12,870	6,388	5,410	56
Germany and Austria .	5,053	5,905	3,227	2,809	27
United Kingdom . .	446	325	105	14	—

Boots and Shoes
Imports : metric tons

Total	41	59	57	49	2
United Kingdom and British Empire . .	3	4	11	6	—

Exports : metric tons

Total	10	192	4,556	2,828	26
Germany and Austria .	—	142	3,470	2,664	15

Sausage Casings
Imports : metric tons

Total	1,077	897	2,324	828	528
United Kingdom and British Empire . .	16	—	20	—	—

Exports : metric tons

Total	697	1,172	2,518	1,177	1,155
Germany and Austria .	484	702	1,883	1,059	1,080
United Kingdom . .	—	—	30	—	—

Rubber (raw and waste, including guttapercha)
Imports . metric tons

Total	1,201	1,131	1,216	1,347	494
United Kingdom and British Empire . .	420	324	754	928	—

Exports : metric tons

Total	671	680	571	788	1,235
Germany and Austria .	76	111	120	487	618

Rubber (manufactures, all kinds)
Imports . metric tons

Total	1,009	954	582	611	180
United Kingdom and British Empire . .	239	215	221	241	13

Exports . metric tons

Total	678	682	395	245	—
Germany and Austria .	129	135	13	—	—

Y

GLYCERINE (raw and refined)

Imports : metric tons

	1913	1914	1915	1916	1917
Total	335	358	472	283	303
United Kingdom and British Empire . .	51	20	29	—	—

Exports : metric tons

Total	184	129	154	124	83
Germany and Austria .	178	97	132	—	40

RESIN (including shellac)

Imports : metric tons

Total	7,077	4,558	6,728	8,987	97
United Kingdom and British Empire . .	89	502	2,341	1,369	14

Exports : metric tons

Total	8	813	939	3,137	1,390
Germany and Austria .	—	519	669	2,944	1,348

TOBACCO (raw and manufactured)

Imports : metric tons

Total	4,768	3,660	3,740	4,812	4,959
United Kingdom . .	259	238	178	199	194

Exports (metric tons)

Total	49	72	77	78	6
Germany and Austria .	—	—	—	—	—

SOAP (all kinds)

Imports : metric tons

Total	374	302	606	954	313
United Kingdom . .	240	191	430	616	179

Exports : metric tons

Total	36	23	3,399	957	2
Germany and Austria .	—	—	2,946	928	—

CANDLES

Imports : metric tons

Total	23	27	145	69	11
United Kingdom and British Empire . .	—	—	139	46	—

Exports : metric tons

Total	35	483	924	4	—
Germany and Austria .	—	422	890	—	—

SWEDISH STATISTICS 323

LUBRICANTS (all kinds)

Imports · metric tons

	1913	1914	1915	1916	1917
Total	24,727	15,865	44,467	24,680	7,635
United Kingdom . .	902	809	2,006	212	206
Denmark . .	—	—	3,353	2,896	288

Exports · metric tons

Total	576	207	737	1,364	634
Germany and Austria .	—	—	476	1,334	630

PETROLEUM (for light and power)

Imports metric tons

Total . .	157,557	129,836	106,958	139,769	44,448
United Kingdom . .	5,689	4,684	4,455	2,033	—

Exports. metric tons

Total	5,070	4,523	2,048	1	18
Austria and Germany .	—	—	52	—	—

SPIRITS

Exports thousands of litres

Total	360	540	3,799	159	—
Germany and Austria .	16	68	3,184	—	—

COAL (all kinds)

Imports. metric tons

Total . .	4,878,854	4,626,932	3,835,687	4,036,452	1,503,757
United Kingdom .	4,654,675	4,385,947	2,723,980	1,659,005	696,666

COKE

Imports. metric tons

Total . . .	495,866	449,576	1,220,161	1,296,446	520,311
United Kingdom .	261,132	296,584	91,750	27,599	8,435

COAL BRIQUETTES

Imports · metric tons

Total . .	24,737	15,146	240,590	885,781	300,827
United Kingdom . .	—	—	—	5,152	—

FODDER MATERIALS (except hay and straw)

Imports : metric tons

Total	184.506	144,503	165,115	80,255	33,602
United Kingdom and British Empire . .	11,699	11,898	13,793	—	—

Exports : metric tons

Total	2,134	623	21	1,700	—
Germany and Austria .	— ·	102	—	1,700	—

Linseed and Rape-seed

Imports : metric tons

	1913	1914	1915	1916	1917
Total	29,789	25,227	30,347	26,526	232
United Kingdom and British Empire . .	—	550	8,132	785	—

Exports : metric tons

	1913	1914	1915	1916	1917
Germany and Austria .	—	698	103	—	—

Raw Phosphates (all kinds)

Imports : metric tons

	1913	1914	1915	1916	1917
Total	123,250	90,864	39,105	85,927	1,752
United Kingdom and British Empire . .	56,266	63,224	3,530	—	—

Cyanamide

Exports : metric tons

	1913	1914	1915	1916	1917
Total	—	4,754	16,553	19,323	2,915
Germany and Austria .	—	3,644	16,203	19,302	2,915

Basic Slag

Exports : metric tons

	1913	1914	1915	1916	1917
Total	21,169	14,428	11,440	1,545	—
United Kingdom and British Empire . .	13,842	8,856	11,400	—	—

Guano and Similar Materials

Exports : metric tons

	1913	1914	1915	1916	1917
Total	663	553	1,168	230	25
Germany and Austria .	357	144	1,053	170	—
United Kingdom . .	—	—	—	—	—

Bone and Horn Meal

Exports : metric tons

	1913	1914	1915	1916	1917
Total	254	496	1,584	1,478	1,191
Germany and Austria .	187	392	50	—	—
United Kingdom . .	—	—	—	—	—

Calcium and Barium Carbide

Exports : metric tons

	1913	1914	1915	1916	1917
Total	13,587	12,714	14,809	14,710	12,930
Germany and Austria .	2,039	1,669	1,922	2,499	6,469

SALTPETRE (all kinds)

Imports : metric tons

	1913	1914	1915	1916	1917
Total	33,891	41,656	37,371	37,393	18,600
Norway and Denmark .	714	3,268	9,065	5,536	2,610
United Kingdom and British Empire . .	—	—	—	—	—

BORAX AND BORIC ACID

Imports metric tons

Total	590	590	1,035	571	222
United Kingdom . .	253	295	759	299	129

Exports : metric tons

Total	4	9	435	88	—
Germany and Austria .	—	—	324	75	—

NICKEL SALTS

Exports metric tons

Total	—	1	194	—	—
Germany and Austria .	—	—	124	—	—

TANNING MATERIALS (all kinds, dry)

Imports : metric tons

Total	6,422	3,834	2,584	2,501	—
United Kingdom and British Empire . .	12	895	376	349	—

Exports : metric tons

Total	1,033	1,349	1,601	121	587
Germany and Austria .	200	634	1,216	—	—

TANNING EXTRACTS (all kinds)

Imports · metric tons

Total	9,158	6,598	11,856	4,962	397
United Kingdom and British Empire . .	1,303	1,250	3,424	329	—

Exports · metric tons

Total	987	924	2,322	524	1,282
Germany and Austria .	426	282	936	95	564

FERROMANGANESE AND FERROSILICON (all quantities)

Exports : metric tons

	1913	1914	1915	1916	1917
Total . . .	9,575	10,047	10,802	16,246	17,983
Germany and Austria .	2,703	5,357	5,472	10,362	14,082

FERROTUNGSTEN AND FERROMOLYBDENUM

Exports : metric tons

	1913	1914	1915	1916	1917
Total	—	1	34	13	11
Germany and Austria .	—	—	34	11	11

LEAD (unmanufactured)

Imports : metric tons

	1913	1914	1915	1916	1917
Total	1,660	2,427	1,984	2,972	70
United Kingdom and British Empire . .	608	1,116	1,780	567	—

Exports : metric tons

Total	369	398	563	359	540
Germany and Austria .	190	124	563	346	519

COPPER (unmanufactured, plate, bar)

Imports : metric tons

	1913	1914	1915	1916	1917
Total	9,559	12,455	13,396	11,257	3,729
United Kingdom and British Empire . .	517	710	1,085	106	5

Exports : metric tons

Total	1,400	4,313	2,483	1,758	519
Germany and Austria .	1,215	3,960	2,304	1,334	184

NICKEL

Imports : metric tons

	1913	1914	1915	1916	1917
Total	150	136	504	125	40
United Kingdom and British Empire . .	27	60	328	78	16

Exports : metric tons

Total	1	—	70	30	7
Germany and Austria .	—	—	70	30	7

TIN

Imports : metric tons

	1913	1914	1915	1916	1917
Total	1,082	1,481	4,189	996	308
United Kingdom and British Empire . .	735	1,130	3,693	972	163

Exports : metric tons

Total	86	517	3,454	35	28
Germany and Austria .	2	306	3,180	35	28

IRON ORE (including concentrates)

Exports : metric tons

	1913	1914	1915	1916	1917
Total . . .	6,439,750	4,787,314	5,992,215	5,536,641	5,818,499
Germany and Austria .	4,977,395	3,677,671	5,124,235	4,298,586	4,861,498
United Kingdom . .	672,836	441,978	499,454	846,222	—

PYRITES

	Exports	metric tons			
	1913	1914	1915	1916	1917
Total	500	3,444	39,998	14,003	29,800
Germany and Austria	100	3,229	39,164	13,992	29,799
United Kingdom . .	—	—	—	—	—

BURNT PYRITES

	Exports ·	metric tons			
Total	40,795	39,643	53,095	72,400	56,490
Germany and Austria	36,113	35,501	50,484	70,360	56,490
United Kingdom . .	—	—	—	—	—

ASBESTOS (raw)

	Imports ·	metric tons			
Total . . .	705	414	506	315	8
United Kingdom and					
British Empire	31	—	134	179	—

	Exports	metric tons			
Total . . .	—	—	259	39	29
Germany and Austria .	—	—	257	39	19

SULPHATE PULP (dry and wet)

	Exports :	metric tons			
Total . . .	98,738	96,419	113,223	148,628	129,215
Germany and Austria	14,801	8,636	21,601	88,356	91,686

CEMENT

	Exports ·	metric tons			
Total	137,073	39,346	60,534	77,717	4,651
Germany and Austria .	450	—	—	—	—
United Kingdom .	—	—	—	—	—
British Empire	540	—	680	—	—

	Imports	metric tons			
Total . . .	12,119	14,769	15,540	15,325	5,220
United Kingdom	—	—	—	—	—
Germany . . .	7,920	8,685	10,565	10,357	5,088

NORWAY

TABLE SHOWING THE EXPORT OF FOOD FROM NORWAY TO THE UNITED
KINGDOM AND GERMANY AND AUSTRIA DURING THE YEARS 1913–1917
(metric tons)

	To the United Kingdom	To Germany and Austria
	Tons	Tons
1913	61,464	81,538
1914	53,715	71,586
1915	69,512	182,630
1916	35,701	215,593
1917	69,680	101,847

In the above table the following are included : Cheese, butter, margarine,
milk (condensed and sterilised), game, canned goods, fish.

FROM NORWAY TO THE UNITED KINGDOM

Exports : tons

	1913	1914	1915	1916	1917
Cheese	10	11	7	4	—
Butter	1,057	676	823	300	—
Margarine	340	231	158	67	—
Milk (condensed)	2,957	2,773	2,917	1,329	7,359
„ (sterilised)	427	1,310	1,685	1,469	1,261
Game	214	73	97	37	—
Canned foods	9,156	9,376	12,273	9,265	13,698
Fish	47,303	39,265	51,552	23,230	47,362
Total	61,464	53,715	69,512	35,701	69,680

FROM NORWAY TO GERMANY AND AUSTRIA

Exports : tons

	1913	1914	1915	1916	1917
Cheese	1	4	115	—	—
Butter	2	4	265	147	—
Margarine	32	15	—	—	—
Milk (condensed)	447	249	100	4	—
„ (sterilised)	282	173	257	498	—
Game	124	63	88	71	2
Canned foods	1,879	3,332	20,396	20,706	18,897
Fish	78,771	67,746	161,409	194,167	82,948
Total	81,538	71,586	182,630	215,593	101,847

CANNED GOODS (all kinds)

Exports : metric tons

	1913	1914	1915	1916	1917
All countries . . .	30,994	34,919	51,669	38,595	39,874
Germany and Austria .	1,879	3,332	20,396	20,706	18,897
Denmark and Sweden .	439	636	4,166	177	454
United Kingdom . .	9,156	9,376	12,273	9,265	13,698

FISH (all kinds other than canned)

Exports · metric tons

All countries . . .	323,716	281,917	370,735	338,323 [1]	204,039 [1]
Germany and Austria .	78,771	67,746	161,409	194,167	82,948
Denmark and Sweden .	50,461	63,016	85,951	40,090	19,732
United Kingdom . .	47,303	39,265	51,552	23,230 [1]	47,362 [1]

FISH OIL (including codliver oil and whale oil)

Exports : metric tons

All countries . . .	24,386	45,077	38,727	18,575	3,454
Germany and Austria .	12,527	27,666	31,258	14,582	2,015
Denmark and Sweden .	1,235	1,102	5,038	101	33
United Kingdom . .	2,815	2,960	1,002	3,024	398

CHEESE

Exports · metric tons

All countries . . .	185	227	308	50	—
Germany and Austria .	1	4	115	—	—
Denmark and Sweden .	10	8	82	4	—
United Kingdom . .	10	11	7	4	—

BUTTER

Exports : metric tons

All countries . . .	1,064	714	1,636	466	—
Germany and Austria .	2	4	265	147	—
Denmark and Sweden .	—	—	532	13	—
United Kingdom . .	1,057	676	823	300	—

MARGARINE

Exports . metric tons

All countries . . .	598	480	396	337	4
Germany and Austria .	32	15	—	—	—
Denmark and Sweden .	12	15	46	120	—
United Kingdom . .	340	231	158	67	—

[1] These would be much larger if the United Kingdom had imported the fish bought under the Fish Agreement, which, however, remained stored in barrels in Norway.

MILK (condensed)

Exports : metric tons

	1913	1914	1915	1916	1917
All countries . . .	15,319	14,405	11,384	8,064	7,853
Germany and Austria .	447	249	100	4	—
Denmark and Sweden .	264	306	602	31	5
United Kingdom . .	2,957	2,773	2,917	1,329	7,359

MILK (sterilised, including cream)

Exports : metric tons

All countries . . .	4,283	5,509	6,188	6,724	2,472
Germany and Austria .	282	173	257	498	—
Denmark and Sweden .	—	—	—	—	—
United Kingdom . .	427	1,310	1,685	1,469	1,261

GAME

Exports : metric tons

All countries . . .	446	192	335	152	2
Germany and Austria .	124	63	88	71	2
Denmark and Sweden .	100	51	147	43	—
United Kingdom . .	214	73	97	37	—

PORK (including bacon and ham)

Imports : metric tons

All countries . . .	2,773	3,505	2,952	5,927	5,110
Denmark and Sweden .	516	1,336	56	106	8

Exports : metric tons

All countries . . .	1,240	1,239	228	11	1
Germany and Austria .	—	—	—	—	—
Denmark and Sweden .	1,233	1,224	205	6	—

LARD (including other animal fats except butter and margarine)

Imports : metric tons

All countries . . .	1,531	1,562	2,195	2,474	2,340
United Kingdom . .	53	94	43	—	16

Exports : metric tons

All countries . . .	1	35	42	2	—

(No details of destination)

HORSES (No. of head)

Exports :

All countries . . .	416	4,590	1,176	1,584	14
Germany and Austria	—	—	—	—	—
Denmark ahd Sweden .	415	4,588	1,175	1,578	14
United Kingdom . .	—	2	1	—	—

VEGETABLE OILS (other than olive, linseed, rape and palm oils)

Imports · metric tons

	1913	1914	1915	1916	1917
All countries . .	8,881	8,877	15,224	13,451	13,433
United Kingdom . .	3,037	2,672	1,971	1,184	84

Exports (including hardened oils) · metric tons

All countries . .	641	1,909	6,349	1,554	—

(No details given of destination)

LINSEED, RAPE-SEED AND PALM OILS

Imports : metric tons

All countries . . .	1,807	1,667	2.821	1.186	2.041
United Kingdom . .	987	1,009	2,590	1,057	565

OLIVE OIL

Imports . metric tons

All countries . . .	1,092	2,428	5,778	3,353	1,752
United Kingdom . .	3	1	69	6	29

ANIMAL OILS AND FATS (including tallow, fatty acids and fish-oils)

Imports metric tons

All countries .	9,698	10,511	13,051	14,169	12,533
United Kingdom . .	1,455	1,300	2,999	2,817	488

Exports as above, including hardened whale fat, but *excluding fish oils.*

All countries . . .	7,274	19,279	20,842	7,078	132

(No details given of destination)

SOAP

Imports · metric tons

All countries . . .	700	800	916	544	1,324
United Kingdom . .	610	704	832	460	747

Exports · metric tons

All countries .	18	22	579	152	—
Germany . .	—	—	363	140	—

COFFEE

Imports · metric tons

All countries . .	13,672	11,898	24,125	24,126	14,954
United Kingdom and British Empire .	440	938	1,725	2,493	1,155

Exports · metric tons

All countries . .	285	330	4.641	4,490	181
Germany and Austria .	7	40	23	37	—
Denmark and Sweden .	257	267	4.505	4,227	1

FISHING-NETS

Imports : metric tons

	1913	1914	1915	1916	1917
All countries . . .	14	43	38	32	16

(No details given of origin)

FISHING-NETS (all materials for)

Imports : metric tons

All countries . . .	124	130	300	604	319

(No details given of origin)

Exports (locally manufactured) : metric tons

All countries . . .	103	119	26	32	17
Germany . . .	2	18	11	—	—

CUTCH AND GAMBIER

Imports : metric tons

All countries . . .	241	225	808	851	289

(No details of origin given)

HEMP

Imports : metric tons

All countries . . .	3,433	4,058	4,417	3,015	3,357
United Kingdom and British Empire . .	1,239	1,540	2,801	1,055	469
Germany . . .	897	591	37	—	—

LINEN AND HEMP YARN (all kinds, including rope)

Imports : metric tons

All countries . . .	2,189	2,100	1,550	2,094	2,348
United Kingdom . .	374	310	455	822	885
Germany . . .	560	439	111	4	269

SAILCLOTH (cotton and linen)

All countries . . .	402	362	411	563	400

(No details given of origin)

PETROLEUM FOR LIGHTING AND POWER

Imports : metric tons

All countries . . .	79,252	87,268	55,945	103,902	51,343
Germany and Austria .	1,859	655	17	206	4,844
United Kingdom and British Empire . .	2,945	2,870	732	1,257	257
Denmark . . .	4,432	1,360	2,363	315	—

LUBRICANTS (including vaseline, etc.)

Imports : metric tons

	1913	1914	1915	1916	1917
All countries . . .	7,567	6,467	10,373	10,725	6,058
United Kingdom . .	1,413	1,491	1,349	1,525	806
Denmark . . .	508	433	990	569	488
Germany and Austria .	2,916	1,763	13	4	221

COTTON

Imports : metric tons

	1913	1914	1915	1916	1917
All countries . . .	3,986	6,581	11,137	5,497	3,688
United Kingdom and British Empire . .	462	2,906	6,615	3,162	1,048

Exports : metric tons

All countries . . .	—	—	643	—	—

(No details given)

COTTON YARN

Imports : metric tons

	1913	1914	1915	1916	1917
All countries . . .	2,017	2,002	2,232	2,711	1,980
United Kingdom and British Empire . .	1,259	1,311	1,794	2,582	1,897

COAL

Imports : metric tons

	1913	1914	1915	1916	1917
All countries . . .	2,276,808	2,504,602	2,758,506	2,467,551	1,059,465
United Kingdom . .	2,227,620	2,441,892	2,648,105	2,328,974	981,980
Germany . . .	10,306	18,046	20,347	92,663	38,872

COKE

Imports . metric tons

	1913	1914	1915	1916	1917
All countries . . .	205,616	259,358	336,438	365,204	167,016
United Kingdom . .	145,131	203,247	200,182	237,403	124,805
Germany . . .	24,242	20,857	112,042	116,059	39,798

NICKEL

Exports metric tons

All countries . . .	594	696	760	722	442

(No details. Practically all went to Germany)

COPPER

Exports : metric tons

	1913	1914	1915	1916	1917
All countries . . .	2,811	3,059	2,984	1,789	1,980
Germany and Austria .	685	406	1,573	1,229	18
Denmark and Sweden .	1,320	1,919	1,411	541	1,734

ZINC

Exports : metric tons

	1913	1914	1915	1916	1917
All countries . . .	10,538	16,517	22,617	28,149	18,394

(No details of export)

TIN

Imports : metric tons

All countries . . .	661	332	1,029	741	99
United Kingdom . .	359	139	898	600	98

TINNED AND GALVANISED IRON PLATES

Imports : metric tons

All countries . . .	34,020	28,239	41,199	29,288	9,805
United Kingdom . .	31,611	25,572	37,869	18,104	6,188

FISH AND WHALE GUANO

Exports : metric tons

All countries . . .	14,214	13,449	10,865	6,447	1,372
Germany and Austria .	13,003	12,620	10,755	6,437	1,372
Denmark and Sweden .	10	210	88	—	—

FISH MEAL (including whale-meat meal)

Exports : metric tons

All countries . . .	8,927	8,978	10,441	5,935	—
Germany and Austria .	5,364	7,634	9,289	5,915	—
Denmark and Sweden .	352	45	562	—	—

SKINS AND HIDES

Imports : metric tons

All countries . . .	7,131	5,910	6,090	5,816	3,101

Exports : metric tons

All countries . . .	7,201	7,958	2,731	7,124	996

(Details of country of destination are not available. Germany got the bulk of the skins of marine animals—seals, etc. Sweden got a good deal of the rest.)

NITRATE OF LIME

Exports : metric tons

All countries . . .	70,926	75,175	38,608	46,001	35,932
Germany and Austria .	45,237	51,649	19,089	19,805	16,279
Denmark, Sweden and Holland . . .	8,977	15,219	10,184	1,132	2,542
United Kingdom and France . . .	13,612	5,519	8,367	25,063	17,110 .

NITRATE AND AMMONIA

Exports . metric tons

	1913	1914	1915	1916	1917
All countries . .	9,107	11.958	26,458	59,639	63,578
Germany and Austria .	No details		4,495	517	—
Denmark, Sweden and Holland . . .	,		279	120	347
United Kingdom and France . . .	,,		17,832	41,357	56,159

NITRATE AND NITRATE OF SODIUM

Exports : metric tons

All countries . . .	10,220	9,262	14,870	20,892	26,247
Germany and Austria .	No details		4,862	3,117	300
Denmark, Sweden and Holland . . .	,,		3,302	1,586	1,069
United Kingdom and France . . .	,,		5,814	14,714	24,271

IRON ORES, CONCENTRATES AND BRIQUETTES

Exports : metric tons

All countries . . .	568,762	467,795	425,892	404,700	197,834
Germany . . .	264,457	265,623	123,134	152,453	135,814
United Kingdom . .	211,146	184,429	253,941	251,982	56,830

PYRITES

Exports metric tons

All countries . . .	425,876	360,228	466,759	253,361	212,908
Germany . . .	40,892	60,729	210,452	84,510	4,105
United Kingdom .	138,134	91,693	75,254	21,844	50,770

MOLYBDINITE

Exports · metric tons

All countries . . .	5	87	101	140	201

(No details of destination available)

CHROME ORE

Exports : metric tons

All countries . . .	20	12	763	2,737	2,395

(No details of destination available)

CARBORUNDUM

Exports metric tons

All countries . . .	1	557	2,002	996	673
Germany . . .	No details		1,077	—	—
Denmark and Sweden	,,		591	738	519
United Kingdom . .	,,		179	20	96

FERROSILICON

Exports : metric tons

	1913	1914	1915	1916	1917
All countries . . .	6,322	6,144	9,307	25,255	29,449
Germany . .	No details	641	3,290	8,997	13,578
Denmark and Sweden .	,,	584	554	1,670	385
United Kingdom . .	,,	1,994	2,626	5,515	6,013

CALCIUM CARBIDE

Exports : metric tons

All countries . . .	66,910	63,722	79,480	58,432	46,066
Germany . . .	20,875	20,317	19,836	29,823	24,386
Denmark and Sweden .	681	593	732	1,098	3,692
United Kingdom . .	9,267	17,000	16,983	18,130	15,836

CYANAMIDE

Exports : metric tons

All countries . . .	22,110	13,719	24,609	13,151	2,312
Germany . . .	12,188	5,462	5,314	—	—
United Kingdom . .	3,598	3,061	7,903	10,172	1,320

ALUMINIUM

Exports : metric tons

All countries . . .	2,177	2,942	2,883	4,488	7,600
Germany . . .	806	350	3	87	1
United Kingdom and France . . .	41	725	1,858	4,339	5,222

INDEX

MADE AND PRINTED IN GREAT BRITAIN. RICHARD CLAY & SONS, LTD.,
PRINTERS, BUNGAY, SUFFOLK.

9 781015 488827